CRIMINAL MOVES

LIVERPOOL ENGLISH TEXTS AND STUDIES 78

CRIMINAL MOVES

Modes of Mobility
in Crime Fiction

EDITED BY JESPER GULDDAL,
STEWART KING AND ALISTAIR ROLLS

LIVERPOOL UNIVERSITY PRESS

First published 2019 by
Liverpool University Press
4 Cambridge Street
Liverpool
L69 7ZU

British Library Cataloguing-in-Publication data
A British Library CIP record is available

ISBN 978-1-78962-058-0 cased

Typeset by Carnegie Book Production, Lancaster
Printed and bound in Poland by BooksFactory.co.uk

Contents

Contributors

Maurizio Ascari teaches English Literature at the University of Bologna (Italy). His publications include books and essays on crime fiction (*A Counter-History of Crime Fiction*, Palgrave 2007, nominated for the Edgar Awards), transcultural literature (*Literature of the Global Age*, McFarland, 2011) and interart exchanges (*Cinema and the Imagination in Katherine Mansfield's Writing*, Palgrave, 2014). He has also edited and translated works by Henry James, Katherine Mansfield, William Faulkner, Jack London and William Wilkie Collins.

Jean Fornasiero is Professor Emerita of French Studies at the University of Adelaide. Her principal area of expertise is the history of ideas in nineteenth-century France. She has worked extensively on French maritime exploration in the Pacific, and is a co-author of two award-winning books on the Baudin expedition: *Encountering Terra Australis* (Wakefield Press, 2004; 2010) and *French Designs on Colonial New South Wales* (Friends of the State Library of South Australia, 2014).

Andrea Goulet is Professor of Romance Languages at the University of Pennsylvania and Co-Chair of the Nineteenth-Century French Studies Association. Her research spans nineteenth- and twentieth-century French fiction and critical theory. She has a particular interest in the nexus of science and literature, on which she has published inter alia *Optiques: The Science of the Eye and the Birth of Modern French Fiction* (University of Pennsylvania Press, 2006). More recently, she has become an authority on the development of crime fiction in France. Notably, she is the author of *Legacies of the Rue Morgue: Space and Science in French Crime Fiction, 1866–2006* (University of Pennsylvania Press, 2016) and guest editor, alongside Susanna Lee, of *Crime Fictions*, a special issue of

Yale French Studies (108, 2006). She is also co-editor of *Orphan Black: Performance, Gender, Biopolitics* (Intellect Press, 2018).

Jesper Gulddal is Associate Professor in Literary Studies at the University of Newcastle, Australia. He has published books and articles on the literary history of anti-Americanism, the nexus of mobility and movement control in the modern novel as well as on detective fiction, including journal articles on Agatha Christie, Ed McBain and Pierre Bayard's 'detective criticism'. Recent essays have appeared in journals such as *New Literary History, German Life and Letters, Textual Practice, Comparative Literature Studies* and *Comparative Literature*. He is currently editing, with Janice Allan, Stewart King and Andrew Pepper, *The Routledge Companion to Crime Fiction* (2020).

Michael Harris-Peyton is an Adjunct Professor at the University of Delaware. His research focuses on transcultural adaptation in world literature, crime fiction and the postcolonial politics of genre. His dissertation, 'Holmes in the Empire', argues for a more rigorous and inclusive model of crime fiction as a global genre. He has contributed to the edited collection *Crime Fiction as World Literature* (2017) as well as the *Routledge Companion to Crime Fiction* (forthcoming, 2020).

Stewart King is Senior Lecturer in Spanish and Catalan Studies and coordinates the International Literatures program at Monash University, Australia. His research focuses on contemporary Spanish and Catalan literatures, including crime fiction, and he has pioneered the study of crime fiction as world literature. He is a member of the editorial board of *Clues: A Journal of Detection*. He is the author of *Murder in the Multinational State: Crime Fiction from Spain* (Routledge, 2019), and is currently editing *The Routledge Companion to Crime Fiction*, with Janice Allan, Jesper Gulddal and Andrew Pepper (2020).

Stephen Knight, a research professor at the University of Melbourne, is a cultural historian who has published widely on medieval and modern literature and is a pioneer in the field of crime fiction studies. He is the author of *Form and Ideology in Crime Fiction* (Macmillan, 1980), *Crime Fiction, 1800–2000: Detection, Death, Diversity* (Palgrave, 2004), *The Mysteries of the Cities* (McFarland, 2012) and *Towards Sherlock Holmes: A Thematic History of Crime Fiction in the Nineteenth Century World* (McFarland, 2017), among other works.

Merja Makinen is Associate Professor in English Literature and Director of Programmes for the Culture and Communications group in the School of Media and Performing Arts at Middlesex University London. She writes on twentieth-century fiction, particularly women's writing, gender and popular fiction. She is the author of *Agatha Christie: Investigating Femininity* (Palgrave Macmillan, 2006), *Jeanette Winterson: A Reader's Guide to Essential Criticism* (Palgrave Macmillan, 2005), *Feminist Popular Fiction* (Palgrave Macmillan, 2001) and *Joyce Cary: A Descriptive Bibliography* (Mansell, 1989). She is also the co-author, with Lorraine Gamman, of *Female Fetishism: A New Look* (Lawrence and Wishart, 1994).

Andrew Pepper is Senior Lecturer in English and American literature at Queen's University Belfast. He has written extensively about crime fiction and is the author of *Unwilling Executioner: Crime Fiction and the State* (Oxford University Press, 2016), *The Contemporary American Crime Novel: Race, Ethnicity, Gender, Class* (Edinburgh University Press, 2000) and co-editor, with David Schmid, of *Globalization and the State in Contemporary Crime Fiction* (Palgrave, 2016). He is also the author of five detective novels set in nineteenth-century Britain and Ireland, all published by Weidenfeld and Nicolson, including *The Last Days of Newgate* (2006), *The Detective Branch* (2010) and *Bloody Winter* (2011).

Heta Pyrhönen is Professor of Comparative Literature at the University of Helsinki, Finland. She has published books and articles on detective fiction, Gothic literature, Jane Austen, the fairy tale tradition in women's writing (*Bluebeard Gothic*, Toronto University Press, 2010), romance fiction, and adaptation. Her many publications on detective fiction include *Murder from an Academic Angle: An Introduction to the Study of the Detective Narrative* (Camden House, 1994) and *Mayhem and Murder: Narrative and Moral Problems in the Detective Story* (Toronto University Press, 1999). Recently she co-edited a volume of essays, *Reading Today* (University College London Press, 2018).

Alistair Rolls is Associate Professor of French Studies at the University of Newcastle, Australia. In the area of crime fiction, he has been guest editor of special issues of the following journals: *Clues: A Journal of Detection*, *Text*, *The Australasian Journal of Popular Culture* and *The Australian Journal of Crime Fiction*. His monographs on the topic include *French and American Noir: Dark Crossings* (Palgrave Macmillan,

2009), which he co-authored with Deborah Walker; *Paris and the Fetish: Primal Crime Scenes* (Rodopi, 2014); and *Origins and Legacies of Marcel Duhamel's Série Noire* (Brill, 2018), which he co-authored with Clara Sitbon and Marie-Laure Vuaille-Barcan. He is also the co-editor, with Rachel Franks, of *Private Investigator* (Intellect, 2016) and, with John West-Sooby and Marie-Laure Vuaille-Barcan, of *Translating National Allegories: The Case of Crime Fiction* (Routledge, 2018).

John West-Sooby is Professor of French Studies at the University of Adelaide. His interests include the nineteenth-century French novel, French and Australian crime fiction, and the history of French maritime exploration in the Pacific. He is a co-author of *Encountering Terra Australis* (Wakefield Press, 2004; 2010) and *French Designs on Colonial New South Wales* (Friends of the State Library of South Australia, 2014).

Introduction

Criminal Moves

Towards a Theory of Crime Fiction Mobility

Jesper Gulddal, Stewart King and Alistair Rolls

Crime fiction, as a constituent member of the field of 'popular literature' and an object of literary criticism, has historically been encumbered by a set of restrictive preconceptions: that the genre does not warrant detailed critical analysis, that genre norms and conventions matter more than textual individuality, and that comparative or transnational perspectives are secondary to the study of the core British-American canon. The present volume challenges the distinction between literary and popular fiction, which we regard as a relic of a previous, elitist view of literature. Also, and more importantly, it posits that this baggage hinders our engagement with what we regard as the inherent *mobility* of crime fiction. It is easy enough to point towards individual crime fiction narratives that validate the critical blueprints. Yet, we argue that crime fiction is nonetheless characterized by a transgressive impulse that actively reflects on and challenges its own generic limitations, thereby potentially recuperating the genre from the stasis of established forms. This is what we understand by mobility: crime fiction, far from being static and staid, must be seen as a genre constantly violating its own boundaries. There is an unacknowledged experimental streak to this genre – an easy slippage between affirming the codes and conventions on the one hand, and on the other hand boldly calling into question and venturing beyond its textual, generic and national traditions. Acknowledging these 'criminal moves', or these modes of crime fiction mobility, enables a comprehensive reinterpretation of the history of the genre that also has profound ramifications for our reading of individual crime fiction texts.

The dynamic, text-based conception of crime fiction that we advocate here responds to elements present in the works of, among others, Gill Plain (2001), Lee Horsley (2005) and Merja Makinen (2006), each of whom has advocated the use of close-reading methodologies as a means of highlighting the sophisticated textual strategies employed in the genre. Maurizio Ascari (2007), moreover, has contested the official canon of crime fiction from the point of view of literary history, calling attention instead to a counter-history of the genre based on very different rules and conventions. Further, Stephen Knight (2015) and Pierre Bayard (2000, 2009), coming from opposing theoretical traditions, have argued for a return to the crime text itself, the former seeking to recover its voice and lost meaning, the latter aiming to unleash its semantic potential beyond the detective hero's authoritative solutions. Finally, studies by Stewart King (2014), Andrew Pepper (2016) and Louise Nilsson, David Damrosch and Theo D'haen (2017) have challenged both the British-American canon and the subset of the national paradigms that dominate the scholarship of their respective language disciplines.

Despite studies such as these furthering our understanding of the genre's textual dynamics, evolution and transnational circulation, a certain taxonomizing tendency has remained the default setting of much crime fiction scholarship. The classic example in this regard is Tzvetan Todorov's 'The Typology of Detective Fiction' (1977). In this essay, Todorov argues that while the masterpieces of 'high' literature are irreducibly individual and transcend the concept of genre, the masterpieces of popular fiction are works that fully embody a set of preestablished genre norms. On this basis, he suggests that detective fiction can be reduced to just three general types, which he defines in terms of plot structure: the whodunnit, the thriller and the suspense novel. The sociological perspective represented by Bourdieu (1996), Gelder (2004) and Boltanski (2014) similarly denies crime fiction the status of 'autonomous' literature, regarding it instead as subject to the commercial imperatives of the marketplace. Finally, the field of cultural studies, while crucial in terms of contextualizing the genre and validating it as a legitimate topic of scholarship, has tended to downplay the textual individuality of crime fiction by viewing the genre in light of higher-order issues of class, gender and sexuality and the social and political problems of the modern metropolis.

Historically, the view of crime fiction as rule-bound is associated with what is commonly known as the Golden Age of crime fiction in the 1920s and 1930s, particularly the two influential rule-sets penned by S.S. Van Dine (1928) and Ronald Knox (1929). These rules explicitly set the genre apart from what is regarded as 'real' literature; as Van Dine states, detective novels should contain 'no long descriptive passages, no literary dallying with side-issues, no subtly worked-out character analyses, no "atmospheric" preoccupations' (1947: 191–92). These rules have come to encapsulate the Golden Age, yet their modelling of the genre has infected other formats and has arguably become ingrained in the DNA of crime fiction studies. Even radical criticisms of the genre, like Raymond Chandler's 'The Simple Art of Murder' (1944), have been diffused and integrated into the canon, becoming themselves a matter of defining types and establishing rules.

The distinction Chandler makes between an effete and feminized English tradition of classic crime fiction and a muscular and masculine American tradition embodied in the works of Dashiell Hammett also serves to entrench a further nationalistic taxonomization, which, in turn, has led to the analysis of different crime fiction traditions along national lines. This is often, of course, the logical result of academic structures, which see English Studies as distinct from, for example, French or Hispanic Studies. These borders are themselves problematic, as attested to by departments of, say, French and Francophone Studies. Thus, studies of 'French' or 'Spanish' crime fiction typically acknowledge the pragmatic necessity, and inherent artificiality, of such classifications. The paradox here, of course, lies in the fact that these studies represent a necessary attempt to redress the overvaluation of the British-American tradition, and thus a mobilization of scholarship, but ultimately reinforce taxonomization. As Stephen Greenblatt has noted (2010: 3–4), albeit in the framework of a manifesto for mobility studies of a far more literal kind, it is all too easy to reproduce established fixities even when trying to account for mobile phenomena; indeed, such self-replication of structures appears to be almost inevitable in the academic model of disciplines and disciplinary differentiation.

The detrimental effects of the view of the genre as static and lacking in originality, depth and autonomy are threefold: first, such a view implies that the individual features of a crime story are coincidental in comparison to the underlying formula and, as a result, that crime fiction does not warrant detailed textual scrutiny; second, it solidifies crime fiction as a genre, making it resistant to innovative analysis, which becomes instead the privileged domain of 'elite' literature; and third, it consecrates specific national traditions of crime fiction and thereby encourages the view that this genre is essentially a British-American phenomenon. Our response to these detrimental effects on the genre forms the basis for the three axes of mobility – meaning, genre and transnationality – that we explore below.

Before we introduce the three axes of mobility in more detail, however, it is important that we acknowledge that, while covering texts from any number of national contexts and adopting a transnational lens as far as possible throughout, our corpus nonetheless privileges the classics of the British-American tradition. This is crucial, for it is precisely this tradition that needs to be mobilized; it is also, and largely for this reason, the one that responds best to the criminal moves for which we are advocating. Indeed, to see mobility as something already achieved in contemporary avatars of crime fiction, which play self-consciously with genre conventions or embrace transnationality (novels set in markedly exotic locales, for example), is to deepen the perceived rift in the genre, moving settings and techniques, and also the study of these, still further from a centre that, in turn, finds itself more rigidly fixed. The challenge that we are setting ourselves in this collection is to explore the mobility that lies at the centre of the genre, in the seminal works of its dominant tradition, as well of course as in its more contemporary manifestations.

This focus on the genre's seminal texts may appear counterintuitive. We argue, however, that a truly mobile conception of the crime genre must begin by demonstrating that mobility is not a fringe phenomenon, characteristic only of texts that purposefully break away from established genre norms, but rather that it manifests itself at the very core of the genre, in classic texts that have only retrospectively been turned into exemplars of genre rules. Poe, Doyle and Christie, for example, wrote narratives of detection that are eminently literary, mobile and worthy of literary analysis. Yet, these same authors have been subsequently fixed as representatives of the genre of crime fiction and their works are seen to coincide with the rules observed by its scholars and critics. From this perspective there is no better place to start mobilizing the genre than in Edgar Allan Poe's genre-defining 'The Murders in the Rue Morgue' (1841). Indeed, as we will demonstrate below, Poe's story is exemplary of each of the three axes of mobility.

Mobility of Meaning

By mobility of meaning we are referring to the fluid, multi-layered and sometimes self-contradictory processes of signification that are crucial in establishing the mystery of the crime story, yet only fully come to light when we bracket the story's authoritative self-interpretation, often presented in the form of the detective protagonist's final reveal.

A distinguishing feature of crime fiction as a literary genre is its strong orientation towards the ending. With mystery as their narrative core, crime novels move circuitously towards a final moment of resolution, clarity and, perhaps, justice – an instance of the desire for denudement (or denouement) that, according to Roland Barthes, makes 'narrative suspense' similar to striptease (1975: 10). This end-orientation in itself is shared by other forms of narrative and can even, as Frank Kermode has demonstrated, be seen as a fundamental way in which human beings make sense of their lives – that is, retrospectively, from a point of view where the beginning, middle and ending of an individual life combine to form a meaningful whole (1967: 7). Yet, the ending of a crime novel is different and goes beyond the narrative function of establishing the coherence of a plot. Rather than simply piecing together the puzzle and tying up loose ends, the crime novel ends with an act of self-interpretation, presented explicitly in the form of the detective protagonist's solution, which replaces mystery with what appears to be complete clarity in regard to actions and motivations. This solution constitutes a first critical reading of the story – one that may well, given the authority invested in the protagonist, be the final and only conceivable reading. If crime fiction is seen as a genre that does not warrant or cannot sustain close critical analysis, this is arguably not only due to the perceived simplicity and formulaic nature of the genre, but also to the fact that the crime story seems to relieve the reader of the burden of criticism by undertaking this criticism itself.

Perhaps unsurprisingly, end-orientation already features prominently in 'The Murders in the Rue Morgue'. When Dupin, at the beginning of the story, uses his extraordinary analytical faculties to lay bare the narrator's complex private musings, this can be read as Poe's attempt to train his readers to accept without question the detective's final, authoritative unveiling of the truth. Yet, the story also contains what could be seen as a warning against the glamour of end-orientation when Dupin, at the tale's conclusion, criticizes the Prefect of Police for being 'somewhat too cunning to be profound'; '[i]n his wisdom', the description continues, 'is no *stamen*. It is all head and no body, like the pictures of the Goddess Laverna – or, at best, all head and shoulders, like a codfish' (Poe 1986: 224). By drawing attention to the uneasy relationship between an overvaluation of the ending, which is associated with cerebral analytics rather than holistic judgement, and a neglect of the textual body, Poe's story arguably anticipates the forms of crime fiction mobility that are the focus of the present volume; and, in doing so, it provides a suitable reference point for a theory of the crime story as a genre that is far from static. While the story's initial example of ratiocination serves to validate the ending, the ending in turn appears to refer readers back to the beginning, inviting us to reconsider the body of the text. Itself an example of textual mobility, this structure redirects attention away from the finality of the solution towards the dynamics of the investigation, including those aspects of the case that Dupin fails to explain fully, such as the two sacks of gold coins that the victims withdrew from the bank on the day of their murder.

To open up crime fiction to the kind of critical scrutiny for which we are advocating therefore requires that we – temporarily, at least, and as a heuristic technique – bracket the ending. It is precisely the end-orientation of crime novels, not only their final solutions, but also the ways in which their narratives appear designed to force readers to rush towards them, that has caused crime fiction, and perhaps most importantly the classics of the genre, to be read only partially. For just as the clues are separated from the red herrings in light of the detective's final solution, so too all other textual meaning is swept aside in favour of those elements that are designed by authors (and retrospectively considered by readers and scholars) to articulate the solution. Bracketing the self-interpretation of the ending makes it possible to engage with crime fiction at the textual level and thus to recognize its full gamut of meaning.

The person who has gone furthest in this direction is French literary critic and psychoanalyst Pierre Bayard. According to Bayard, the history of crime fiction is the history of repeated miscarriages of justice whereby innocent characters have been accused and sentenced in spite of the state of the evidence. He therefore advocates that we develop a close-reading methodology that is as rigorous and attentive to detail as the investigative technique of the detectives. Applying this method of *critique policière*, or 'detective criticism', to crime fiction classics such as Christie's *The Murder of Roger Ackroyd* and Doyle's *The Hound of the Baskervilles*, Bayard not only challenges the final resolutions presented by the detectives, but also gathers evidence against other characters and thereby aims to identify the real murderers whom the detectives themselves were incapable of exposing. Underlying this style of analysis is a theory of crime fiction characterized by a double movement: it puts forwards a plethora of competing, virtual narratives that could all be true, only to conclude by privileging a single storyline that is sanctioned by the detective. However, as Bayard argues, this final act of narrative reductionism cannot fully contain the proliferation of virtual storylines that create the mystery of the plot, and this enables critical readers to reactivate some of the forgotten possibilities and ultimately to arrive at an alternative solution.

This approach has been criticized as 'sensational' (Knight 2015: 104–05). and 'more mischievous than serious' (Horsley 2005: 243). It is true that Bayard presents it tongue-in-cheek. Yet, while its most surrealist conclusions – for example, the treatment of fictional characters and murder cases as though they were real – may not be acceptable to every reader, Bayard's detective criticism demonstrates how an approach that challenges end-orientation can lead to new critical insights as well as a new appreciation of the textual complexity of crime fiction. His idea of crime fiction's initial 'opening of meaning' and ultimate 'foreclosing of meaning' (2000: 67) is one such insight, which usefully considers crime fiction from the point of view of its textual mobility rather than its final investigative resolution. Another is his analysis of the multifarious strategies of concealment through which crime writers keep their readers from guessing the truth. However, the point extends further still. Suspending the streamlined teleology of the crime plot also, more generally, enables what might be called a whole-text approach to the individual story (Pepper 2000; Makinen 2006). While end-orientation by definition reduces the textual complexity of crime fiction, a whole-text investigation restores it by bringing to light the mobile and multi-layered semantics of the crime text. Such an approach recognizes that 'more questions are raised in the narrative than are answered by formal closure' (McCracken 1998: 50).

Ultimately, the concept of the mobility of meaning is predicated on the view that genuine innovation in crime fiction studies must come about as a result of detailed critical analysis of individual texts. If the field of literary studies has in recent years pivoted towards contextual and 'distant' reading, this has been due to an increasing sense that the close-reading practices that dominated literary studies throughout the second half of the twentieth century have exhausted their potential (Moretti 2013). Yet, this is not the case in the context of crime fiction where, on the contrary, distant reading was always the norm, and Knight is correct in pointing out that scholarship in this field has traditionally taken the form of large-scale historical, generic or author-based surveys and has contented itself with 'inherently dominating the form and asserting its simplicity by never allowing it to speak up for itself' (2015: 4). As becomes particularly obvious in studies using computational methodologies to find the 'Agatha Christie Code' (ITV 2005), identify the 'Whodunit Formula' (Siddique 2015) or break the 'bestseller code' (Archer and Jockers 2016), reading crime fiction distantly tends to reinforce the idea of its static and formulaic nature. The problem with such an abstract methodology is, as with Poe's Prefect of Police, that it is 'all head and no body': it does away with the textual flesh that makes individual crime stories infinitely more exciting than any generic skeleton. In order to go beyond the constraining notion of 'genre fiction' and all the critical assumptions that accompany it we therefore need to develop contemporary forms of textual analysis that do justice to the complexity and mobility of the crime story.

The essays in the 'Mobility of Meaning' section of this volume contribute to this project while also showing how an overall commitment to mobility can result in a range of different critical and analytical practices. In their chapter on the social anxieties of the belle époque, Jean Fornasiero and John West-Sooby cast doubt on prevailing assumptions about the pioneering crime fiction of late-nineteenth- and early-twentieth-century France, revealing that the novels of Maurice Leblanc and Gaston Leroux not only depict the Golden Age that preceded the First World War, but also offer a critique of the dominant paradigm of the day, revealing the counter-currents that were already simmering in that period of glorious optimism. Complexities and doubts traverse these novels, ensuring a double critique – of society via the tropes of the novel, and of the plot made complex by the social networks and genealogies of ambiguous, even damaged, protagonists. Interestingly, too, the important place of psychoanalysis – that theory of the other side – in twentieth-century literature is shown to be ushered in here with extraordinary prescience. In his chapter on *The Mystery of a Hansom Cab*, written by Fergus Hume in Australia at the time of the belle époque, Alistair Rolls demonstrates how the physical mobility, on which the readability of the modern city is founded and around which much of the critical discussion of this foundational crime novel has revolved, is in fact surprisingly lacking; in its place, and around the focal points of its absence, not least of which is the eponymous cab itself, rich veins of metaphorical mobility spread out, leading to an alternative mapping of the novel's signs, including the potential for a Bayardian re-solution. In the third chapter of this section, Heta Pyrhönen offers a new engagement with another classic, Raymond Chandler's *The Big Sleep*. Pyrhönen's focus here is the spectrum of emotions at play in readers' negotiation of the crime text. With this lens, she is able to challenge the idea that a genre can be neatly mapped onto a corresponding emotional range. By questioning the responses that the reader picks up from and projects onto Chandler's novel, Pyrhönen is also able to challenge the status of its official solution. Finally, the quest for crime fiction's other side begun in chapter one continues in Merja Makinen's rereading of the genre's most famous practitioner, Agatha Christie; indeed, Makinen argues that it is precisely because Christie is synonymous with crime fiction, and more precisely the Golden Age and the whodunnit format, that her novels have been neglected, and further delimited, by literary criticism. For Makinen, Christie's work offers the literary range and textual pleasures of Modernism on the one hand, and, on the other, genuine social interventionism, including a surprising focus on world politics.

Mobility of Genre

The concept of genre mobility refers to an attempt to go beyond the idea that popular fiction genres are 'heteronomous' constructs, subject either to prescriptive genre conventions or to commercial imperatives that lead authors to replicate patterns that have proven successful in the marketplace. The mobile approach to crime fiction – and potentially to other popular genres – questions the stasis of established forms and focuses instead on the dynamism of a genre that keeps evolving and seemingly knows no convention or device that cannot be challenged.

In our attempt to 'mobilize' the genre concept, we are contesting what we regard as a certain restrictiveness in the use of this concept in crime fiction criticism. At the most general level, this restrictiveness manifests itself in the form of a taxonomical endeavour to define and classify the genre and its various subsets, and in a strong critical focus on the relationship, often seen as purely participatory, between the individual text and the genre as a body of rules, norms and patterns. Such an approach implies that the foremost aim of crime fiction criticism is to elucidate the individual crime story's embodiment of a given genre pattern, and only secondarily to characterize that story in its individuality, including all the meat that attaches to the bare bones of the formula. The problem is, however, that 'pure' examples are arguably rare, and that in recent years hybrid forms, including those that result from transnational mobility, have become the norm within the genre. The crime fiction genre, in other words, is fluid, and more so today than ever before. Taxonomical criticism has responded to this process of hybridization by increasing the level of conceptual granularity and increasing the number of crime genres from Todorov's three to a plethora of more and more specialized descriptors – mystery, whodunnit, cosy, hard-boiled, psychological, procedural, metaphysical, historical, literary – which are further expanded through the introduction of adjectivized or hyphenated forms such as neo-noir, scandinoir, tartan noir, weird noir, bush noir, Euro crime, femicrime, among many others. The quality of such studies notwithstanding, this fine-meshed web of genre designation seems to be, to borrow a phrase from Claudio Guillén, the work of a 'deluded keeper of archives' (1993: 37). The proliferation of genre terms certainly suggests that the real problem is not the lack of sufficiently precise language, but rather the taxonomical project itself, particularly its attempt to contain and stabilize the mobility of the crime fiction genre.

A mobile concept of genre resists taxonomy and attunes itself instead to the fluid, hybrid and mutative aspects of crime fiction. Based on detailed critical analysis, it emphasizes, not how individual crime narratives embody pre-existing patterns, but, on the contrary, how they transform these patterns through processes of negation and adaptation. Our contention is that the relationship between the individual text and the genre is never simply one of genre affirmation, although some instances of crime fiction may come close to operating in this way; nor is it ever one of genre negation, even though the self-reflexivity of the genre at times seems to undermine even the most entrenched conventions (cf. Gulddal 2016). It may be that not every crime novel transforms the genre, yet not even the most genre-conforming novel can avoid performing its genre in an individual way. If this is the case, then crime fiction criticism should aim to elucidate the mobile textual practices that bridge the gap between genre structure and genre performance.

A mobile theory of crime fiction also needs to address the restrictiveness of the way in which crime fiction is delimited as a genre. A key question in this regard concerns the genre's origins and evolution. Introductions and textbooks, with characteristic anglophone bias, have typically cast Poe as the father of crime fiction. This assessment is not altogether untrue given that Poe's Dupin trilogy, especially 'The Murders in the Rue Morgue', uses a number of devices that would later, retrospectively, come to be seen as central to the genre. Yet, most of these devices can be found both in earlier literature and in literature in languages other than English, not least in the French and German traditions with which Poe was intimately familiar. More importantly, this foundational myth cuts 'The Murders in the Rue Morgue' off from the gothic, supernatural and sensationalist currents of early nineteenth-century literature, which as a consequence come to be seen as transgressive, and obscures references to these currents that appear in this story. Two of the contributors to this book, Stephen Knight and Maurizio Ascari, have been instrumental in presenting a more inclusive and nuanced account of the genre, the former by calling attention to the roots of crime fiction in sensationalist literature and true crime writing around 1800, and the latter by presenting an ambitious 'counter-history' of crime fiction that includes some of the historical modes of crime narrative that have been obscured by the early canonization of Poe, Doyle and Christie.

Franco Moretti's Darwinian approach to the evolution of the clue sheds light on these processes of canonization by highlighting the wealth of mutations that finally – in some, but not all, of Doyle's Sherlock Holmes stories – led to the development of a prototypical whodunnit format with clues that are necessary to the plot as well as visible and decodable from the point of view of the reader (2013: 63–90). Emphasizing the experimentalism of crime fiction, Moretti's evolutionary trees provide a compelling model for exploring the mobility of the genre. The problem is, however, that Moretti seems to argue that the genre mutations tend teleologically, and are driven by market forces, towards final and prescriptive forms (for example, the clue puzzle). Yet, the mobility of the crime genre is not limited to threshold periods. On the contrary, crime fiction as a genre is constantly evolving, and mobility, as demonstrated in several chapters in this book, is ingrained in even the most highly canonized, genre-defining works.

Another way of delimiting the genre involves the exclusion, or rescuing, of works that clearly include crime elements, yet are perceived as serious, literary and hence capable of sustaining detailed critical analysis. Categorizing these works as 'literary fiction' supports the idea that crime fiction is simple and conventional, and helps uphold a neat distinction between high and low forms of literature. Richard Bradford, for example, suggests that a number of literary classics whose plots focus on murder and subsequent investigation should not be considered crime fiction, because, in these cases, the criminal act serves simply as a 'thematic hinge for the exploration of more fundamental issues' (2015:

3); reading Dostoyevsky's *Crime and Punishment* (1866) as a crime novel would therefore be 'an act of interpretative vulgarity' (2015: 72). The mobile account of crime fiction challenges this view. If these classics seem to foreshadow the narrative patterns of modern crime fiction, we should try to understand why this is, and how this type of plotting might have enabled the thematic explorations that Bradford privileges. There is nothing inherently vulgar in reading *Oedipus Rex* or *Hamlet* as crime stories, as Bayard does (2000: 77–84; 2002); on the contrary, it takes a certain elitism to discount the possibility that such an approach may be illuminating. Equally, Paul Auster may believe that his *New York Trilogy* (1987) makes use of crime fiction conventions only 'to get to another place, another place altogether' (Mallia 1988: 23); the literary critic may nonetheless still reasonably ask how this view replicates the modernist insistence on differentiating between the popular and the literary and explore how the crime format is not just a pretext, but a crucial means of getting to that other place.

Just as importantly, it would be easy to amass examples of crime stories that explore 'more fundamental issues'; think, for example, of the rich explorations of politics, power, urban life, gender and sexuality in twentieth-century crime fiction. However, the key issue here is that fixed ideas about genre tend to be self-confirming: one is unlikely to find complexity, for example, if approaching the genre with the assumption that it is thematically simple. A mobile approach, on the other hand, remains open to discovery beyond the fixities of genre. It acknowledges crime fiction's potential for engaging with its historical environment in complex and productive ways, and it accepts that crime fiction, like all literature, can be actualized through a variety of different interpretative modes, each highlighting different aspects of the text. It challenges the binary of 'genre fiction' *versus* 'literary fiction', not discounting the existence of genre-conforming texts, yet assuming that a fluid interplay of modes constitutes the real norm of crime fiction.

The various aspects of genre mobility discussed in this section ultimately represent a challenge to the concepts of 'genre fiction', 'formula fiction' or 'popular literature' understood as types of writing categorically distinct from 'Literature' with a capital L (Gelder 2004: 11),[1] in which the prescriptiveness of established patterns and formulae takes primacy

---

1 For an astute critique of Gelder that in part supports the notion of mobile genres and challenges the divide between so-called popular and literary forms, see Milner (2012: 9–14).

over individual forms of expression. A legacy from the modern aesthetics of originality, and from Modernism in particular (Carey 1992), this distinction between popular fiction and literature was an apt way of protecting the allegedly sacred realm of literature against what Ortega y Gasset (1993) called 'the rise of the masses'; yet, it has failed singularly to capture the complexity and mobility of crime fiction as well as of other popular genres. Calling attention to the genre's mobility is a way of going beyond the prejudices embedded in the notion of 'genre fiction', namely that writing of this kind is unambitious and simple, driven by the logic of the marketplace (which is seen, questionably, as a logic of uniformity rather than differentiation) and offering little more than escapist entertainment for the masses.

Against these critical predispositions, the present volume argues for a fluid, inclusive and multifaceted conceptualization of crime fiction as a genre. At the level of literary history, it foregrounds crime fiction's self-reflexive experimentalism as well as its evolution through waves of genre affirmation and negation; while not discounting the concept of genre in itself, it places its main emphasis on the breaking rather than observance of genre rules. At the level of critical analysis, it aims to develop reading practices that do justice to the mobile ways in which individual crime narratives use the conventions and formulae of the genre as a springboard for innovation.

The 'Mobility of Genre' section opens with Maurizio Ascari's chapter on the archaeology of the 'psycho-thriller', which emerged as a named, self-identifying genre in the postwar period and was popularized by the films of Alfred Hitchcock, most notably *Psycho* (1960). Scholars have pointed out links back to American noir of the 1930s and 1940s, but Ascari goes further by presenting a full prehistory of the genre, arguing that it has roots in late-eighteenth- and nineteenth-century theories of the conflicted, often irrational mind. Beginning with William Godwin's psychological philosophy, including its application in the novel *Caleb Williams* (1794), and ending with novels and films inspired by Freudian psychoanalysis, Ascari not only uncovers an alternative history of the genre that crosses boundaries between genres and media, he also articulates a theory of genre predicated on hybridization and mobility rather than outlived notions of origin, stasis and purity. Jesper Gulddal's chapter on Dashiell Hammett's *The Dain Curse* takes a narratively unmotivated car accident as the starting point for a discussion of genre negation as a force of innovation in Hammett's writing. As a violent interruption of preestablished modes of operation, the accident embodies the way in which the novel relates to the conventions of popular fiction only to wreck and overturn them. Thus, the linearity of the investigative process is replaced with a circular structure; the purity of genre is replaced with references to a catalogue of popular fiction templates, none of which are fully executed; narrative closure is replaced with ambiguity; and the classic figure of the 'sidekick' is literally blown to pieces in what Gulddal reads as another emblematic representation of the principle of genre mobility. Andrea Goulet's chapter on Léo Malet shares this focus on cars and equally, although in a very different way, draws a connection between automobility and genre mobility. Through the lens of the automobile revolution in postwar France, Goulet discusses four novels in Malet's *Les Noveaux Mystères de Paris* cycle (1954–59), demonstrating how cars and transportation infrastructure inform the unfolding of the plot while also defining a prose rhythm of alternating stasis and mobility. More broadly, the motif of the car in Malet's novels facilitates an ambivalent experience of Paris as torn between nostalgia for the past and commitment to modernity. In the section's final chapter, Andrew Pepper analyses Hideo Yokoyama's *Six Four* (2012), drawing on Clare Birchall's theory of transparency and secrecy to complicate the classic understanding of crime fiction in terms of a progressive uncovering of the truth. For Pepper, Yokoyama's novel evokes instead a world where transparency is only ever partial, where secrecy is used tactically or as a mode of resistance within bureaucratic units as they engage in territorial struggles against other units, and where the investigation inevitably leaves a residue of what is 'unknowable'. If these manoeuvres challenge the value placed on transparency in liberal democracies, they also trouble, and mobilize, some of the epistemological certainties on which the detective novel is often taken to rely.

Transnational Mobility

The concept of transnational mobility posits that crime fiction, far from being a British-American invention that has been adopted on a global scale, is inherently a transnational practice characterized by the multidirectional transmission and adaptation of styles, structures and themes across national borders.

Crime fiction in all its multiple manifestations, its global production and readership and its transmedia adaptation and circulation is one of the most widespread of all literary genres. Indeed, the international success of writers like Stieg Larsson, Henning Mankell, Andrea

Camilleri and Natsuo Kirino over the past decade or so has done much to draw attention to the existence of crime fiction traditions beyond the British-American canon with which we are all familiar. The emergence of these 'new' traditions – at least to an international readership – presents challenges to the study of crime fiction as it has been traditionally conceived as well as opportunities for imagining the genre's historical development in innovative ways. These challenges and opportunities, however, have so far been underexplored in much crime fiction scholarship, as argued by Stewart King in his contribution to this volume. The *Cambridge Companion to Crime Fiction* (Priestman 2003), for example, contains only one chapter on non-anglophone – in this case, French – crime fiction. Another companion, published by Wiley-Blackwell (Rzepka and Horsley 2010), does a little better, as it dedicates one chapter to the metaphysical crime stories of the Argentine international writer, Jorge Luis Borges, while another provides an overview of recent (mid-1990s onwards) European crime fiction available in English translation. Richard Bradford's *Crime Fiction: A Very Short Introduction* (2015) likewise devotes just a single chapter to international crime fiction.[2]

As previously suggested, the limited engagement with the genre's international dimensions in these studies is amply made up for in the work of literary historians working on distinct national or regional crime fiction traditions, such as Australian (Knight 1997), Cuban and Mexican (Braham 2004), French (Gorrara 2009), German (Hall 2016), Italian (Pezzotti 2014), Japanese (Seaman 2004), Spanish (Vosburg 2011), and Swedish (Bergman 2014) or Scandinavian (Stougaard-Nielsen 2017), to cite only English-language examples. While these studies point to the genre's global expansion, they have done little to challenge the dominance of the British-American canon. Instead, like the single chapters in the abovementioned companions and introductions, they sit largely apart. The national focus of these studies, moreover, while understandable, does little to facilitate critical engagement between different traditions, as King has argued (2014: 9–10). Instead, national approaches to the study of the genre tend to restrict meaning to what is comprehensible exclusively within a national context.

Although the contemporary cosmopolitan dimensions of the genre

---

2 To be fair to Bradford, the chapter on international crime fiction includes brief references to East Asian and Latin American writers and constitutes over one-fifth of his study (25 of 122 pages).

have attracted a great deal of critical attention in the past few years (Sulis 2017; Pepper and Schmid 2016), perhaps facilitated by current globalizing practices (translation, circulation and marketing by publishers), this transnationality has a remarkable history (Pepper 2016; see also Knight in this collection). Poe's 'The Murders in the Rue Morgue' again serves as an emblematic text of mobility, as the so-called birth of crime fiction was the result of a transnational conception made possible by an American writer who set his crime narrative in Paris and gave it a French detective and a possibly American narrator. In so doing, Poe seemingly inaugurated a trend for setting crime stories in foreign climes. Indeed, foreign settings and characters have become so prevalent that from Belize to Botswana, China to Cuba, the Netherlands to New Zealand, there are few parts of the world that have escaped non-native crime writers. Like 'The Murders in the Rue Morgue', such works are born transnational, as a non-national writer produces a text that moves back and forth between the foreign other (place, people and culture) and a domestic reader.

Poe's choice of setting, however, produced a more radical form of transnational movement. If Poe is the father of American crime fiction, then it must be acknowledged as well that Paris – rather than the Los Angeles or San Francisco that we associate so closely with the American genre – is its birthplace, thus fracturing the alleged symbiosis between the setting and the national tradition (cf. Rolls et al. 2018). At the same time, for Goulet (2016), Poe is the inventor of French crime fiction. In Goulet's analysis, Poe invented crime fiction, not because Baudelaire – Poe's French transcreator – was a passive vehicle for the reproduction of his stories in France, but rather because 'The Murders in the Rue Morgue' 'registers a specific spatial imaginary' that is Parisian in its poetics of modernity (2016: 3). Moreover, while seemingly fixed in France, the story rejects the sort of closure that national approaches effect on texts. The Maltese ship, the Bornean orangutan, and, importantly, *Le Monde* – the newspaper that links Dupin to the seemingly disparate elements that made this double murder possible – are all traces of the world within the nation itself, expanding meaning beyond France's borders.

'The Murders in the Rue Morgue', moreover, reveals within the investigation itself some of the underexplored complexity of the genre's transnational and multilingual history. Here, Ascari's counter-historical argument, which has been discussed above, on the suppression of an alternative, gothic and sensationalist, crime fiction tradition, can be expanded to include the erasure of the transnational origins of the genre. Indeed, after reviewing the evidence of the witnesses of diverse nationalities, Dupin embarks on a criticism of the methods used by the French police and, in so doing, he makes Eugène François Vidoq, a real-life criminal who became the head of the Paris Sûreté, the target of his censure. While such criticism has become something of a cliché in subsequent crime fiction, Dupin's identification of Vidocq is also an acknowledgement of Poe's literary debt to the author who, with the publication of his own crime narrative memoirs (1828), was Poe's immediate precursor. In a further transnational turn, Poe described his fiction as 'phantasy pieces', his translation of E.T.A. Hoffman's term *Fantasiestücke* (Clark 2009: 254), thus acknowledging another literary debt, this time to the German author of an earlier, transnational crime novella, *Das Fräulein von Scuderi* (Mademoiselle de Scuderi, 1819), set – like 'The Murders in the Rue Morgue' – in the French capital. These two references point to the emergence of a genre that is always already transnational and translational. To explore the genre's transnational mobility is to acknowledge that crime fiction is a genre 'born in translation' (Walkowitz 2015; King and Whitmore 2016).

The complex transnationality that we have identified in 'The Murders in the Rue Morgue' highlights the limitations of national-bounded approaches to the study and interpretation of crime fiction. To embrace the genre's transnational mobility is to acknowledge that crime fiction is world literature, not just in its global reach or in the ease with which this genre travels beyond its original context, but also in the existence of a vast and ongoing dialogue between crime fiction writers, texts and readers across national, cultural, linguistic and temporal borders (King 2014; Nilsson et al. 2017).

Recognizing transnational mobility has important implications for how we approach and make sense of the genre. First, to read crime fiction – or, indeed, other popular fictions – as world literature is to blur the seemingly rigid borders between a world literature that has traditionally been defined by, among other things, its 'originality, complexity, closure, autonomy, personality, multilayeredness, timelessness, and so on' and popular fiction characterized by 'format and genre (and, on a more micro-stylistic level, formulaic writing), sensationalism and voyeurism [...], and finally heteronomy' (Baetens 2011: 336–37). To read crime fiction as world literature, then, challenges the distinction between literary and popular fiction that we have identified above while also expanding the field of world literature beyond its established focus on high-cultural forms. Second, and perhaps more importantly, to recognize the cultural transfer and the transculturation of styles and genre conventions across different national and linguistic settings requires us to imagine a very different literary history of the genre. Do we continue, for example, to silo the expanding world of crime fiction in separate chapters, treating novels that fall outside the British-American canon as exotic, linguistically distinct curios or do we 'break the obsession with national particularity' and engage in a more radical revision of the genre's historical development (Pepper 2016: 7)? In advocating for the genre's transnational mobility we argue that it is no longer possible to dismiss foreign forebears, as Poe and Doyle have their detectives Dupin and Holmes do, or to treat non-anglophone crime fiction traditions as operating exclusively in parallel to, in or derivation from, the British-American canon. Instead, we propose a critical practice that develops a more nuanced, mobile understanding of this truly global genre.

This section opens with Stephen Knight's investigation into the profound international connections between and in nineteenth-century crime fiction. In tracing the emergence of the genre from the 1700s through legal narratives and Romantic preoccupations and aesthetics in France, Germany, England, the US, Scandinavia and Australia, Knight places doubt on the supposed centrality of the genre's British and American genealogy. In so doing, he challenges the dominant perception that the genre's transnationality is a consequence of twentieth- and twenty-first-century globalization and, as such, that it is largely a contemporary phenomenon. Michael B. Harris-Peyton's chapter on 'Brain Attics and Mind Weapons' extends this investigation into the complexity of crime fiction's international connections. Harris-Peyton brings together three crime writers whose various takes on Sherlock Holmes seemingly embody the distinction between original and reproduction. In demonstrating the ways in which Satyajit Ray and Cheng Xiaoqing adapt what is typically considered an archetypically British genre to their local settings, Harris-Peyton deconstructs the preeminent position granted to Holmes as the originator and, instead, draws attention to how Doyle himself adapted the genre in a transnational dialogue with his literary forebears. Finally, Stewart King reflects on the tension between national-focused and more worldly readings of crime fiction. Following Jorge Luis Borges, King argues that the transnationality of the crime genre does not reside exclusively within the text, but rather emerges through the interaction of the reader and the text. What emerges is a transnational and trans-historical reading practice, one that respects the local but that also allows for innovative connections and new paradigms to be forged when texts are read beyond the national context.

* * *

The concept of the mobility of crime fiction and the three axes of semantic, generic and transnational mobility present a new way of engaging critically with a genre whose scholarly reception has tended to be constrained by prejudices and preconceptions – a genre that has been paraphrased, categorized and surveyed more often than it has been read on its own terms as complex literature. The new reading practices that we propose in this collection at times, as some of the contributions make clear, have an experimental flavour and present readings of crime narratives that take us, and the texts in question, far beyond the notion of 'genre fiction'. However, the main aim of this volume is to initiate a critique of the assumptions that shape the interpretation of the genre. We posit that crime fiction studies has been, although with numerous individual exceptions, characterized by a certain intellectual laziness and a tendency on the part of scholars to dismiss as unliterary or formulaic what has not been carefully read. To propose, as we do, a redefinition of crime fiction that emphasizes its inherent mobility, we need to pose a new set of questions: How can we imagine a new, mobile reading practice that realizes the genre's full textual complexity, without being limited by the authoritative self-interpretations that crime narratives tend to provide? How can we venture beyond the restrictive notions of 'genre', 'formula', 'popular' or 'lowbrow' to develop instead a concept of genre that acknowledges its mobility? Finally, how can we establish a global and transnational perspective that challenges the centrality of the British-American tradition and recognizes that the global history of crime fiction is characterized, not by the existence of parallel, national traditions, but rather by processes of appropriation and transculturation?

One might legitimately query whether all crime fiction is mobile, or whether this notion, and hence any mobile criticism, applies only to a relatively small subset of the genre – 'literary crime fiction' – which rises above the genre in terms of sophistication and therefore warrants closer scrutiny? Further, does the idea of mobility not simply amount to a 'postmodern' take on the genre? Or is it not true, at least, that the reading practice we advocate projects onto crime fiction a set of theoretical assumptions that are alien to it both historically and generically? Our answer to these questions is a qualified no. Beginning with the last question, we would do well to recall that some of our most strongly held assumptions about literature have evolved historically, as a result of transformations and ideologies that are exterior to the literary field, and only habit and tradition shield them from being exposed as archaic. The danger, if there really is one, of rereading the crime fiction tradition unhistorically, through the lens of mobility is, we argue, much less than that of staying true to outmoded critical ideologies. The idea, for example, that the *nation* is the natural and privileged framework of literature harkens back to Johann Gottfried Herder and the rise of nationalism in the late eighteenth and early nineteenth centuries; it is hardly a productive approach in the age of globalization. Further, the critical distinction between 'literary' and 'genre' fiction, as we have discussed, is historically tied to modernist anxieties about mass culture, and the legacy of this perspective has remained in spite of a wealth of critical and artistic attacks. Even though these assumptions, particularly the Herderian worldview of literary studies, have attracted considerable criticism, crime fiction studies still needs to discard some of its ideological baggage. This book attempts to hasten this process by introducing a more dynamic conception of the genre.

Further, in response to the issue of 'literary crime fiction', we contest the distinction between literary and popular fiction. There seems to be little textual evidence to back the claim that literary fiction is original, complex and written without commercial concerns whereas crime fiction, and popular fiction in general, is conventional, simple and ultimately aimed at success in mass-market ventures. Formulaic crime fiction certainly does exist, but the category of literary fiction also includes many examples of clichéd writing and arguably has its own repertoire of narrative formulae, the only difference being that readers are not trained to spot them. Conversely, so-called popular fiction may well, as we have argued, exhibit higher levels of originality than is commonly assumed, yet readers are encouraged to identify patterns and cross-genre commonalities. It makes more sense, we argue, to conceive of literature as a single field where innovation and tradition blend in complex and sometimes unpredictable ways. Moreover, the mobile crime fiction criticism we propose here is in essence a reading strategy, and as such it can be applied equally to any form of crime fiction, however original or conventional. And, as we have stated, the crime fiction texts that lend themselves to the most interesting and productive analyses are often those that are typically considered exemplary of the genre, which is to say, those, like Christie's, that have come to embody the familiar rules and conventions. To distinguish between these texts and other texts that are deemed, by some, more 'literary', or indeed to elevate Christie's works to such a subcategory but not other classic crime texts would be simply to introduce one more unhelpful subgenre and would fail to address the fundamental mobility of the genre as a whole. The aim of our approach is to redirect critical attention to those aspects of the crime narrative that cannot simply be reduced to genre or tradition – all the aspects, in other words, that keep crime fiction alive.

Crime fiction itself is developing rapidly, driven by the globalization of the genre and the increasing hybridization and blending of forms. Crime fiction studies would do well to catch up with these developments and embrace the mobility of its object of study. We must recognize that the critical vocabulary developed to describe British-American crime fiction and to reinforce the dichotomy of literary and popular fiction is no longer adequate. As the contributions to this volume argue in their various ways, crime fiction studies need to look beyond the self-interpretation of the text, beyond the prescriptiveness of the genre and beyond the narrow framework of the nation. Crime fiction is mobile; it is now up to us, readers and critics, to move beyond the locked rooms of the critical tradition.

Works Cited

Archer, Jodie and Matthew L. Jockers (2016). *The Bestseller Code. Anatomy of the Blockbuster Novel* (New York: St. Martin's Press).

Ascari, Maurizio (2007). *A Counter-History of Crime Fiction: Supernatural, Gothic, Sensational* (London: Palgrave/Macmillan).

Baetens, Jan (2011). 'World Literature and Popular Literature: Toward a Wordless Literature?', in Theo D'haen, David Damrosch, and Djelal Kadir (eds), *The Routledge Companion to World Literature* (London/New York: Routledge), 336–44.

Barthes, Roland (1975). *The Pleasure of the Text*. Trans. Richard Miller (New York: Hill and Wang).

Bayard, Pierre (2000). *Who Killed Roger Ackroyd?* Trans. Carol Cosman (New York: The New Press).

— (2002). *Enquête sur Hamlet. Le dialogue de sourds* (Paris: Minuit).

— (2009). *Sherlock Holmes Was Wrong*. Trans. Charlotte Mandell (New York: Bloomsbury).

Bergman, Kerstin (2014). *Swedish Crime Fiction: The Making of Nordic Noir* (Milan: Mimesis).

Boltanski, Luc (2014). *Mysteries and Conspiracies. Detective Stories, Spy Novels and the Making of Modern Societies* (Cambridge: Polity).

Bourdieu, Pierre (1996). *The Rules of Art. Genesis and Structure of the Literary Field* (Stanford: Stanford University Press).

Bradford, Richard (2015). *Crime Fiction. A Very Short Introduction* (Oxford: Oxford University Press).

Braham, Persephone (2004). *Crimes against the State, Crimes against Persons: Detective Fiction in Cuba and Mexico* (Minneapolis, MN: University of Minnesota Press).

Carey, John (1992). *The Intellectuals and the Masses. Pride and Prejudice Among the Literary Intelligentsia, 1880–1939* (London: Faber and Faber).

Chandler, Raymond (1944). 'The Simple Art of Murder'. *The Atlantic Monthly* 174: 53–59.

Clark, Robert (2009). '1841: "The Murders in the Rue Morgue"', in Greil Marcus and Werner Sollors (eds), *A New Literary History of America* (Cambridge, MA: The Belknap Press of Harvard University Press), 254–59.

Gelder, Ken (2004). *Popular Fiction. The Logics and Practices of a Literary Field* (Milton Park, Abingdon: Routledge).

Gorrara, Claire (ed.) (2009). *French Crime Fiction* (Cardiff: University of Wales Press).

Goulet, Andrea (2016). *Legacies of the Rue Morgue: Science, Space, and Crime Fiction in France* (Philadelphia: University of Pennsylvania Press).

Greenblatt, Stephen (ed.) (2010). *Cultural Mobility: A Manifesto* (Cambridge: Cambridge University Press).

Guillén, Claudio (1993). *The Challenge of Comparative Literature*. Trans. Cola Franzen (Cambridge, MA: Harvard University Press).

Gulddal, Jesper (2016). 'Clueless. Genre, Realism and Narrative Form in Ed McBain's Early 87th Precinct Novels', *Clues: A Journal of Detection* 34.2: 54–62.

Hall, Katharina (ed.) (2016). *Crime Fiction in German: Der Krimi* (Cardiff: University of Wales Press).

Horsley, Lee (2005). *Twentieth-Century Crime Fiction* (Oxford: Oxford University Press).

Kermode, Frank (1967). *The Sense of an Ending. Studies in the Theory of Fiction* (Oxford: Oxford University Press).

King, Stewart (2014). 'Crime Fiction as World Literature', *Clues: A Journal of Detection* 32.2: 8–19.

King, Stewart and Alice Whitmore (2016). 'National Allegories Born(e) in Translation: The Catalan Case', *The Translator* 22.2: 144–56.

Knight, Stephen (1997). *Continent of Mystery: A Thematic History of Australian Crime Fiction* (Melbourne: Melbourne University Press).

— (2015). *Secrets of Crime Fiction Classics: Detecting the Delights of 21 Enduring Stories* (Jefferson, NC: McFarland).

Knox, Ronald (1929). 'Ten Commandments for Detective Stories', in Henry Harrington and Ronald Knox (eds), *Best Detective Stories of the Year 1928* (London: Faber and Faber).

McCracken, Scott (1998). *Pulp: Reading Popular Fiction* (Manchester: Manchester University Press).

Makinen, Merja (2006). *Agatha Christie: Investigating Femininity* (London and New York: Palgrave Macmillan).

Mallia, Joseph (1988). 'Interview with Paul Auster'. *BOMB Magazine* 23: 24–27.

Milner, Andrew (2012). *Locating Science Fiction* (Liverpool: Liverpool University Press).

Moretti, Franco (2013). *Distant Reading* (London: Verso).

Nilsson, Louise, David Damrosch and Theo D'haen (eds) (2017). *Crime Fiction as World Literature* (New York: Bloomsbury).

Ortega y Gasset, José (1993) [1930]. *The Revolt of the Masses* (London and New York: W.W. Norton).

Pepper, Andrew (2000). *The Contemporary American Crime Novel: Race, Ethnicity, Gender, Class* (Edinburgh: Edinburgh University Press).

— (2016). *Unwilling Executioner. Crime Fiction and the State* (Oxford: Oxford University Press).

Pepper, Andrew, and David Schmid (eds) (2016). *Globalization and the State in Contemporary Crime Fiction* (London: Palgrave Macmillan).

Pezzotti, Barbara (2014). *Politics and Society in Italian Crime Fiction: An Historical Overview* (Jefferson, NC: McFarland).

Plain, Gill (2001). *Twentieth-Century Crime Fiction: Gender, Sexuality and the Body* (Edinburgh: Edinburgh University Press).

Poe, Edgar Allan (1986) [1841]. 'The Murders in the Rue Morgue', in *The Fall of the House of Usher and Other Writings* (London: Penguin), 189–224.

Priestman, Martin (ed.) (2003). *The Cambridge Companion to Crime Fiction* (Cambridge: Cambridge University Press).

Rolls, Alistair, Clara Sitbon and Marie-Laure Vuaille-Barcan (2018). *Origins and Legacies of Marcel Duhamel's Série Noire* (Leiden and Boston: Rodopi/Brill).

Rzepka, Charles J. and Lee Horsley (eds) (2010). *A Companion to Crime Fiction* (Chichester and Maldon, MA: Wiley-Blackwell).

Seaman, Amanda C. (2004). *Bodies of Evidence: Women, Society and Detective Fiction in 1990s Japan* (Honolulu: University of Hawai'i Press).

Siddique, Haroon (2015). 'How to Spot Whodunit: Academics Crack Agatha Christie's Code'. *Guardian* 3 August 2015.

Stougaard-Nielsen, Jakob (2017). *Scandinavian Crime Fiction* (London and New York: Bloomsbury).

Sulis, Gigliola (2017). 'Introduction: Crime Fiction: A Polymorphic Genre and the Challenge of Globality'. *The Australian Journal of Crime Fiction* 3.1.

Todorov, Tzvetan (1977). 'The Typology of Detective Fiction', in *The Poetics of Prose*. Trans. Richard Howard (Oxford: Basil Blackwell), 42–52.

Van Dine, S.S. (1947) [1928]. 'Twenty Rules for Writing Detective Stories', in Howard Haycraft (ed.), *The Art of the Mystery Story* (New York: The Universal Library), 189–93.

Vidocq, Eugène François (1828). *Mémoires de Vidocq, chef de la police de Sûreté, jusqu'en 1827* (Paris: Tenon).

Vosburg, Nancy (ed.) (2011). *Iberian Crime Fiction* (Cardiff: University of Wales Press).

Walkowitz, Rebecca L. (2015). *Born Translated: The Contemporary Novel in an Age of World Literature* (New York: Columbia University Press).

Warwick, Ben (prod. and dir.) (2005). *Agatha Christie Code* (3DD production: ITV1).

PART I

Mobility of Meaning

CHAPTER ONE

Behind the Locked Door

Leblanc, Leroux and the Anxieties of the Belle Époque

Jean Fornasiero and John West-Sooby,
University of Adelaide

Formula-driven works of crime fiction, and particularly the mystery novel, have often been cast as those versions of the genre that are the least adaptable to new forms of enquiry, or the least permeable to the influence of the major issues of their day. This judgement was certainly given some authority by the rules of the mystery novel that were drafted by practitioners like S.S. Van Dine (1928) and by the writers whose popular success was built upon the respect of the traditions of the genre. However, rules are meant to be broken, especially in the criminal sphere (Dubois 1992: 157), and nowhere is this more apparent than in the forms of the genre that were practised in France by Maurice Leblanc and Gaston Leroux. Far from being narrowly driven by the resolution of enigmas, their novels present multiple layers of meaning that work to undermine the sense of closure they appear to promise. Theirs is a dynamic and shifting world that is much more in tune with the complexities of real-life concerns than might first be suspected. The reasons both writers opened their works, if not overtly to social or political commentary, at least to the tensions and undercurrents of contemporary life, can be attributed to the momentous times in which they exercised their craft. This was the France of the dawn of the twentieth century, a period of stark contrasts, characterized by boundless energy and dark despair.

For those who had lived through the Great War, the decades that immediately preceded it took on retrospectively the aura of a Golden Age. The belle époque, as this period was nostalgically named, was indeed a time of prosperity and progress. Thanks to the extended peace that followed the Franco–Prussian War (1870–71), Europe's economy eventually recovered from the depression of the final decades of the nineteenth century, and by the middle of the 1890s a new-found confidence began to emerge. This was fuelled by the technological marvels of the time: moving pictures, flying machines, motor cars, underground rail transport and the mastery of electricity. In France, republican values were being enshrined through legislation: the adoption of the *Marseillaise* as national anthem in 1879 and the nomination of 14 July as France's national day in 1880 were important symbolic decisions, but the fabric of society would be irrevocably altered by other acts of parliament such as Jules Ferry's bills on education and the secularization of state schools. Social progress was evident in all sections of society, but above all among the urban middle classes, one of the enduring images of the belle époque being that of well-to-do Parisians parading elegantly down the boulevards of the capital. This sense of confidence and prosperity was also reinforced by France's colonial empire, which was then at its zenith. Nothing captures better this triumphalism and positivist spirit than the Expositions universelles held in Paris in 1889 and 1900.

There was nonetheless a more sombre side to the period, which prolonged the *fin de siècle* anxieties and divisions of the late nineteenth century. The Boulanger Affair, for example, or the Panama Scandal, not to mention the Dreyfus Affair, which exposed the virulent strain of xenophobia and anti-Semitism that infected all sections of society and the political classes. Various radical political groups emerged, sometimes in response to these affairs; the left-wing anti-parliamentary movement, which developed in reaction to the Panama Scandal, is one such example. The 1890s also saw the rise of anarchism, with bombs being planted across Paris, including the National Assembly. The citizens of the nation's capital were further unsettled by the lurid descriptions in the popular press of the violent acts perpetrated by the city's petty criminals and delinquents, whose menace was all the more chilling because of the name by which the newspapers designated them: the *Apaches*. Behind the glittering façade, dark forces were working to unsettle and destabilize French society and its institutions.

It is in this context that two of France's most popular and enduring authors of crime fiction rose to prominence: Maurice Leblanc, whose

Arsène Lupin character first appeared in 1905, and Gaston Leroux, whose first novel, *Le Mystère de la chambre jaune* (The Mystery of the Yellow Bedroom),[1] was published in 1907. On one level, these works can be read as stylish and playful manifestations of the developing crime genre: Leblanc's gentleman thief is a debonair figure whose use of disguise and mechanical devices both confounds the police and amuses the 'gallery'; Leroux's novels are similarly ludic in nature and have a decidedly whimsical element. In both cases readers are presented with 'classic' locked-room mysteries and intriguing enigmas whose resolution appears to provide closure. The novels of Leblanc and Leroux might thus be seen as entertaining and unthreatening stories entirely in keeping with the apparently carefree ambiance of the period. As Jean-Paul Colin reminds us, however, French crime novels of the pre-war period are not objects of 'pure entertainment' or 'gratuitous escapism': they function within a set of socio-cultural and ideological forces which they both reflect and, in some ways, inflect (1999: 27). In this re-examination of the novels of Leblanc and Leroux, we do not propose that these authors necessarily set out with the deliberate and conscious aim of portraying the socio-political complexities of their time; what we hope to show is that these witty and exuberant narratives are not just a source of escapist fun, but that they exhibit destabilizing features which undermine the sense of finality they appear to provide, thereby producing a malaise that resonates with the sombre undercurrents which traverse the belle époque.

Constructing and Deconstructing Meaning: The Case of Arsène Lupin

Maurice Leblanc's Arsène Lupin, whose first adventure was published in the magazine *Je sais tout* in 1905 under the title 'L'Arrestation d'Arsène Lupin' (The Arrest of Arsène Lupin), was not the first manifestation of the gentleman thief in literature. His cross-Channel contemporary, E.W. Hornung's Raffles, was first introduced in 1899. In France, as Yves Olivier-Martin notes (1979), we can find antecedents as far back as L.T. Gilbert's 1824 novel *Fortune et revers, ou l'Aventurier portugais* (Good Fortune and Setbacks, or the Portuguese Adventurer), which featured a protagonist by the name of don Coriza who displayed many

---

1 *Chambre* is often translated as 'room', but the contents of the novel make it clear that the action takes place in a bedroom and that this site is of prime importance in both physical and metaphorical terms.

of the characteristics that Arsène Lupin would later exemplify. It might nevertheless be argued that the figure of the gentleman thief, whose anarchical tendencies are reassuringly offset by his debonair ways and often chivalrous intentions, was tailor-made to appeal to a belle époque society preoccupied with elegance (Thiesse 1985: 36) and 'beset by deliquescence' (Deleuse 1991: 50).[2]

The rise to popularity of the gentleman thief also corresponds to a distinct shift in literary preoccupations with criminality. As Nelly Wolf notes, novels focusing on crime in the second half of the nineteenth century generally associated delinquency and criminality with poverty and social disadvantage. The figure of the *misérable*, which so inspired the Romantics, was as much a victim of society as a threat to it. Wolf argues, however, that at the turn of the twentieth century a significant change took place in terms of the representation of the felon: the link between criminality and poverty became less compelling as attention gradually turned to the connection between crime and various forms of social and political protest, fuelled notably by the rise of anarchism and other militant movements (1989: 11). A space thus opened up for a new type of wrongdoer whose transgressions were in some sense legitimized by social and political motivations. In the case of the gentleman thief, this process was taken one step further, his misdemeanours being presented not only as legitimate but as worthy in some way of our approval. This is a fundamentally destabilizing development, for it blurs previously accepted lines between good and evil and undermines our reading of crime fiction as a confrontation between the criminal as fomenter of social disruption and the detective or sleuth as protector/ restorer of social order.

In the belle époque novels of Leblanc, this ambivalence plays out in a variety of ways, beginning with the duality inherent in Arsène Lupin's status as both a criminal and a gentleman, that is to say as someone who transgresses social conventions while at the same time appearing to uphold them. This might be harmless enough if, as can be the case with Lupin, his misdemeanours serve a higher purpose and ultimately redress injustices that the police and the law seem incapable of correcting. But to what extent is Arsène Lupin in fact a gentleman thief? To put it simply, is his behaviour always 'gentlemanly' and, conversely, are his energies primarily devoted to theft and its associated misdeeds? Any ambiguity

---

2 All translations from French sources, including the novels themselves, are our own.

in either of these two defining features would destabilize his status, thereby undermining the already unsettling notion that transgression can be acceptable if it works to re-establish order – and is performed with panache.

With respect to Arsène Lupin's status as a gentleman, it is important to note that, despite his mixed origins – his mother was a fallen aristocrat and his father a commoner – he moves almost exclusively in well-to-do circles in which he is perfectly at ease, his adventures taking place either in the châteaux of his native Normandy or in the wealthy quarters of Paris and its surrounds. This is not to say that he looms as a purely benign presence. On the contrary, he has a cruel and even sadistic streak that emerges when under pressure. Take, for example, the pleasure he derives from taunting his young adversary, Isidore Beautrelet, in *L'Aiguille creuse* (The Hollow Needle), when he reveals the trick he has played by masquerading as the academician Massiban. There is a strong degree of narcissism in his sense of triumph, and much cruelty in his promise to make Beautrelet cry. Lupin even goes so far as to shake the young student 'in order to enforce his will upon him' (Leblanc 1964: 202–03). When his indomitable will encounters resistance, he often explodes into acts of great physical violence that are anything but gentlemanly – as, for example, when he breaks the chains of his handcuffs by stretching his wrists apart, the veins in his forehead swelling, in *Arsène Lupin contre Herlock Sholmès* (Arsène Lupin Versus Herlock Sholmès) (Leblanc 1963: 169), or when he suddenly and effortlessly breaks a steel ruler in half during an earlier violent confrontation with Beautrelet in *L'Aiguille creuse* (Leblanc 1964: 115). These eruptions of violence reveal a primal brute force in which he takes some pride: as he says in reproach to Beautrelet, 'you don't have the primitive impulse' (Leblanc 1964: 202). We should not forget either that, in addition to his glamorous accomplices, such as the mysterious 'dame blonde', Arsène Lupin has a close association with a number of very shadowy figures who serve as his henchmen on occasions when an assertive physical presence is required – a reminder for contemporary readers of the violent threat posed by certain marginal elements of the lower classes. There is a darkness in Arsène Lupin's character that works in counterpoint to his genteel and elegant appearance, and that harks back to associations of crime and lowly origins.

Can we say, as a counter to this, that Arsène Lupin's motivations and the causes he defends are always noble and worthy of a gentleman, and that this somehow serves to redeem him? Are his transgressions always 'committed in the name of establishing a new and more perfect order', as Emma Bielecki has claimed (2014: 60)? There can be no doubt that, as a result of his machinations, many mysteries are elucidated and (other) criminals punished. He also intervenes on occasion with chivalrous intentions, as in the final episode of *Arsène Lupin contre Herlock Sholmès*, 'La Lampe juive' ('The Jewish Lamp'). Here, he is pitted against the dogged Sholmès whose indiscretion in revealing the solution to the enigma puts an end to an otherwise happy marriage, foiling the attempts of Lupin, who has already unlocked the secret to the mystery, to keep the minor transgression of Mme d'Imblevalle a secret (Leblanc 1963: 185–253). The gentleman thief in this case attempted to preserve conjugal harmony, whereas England's star detective is responsible for destroying it. Arsène Lupin's status as the French people's 'voleur national' ('national thief') (Leblanc 1963: 15) is due in part to such displays of elegance and finesse. It is reinforced by the fact that his personal interests at various times are congruent with those of the nation. In the novel *813*, for example, his pursuit of the secret papers in Robert Castleback's possession is primarily motivated by his desire to prevent Castleback from becoming a ruling force in Europe and to ensure the papers do not fall into German hands. Likewise, in *L'Aiguille creuse*, there is a sense in which, as the custodian of a treasure passed down from Louis XIV, he is presented as the guardian of the nation's heritage. And his theft of the desk in 'Le Numéro 514 – Série 23' ('Lottery Ticket No. 514'), the first episode in *Arsène Lupin contre Herlock Sholmès*, can similarly be construed as a gesture of national significance, as it had been given to Marie Walewska by Napoleon himself.

Yet even in these cases, Lupin is always pursuing his own agenda. The fact that he is said to be a descendant of Louis XIV is surely behind his efforts to reconstitute the king's treasure in *L'Aiguille creuse*, a treasure which he has hoarded away for his own enjoyment. His personal need to disculpate himself of the murders of Castleback, his secretary and a hotel porter similarly puts into perspective the altruism of his quest for Castleback's papers in *813*. And no amount of narrative manipulation can hide the fact that he has stolen someone's rightful property in 'Le Numéro 514 – Série 23'. More generally, there is a strongly narcissistic element to his constant mystifications, which at times appear to have no other purpose than to allow him to display his talents. Even when pursuing causes that ultimately prove to be worthy, Lupin's methods can be profoundly unjust; and yet, the narratorial perspective is almost always sympathetic to him. This narrative sleight of hand serves to blur our vision of what is right and wrong. Anyone who has the misfortune of getting in his way, for example, is generally portrayed in highly negative terms, even if they are not guilty of any wrong-doing other than presenting an obstacle to Lupin's plans. In one example, the unfortunate Monsieur Gerbois, in 'Le Numéro 514 – Série 23', is a simple mathematics teacher from Versailles whose only mistake is to buy for his daughter a second-hand mahogany writing desk that Arsène Lupin had in his sights. In purely objective terms, Gerbois is the innocent victim of a predatory and intimidating criminal. And yet, these events are portrayed in such a way as to elicit our disapproval of his actions and our sympathies for those of the thief. In refusing to sell the desk, and then rejecting Lupin's offer of a compromise regarding the winning lottery ticket it contains, Gerbois comes across as stubborn, avaricious, proprietorial and unreasonable. Although, in the face of Lupin's threats, he subsequently displays these characteristics, the fact remains that he is the victim of a cunning and ruthless criminal.

It is clear from these and other examples that Lupin is frequently involved in acts of larceny. His status as thief is nevertheless constantly undermined. Even though, as Colette Windish notes, his overall objective remains anarchical, or at the very least disrespectful of authority and order – an attitude which, for Windish, reflects the ingrained mistrust of the French people with respect to those in power and their equally entrenched desire to be protected from Evil (2001: 152) – Arsène Lupin spends as much time solving enigmas as he does creating them. Indeed, as the series evolves, his criminal activities diminish and he becomes more and more engaged in detecting crimes, even though he still has to commit the occasional misdemeanour to elucidate them. The rejection of authority remains a constant, but this is offset by the dominant role he plays when he uses his talents and ingenuity to resolve the crimes. In *813*, this transformation finds concrete expression when, under the guise of 'Monsieur Lenormand', he is promoted to the position of Head of the Sûreté – a nod, no doubt, to the real-life trajectory of Vidocq and to Balzac's Vautrin, except that Lupin does not then abandon his true identity or his practice as thief. Maintaining this ambivalent status is essential to his persona, even as his criminal activities diminish with the post-First World War novels.

Finally, the same instability or ambiguity can be identified in the portrayal of the business of detection itself. One of the defining characteristics of the crime novel is the reliance on observation, clues and logic. This scientific approach to detection is prominent in the Lupin saga and is shown to be generally effective; however, it is counter-balanced by a more imaginative and intuitive approach that is considered far superior in the value system encapsulated by the novels. This is in fact an uneven contest, as is made clear by the opposition between Sholmès and Lupin. To quote Emma Bielecki, 'Sholmès relies heavily on a painstaking process of gathering physical evidence to build his cases, in sharp contrast to Lupin, whose detective work is characterized by ingenuity and intuition' (2014: 53). And there is no prize for guessing who solves the enigma first. The meaning we ascribe to the crime genre is typically dependent on the reassurance provided by rational thinking, and the fact that this kind of approach to detection is continually undermined is a sign of the mobility of these novels. There is, indeed, an astonishing admission on the part of the methodical and rational Sholmès that the traditional approach to detective work is inadequate when it comes to solving the mysteries created by Arsène Lupin. When his long-suffering companion Wilson wonders why he is doing so much talking and taking so little action, Sholmès responds: 'Why? [...] because with this Lupin fellow one is working in the dark, randomly, and instead of extracting the truth from precise facts, one must draw it out from one's own brain before then verifying whether it properly fits the facts' (Leblanc 1963: 101). The equally brilliant and clear-thinking sleuth, Beautrelet, comes to exactly the same conclusion in *L'Aiguille creuse*. When the magistrate learns that the young man is cogitating, he responds by reminding him of the method he should be adopting to solve the mystery: 'It's not a question of thinking! One must look into things first, study the facts, look for clues, establish links. It is only after having done this that, through reflection, one puts everything together and discovers the truth' (Leblanc 1964: 69–70). This could be the textbook description of the work of both real-life and fictional detectives. In his response, however, Beautrelet demurs:

> Yes, I know... that's the usual method... the correct one, no doubt. But I have another... I think first, I try above all to come up with a general idea about the case, so to speak. I then imagine a reasonable and logical hypothesis which accords with this general idea. And it is only then that I examine whether the facts fit my hypothesis. (Leblanc 1964: 70)

The similarity between the pronouncements of Beautrelet and Sholmès is striking: both have come to see 'facts' as deceptive when it comes to Lupin and have therefore been forced to adopt a 'top-down' rather than the traditional 'bottom-up' approach. The doubt that is cast here on the reliability of factual evidence clearly undermines one of the most important conventions of crime detection, and in terms of the positivist spirit of the belle époque, it is profoundly unsettling.

Equally unconventional, and unsettling, is the fact that crime and its detection are put on public display in the Lupin novels. Most criminals go to great lengths to maintain secrecy – for obvious reasons. The work of detection likewise relies on discretion. What is unusual in the Arsène Lupin novels, however, is that the battle between criminal and detective is played out in the public arena, through the press. The notion of the 'gallery' thus emerges and in fact becomes a peculiarity of belle époque crime fiction. It is a key element in the Lupin saga, but also plays an important role in Gaston Leroux's Rouletabille series. In the same way that the increased circulation of newspapers gave the belle époque public ready access to stories of crime and its elucidation, so too does the gallery enjoy the spectacle of criminal investigations in the detective novels of the period. Many commentators have noted that the adventures of Arsène Lupin are inherently theatrical (Bielecki 2014: 49; Marill Albérès 1979: 17). His many disguises and personas are of course key elements of this theatricality. The public 'performance' of the ordinarily private work of crime and its detection also contributes significantly to it.

What we have in the Lupin saga, then, is a thief who works to elude detection but also engages regularly in detective work, whose dark and cruel character is at odds with his gentlemanly persona, and whose adventures, which blur the lines between right and wrong, are played out on the public stage and defy the rational and scientific methods which society has come to understand as essential to the resolution of crime. These novels are thus a reflection of the moral ambivalence of the period itself. Far from being a simple 'moment' in the history of French crime fiction, they are the very expression of the uncertainties that lurked beneath the glittering surface of belle époque France.

Gaston Leroux's Rouletabille Series: Meet the Ancestor

If Arsène Lupin's unsettling and risky behaviours capture the ambiance of their time, they can also be seen as a dynamic response to the undercurrent of fear that marked the late nineteenth century and found its expression in *fin de siècle* decadence, during which in France, and in Europe more generally, obsessions and anxieties became a prime feature of literary, medical and scientific discourses alike (Shuttleworth 2018: 178). Unsurprisingly, these anxieties are a strong feature not only of Leblanc's writings, but also of Gaston Leroux's Rouletabille series.

Françoise Gaillard's (1986) study of the fear of the 'ancestor', and the thin divide between the 'civilized' and the 'primitive' or 'animal' self, provides great insight to Lupin's persona and his mission. His own mixed origins dictate his will to survive at all costs; just as he clings to his high social status, he covers up the crimes and peccadillos of his friends to help them to do the same. In this survival of the fittest, he harnesses both his 'civilized' and 'primitive' sides, having no fear of falling across the social divide: his less than gentlemanly behaviour helps him to perfect this balancing act. However, the pride he takes in harnessing his 'primitive impulse' is also an act of defiance: in embracing it, he is refusing to succumb to fears of the irrational. Far from being the passive prey of his worst instincts or of the beast that lurks within him, he renders these impulses useful to him. He is as immune to the irrational fears of his contemporaries as he is to the comfort to be derived from the rational approach to resolving crime and social disorder. Hence his determination to triumph over the rigid methodology espoused by Herlock Sholmès. Through his power to mock and to overcome his detractors he is the bastion against *fin de siècle* malaise – both the irrational fears that inspired it and the rational solutions it engendered.

It is precisely this thread that links Lupin's persona to Rouletabille, an orphan whose exploits as an investigative reporter brought him notoriety, but also pitted him against the establishment, in particular its police force. Although Rouletabille's virginal existence sets him apart from Lupin, as does his day-to-day existence as a paid employee, he has in common with his contemporary supersleuth a form of celebrity which allows him to perform his exploits in the public eye, to the acclaim of the 'gallery'. But beyond these tropes of the ludic and performative crime fiction of the belle époque, Rouletabille's adventures involve such a determined pursuit of the primitive ancestor as to distract the reader entirely from the mechanics of crime-solving that ostensibly drive the narrative. Despite the distancing effects of humour and irony, Leroux creates a scenario in which he, like Zola, 'plunges into the ancestral abyss' while pursuing, through Rouletabille's criminal investigation, a form of enquiry, even an initiatory quest, 'which tracks down its quarry through its scent, its trail, its remains' (Gaillard 1986: 16). And, unsurprisingly, in this search for the 'ancestor' – the beast within, who, in Rouletabille's case is none other than his father – Leroux finishes by casting his narrative into pre-Freudian territory.[3]

3 Freud did not publish the first version of his essay 'Family Romances' until 1908, and the definitive version dates from 1909.

Critics have not failed to identify the oedipal narrative within the first two volumes, *Le Mystère de la chambre jaune* (The Mystery of the Yellow Bedroom) and *Le Parfum de la Dame en noir* (1908, The Perfume of the Lady in Black), in which the complicated genealogy of the Stangerson family is teasingly revealed. Indeed, the complex familial relationships between the protagonists, but also the unravelling of their intertwined social and professional destinies, is what is really at stake in these novels, all the more so since the crime narrative per se implodes as the author knowingly dispenses with most of the rules of the genre.[4] Few critics would disagree that Rouletabille's interests lie in disposing with conventional detecting. By his mocking remarks about crime novels and their obsession with material evidence, Rouletabille 'relegates an entire tradition of detective fiction methodology to antiquated, fictional past' (Ross 2000: 145). Indeed, like Lupin, the young reporter rejects the model of Conan Doyle and relies completely on his own powers of reasoning, thus putting up a spirited 'resistance to the newly dominant paradigm of evidential, observation-based logic' (Goulet 2005: 41).[5]

Rouletabille's chosen methodology is derived from personal experience: raised as an orphan he had made his own way in the world by the sheer force of his brain power. It had served him well, as revealed by his early rise to fame as a journalist. By resolving the 'mystery of the yellow bedroom' and bringing about the downfall of his rival, the famed detective Frédéric Larsan, Rouletabille scores his most notable triumph to date. And yet, since Larsan is revealed to be not only his father, but also the arch-criminal Ballmeyer, the triumph Rouletabille obtains can only be a source of future regret and disorder. Far from reuniting the Stangerson family from which he was excluded at birth, he has hastened its destruction, thus cementing his status as eternal orphan. The subsequent novels in the Stangerson cycle confirm his exile from the comfortable existence to which the childhood reminiscence of his mother, the perfume of the 'Lady in black', had once lured him. The later novels are often seen as works from which the crime genre has been completely evacuated (Deleuze 1991: 51), but there is still a case to

---

4 Dubois sets out these structural defects in order to demonstrate that Leroux has constructed a utopian project rather than a crime investigation (1992: 159–60). While the first two Rouletabille novels produce the positive outcome on which Dubois's conclusion is founded, the same cannot be said for the entire Rouletabille cycle, as Couegnas demonstrates (1981: 125).

5 David Platten (2001) has also made this point in his discussion of Rouletabille's attitude to the science of his day.

be made for their relevance. Since the first two novels already subvert both the detective and 'locked door' paradigms, and since Rouletabille actually continues his criminal investigations throughout the series, albeit in faraway lands, there appears little reason to reject these later works. On the contrary, the narratives of *Les Étranges Noces de Rouletabille* (1914, Rouletabille's Strange Wedding) or *Le Château noir* (1914, The Black Castle) are pertinent to the analysis of Leroux's version of detecting in the belle époque. It is through a greater number of Rouletabille's novels that we can elucidate what Christian Robin (1976) has called the 'real mystery' confronting Rouletabille and determine the nature of the scent that leads him from crime to crime and not to revelation: that heady mix of sex and science so tantalizingly promised and withheld by the 'Lady in black'.

As the daughter and assistant of a famous scientist and future bride of her father's most trusted colleague, on the one hand, and former wife of a criminal and mother of Rouletabille, on the other, Mathilde Stangerson, or the 'Lady in black', occupies several sets of conflicting spaces within the novels, notably the licit and the illicit, the incarnate and the carnate. This latter duality is all the more important in that the object of Professor Stangerson's research is the 'dissociation of matter', while his daughter Mathilde's former husband is the ubiquitous criminal known for his ability to vanish into thin air (Leroux MCJ 1907: 111). Using this metaphor, Leroux quickly establishes that, through Mathilde, the boundaries between spaces have been blurred, with the result that the powers of science have been transferred to an illegitimate claimant, rather than to her fiancé Robert Darzac, the scientific heir designated by the Father. And not just metaphorically, for Mathilde has inadvertently allowed Ballmeyer, her criminal spouse, to come into possession of her father's scientific papers. In this context she becomes the victim of a series of aggressions perpetrated by Ballmeyer. Not simply crimes of passion, these violent acts are also designed to overthrow the scientific order to which she aspires to return by marrying Darzac.

Rouletabille, whose origins also place him on the boundaries of the worlds of science and crime – thus predisposing him to a kind of semantic mobility – must choose whether to restore the scientific hierarchy, to save his mother's life, or to subvert it, by adopting his father's illegitimate claims and allowing Darzac, the true scientific heir, to be eliminated. His chief difficulty comes from the metamorphosis of Ballmeyer into the revered practitioner of scientific investigation, Frédéric Larsan, whose forensic method has led him to designate Darzac as the principal suspect in the crimes against Mathilde. Rouletabille categorically rejects Larsan's seemingly irreproachable science in favour of his own method of logical deduction. In doing so, his science is put to the service of his mother and the restoration of scientific order. Nonetheless, Rouletabille's action does not mean that he has chosen the Stangerson career path.

In his subsequent adventures he remains a solitary figure, with no institutional or domestic attachments. He is no more capable of entering his mother's universe than he is of reuniting with his father – whom he encourages to escape and later to commit suicide. Once Mathilde has married Darzac and stepped back into the scientific space, Rouletabille becomes an international adventurer, like his father. He achieves notoriety, rather than institutional recognition, for his sensational stories of crime and mayhem. Both 'bandit' and 'artist', like Ballmeyer, he lives by his wits while remaining perfectly unmoved by the carnage his acts entail. While he prefers to protect damsels rather than destroy them, he aspires to ubiquity rather than domesticity, as his very name – the wanderer (*roule-ta-bosse*), or even, by wordplay, the wandering brain (*roule-ta-bille*) – would indicate. He remains an outsider, in spite of fame and fortune, for he seems unable to forget how, as a child, he was abandoned, then obliged to make his own way in the world, a victim of his mother's fear and shame. Besides, the community of science is no longer the ordered world over which Stangerson, the patriarch, had once held sway. Not only is it too late for the middle-aged couple formed by Mathilde and Darzac to continue the line, even if they were talented enough to take over the research, but the patriarch himself dies, leaving the scientific world bereft of the philanthropic version of scientific endeavour (Stangerson had sought to leave his inventions in the public domain, for the greater good of society).

A now sterile world, marked by petty rivalries between ageing monomaniacs, can hold no attraction for Rouletabille, for whom intellectual activity is insufficient in itself, being inseparable from physical action and chivalrous gesture. In fact, we are entitled to ask whether Rouletabille's vocation had much to do with science at all. He may well possess an instinctive capacity for reasoning that enabled him to work out Euclid's theorem (Leroux PDN 1908: 213), but, in contrast, he does not know his tables and can only count on his fingers. His father's destiny beckoned him early when he was falsely accused of theft while still at school, but he managed to explain away the false logic of his accusers, and later to exploit his insider knowledge of the criminal mind, not by succumbing to the lure of crime but by becoming a criminal reporter.

His knowledge is committed to the service of his own advancement, his efforts directed at obtaining the respect of which he was deprived as a child. He nonetheless despises the institutions which had once excluded him: academies, courtrooms and royal palaces. Figures of power, from the Chief of the Secret Police, to the Russian Czar, are figures of fun. Even the one respectable scientific figure – Robert Darzac – is only truly admirable when he has been replaced by Ballmeyer in disguise and suddenly appears transformed, 'taller and more handsome' (Leroux PDN 1908: 198). Does Rouletabille even have recourse to scientific method? We quickly come to realize that his methods are as partial as those employed by his father, in that they are largely directed at eliminating a rival or obtaining power over the object of his desire. Where women are concerned '"the good way of reasoning" is no good to him at all' (Leroux CN 1914: 829).

As Rouletabille's trajectory has shown us, there is little to suggest, as Jacques Dubois has done (1992: 170), that he represents a renewal of the class, the profession, or the patriarchal order from which he descends. Instead, Leroux highlights through Rouletabille's career path that it is the press which offers new possibilities for individual advancement. As Rouletabille's 'heroic brain' acquires celebrity, his capacity to control those around him and mock those who resist him increases in direct proportion. However, this positive social victory is precarious, not only because the press gallery before which the struggle for ascendancy is being played out is notoriously fickle, but also because the young reporter must contend with darker forces within himself if he is to avoid the spectacular fall from grace experienced by his own diabolically clever father. In short, Rouletabille must avoid entrapment by the opposite sex, the fatal attraction of the 'perfume of the Lady in black', that very attraction that had brought Ballmeyer to his death.

When Rouletabille is first confronted with the mystery of the yellow bedroom, it rapidly becomes apparent that, through the 'crime' he discovers there, he faces the drama of his own origins. Once Rouletabille sees the 'monstrous back' of Mathilde's would-be assassin in the 'yellow bedroom' and the presence of 'the man bent over her' (Leroux MCJ 1907: 111), he is witness, in the figurative sense, to the sexual act between his parents. As a dutiful son, he is thus bound to liberate Mathilde from this 'latent murder' (Leroux MCJ 1907: 128), liable to recur at any time, with grave consequences for the social order. This is so because Ballmeyer's real claim to criminal status is that he has ravished a young virgin, removed her from the paternal home and corrupted the bloodline.

Mathilde's father tries to protect his domain and his legacy by sleeping in his daughter's bedroom, but the attacks persist. After one such attack has been averted, 'her father took her in his arms, kissed her passionately, seemed to win her back once more' (Leroux MCJ 1907: 128). Ballmeyer later understands that he has lost the struggle for possession to the Father: 'I have been waiting for her for twenty years, and when finally I think she has arrived, her father snatches her away from me!' (Leroux PDN 1908: 332).

And yet, it is not just the will of the Father that is accomplished by the eviction from the ranks of the bourgeoisie of the 'primitive brute' and, with him, sexual anarchy. The daughter too has played a key role in preventing the return of the beast. After first being an accomplice to the 'crime', she then uses all the powers in her arsenal to restore the social order she has disturbed. Thanks to her beauty and the captivating scent exuded by her sexual persona, she has recruited to her cause all the men in her vicinity: Darzac, her sexually deprived fiancé; the cerebral and juvenile Rouletabille; and his dim-witted assistant Sainclair. By initially consenting to, and subsequently withdrawing from, sexual relations, Mathilde becomes the powerful matriarch who has aroused then metaphorically castrated all the males in her entourage, as they become her hapless suitors or unrewarded devotees. Darzac, the eternal fiancé, fares even worse than the others: partially blinded and irremediably weakened by the aggressions of Ballmeyer, he comes to represent a figure of impotent desire, doomed to find the wedding chamber as frustrating as the antechamber.

This representation of woman reappears throughout the Rouletabille series, and much of Rouletabille's art seems to lie in closing Pandora's box before the full horrors of sexual anarchy have been unleashed. In any case, he does not experience those particular horrors on his own account. When he falls in love for the first time, it is to the model of the sterile union of Mathilde and Darzac that he seems to aspire, as he speaks of his desire for 'calm domesticity, with this lady doctor' (Leroux CN 1914: 606). But his adored Ivana had deceived him with her 'scientific commonsense' and kept well hidden her savage nature, her true self as a 'tigress' rather than a 'doctoress' (Leroux CN 1914: 606). She is far more intent on avenging the harm done to her family, and Rouletabille is obliged, like Darzac before him, to help her both to save and destroy the assailant she has married. Although Ivana, like Mathilde, is eventually freed by the death of Gaulow, the spouse-cum-assailant, and her 'strange' and persistently deferred wedding to Rouletabille can take place, the experience of nuptial bliss is fleeting, produces no offspring and is constantly threatened by the presence of would-be candidates for Ivana's favours. In *Le Crime de Rouletabille* (1921, Rouletabille's Crime), Ivana is murdered for her devotion to, and flirtation with, an eminent scientist. While Rouletabille brilliantly defends himself against the murder accusation levelled against him and reveals the assassin as the scientist's jealous wife, it is clear that the combination of sex and science that Rouletabille had first come to know through Mathilde and the mystery of his parents' nuptial chamber is lethal for all who are subjected to it. Through this metaphor, we can also glimpse a society that fears the re-emergence of the primitive impulse and its capacity to destroy the dream of civilization that scientific progress represents. Sainclair, the narrator of *Le Crime de Rouletabille*, is only too aware of the dangers of sexual anarchy and the illusion of happy marriage, speaking of the threat of returning to 'the age of the caveman' or of succumbing to 'the impulse of the beast' (Leroux CR 1921: 178, 198).

For Rouletabille, the loss of his mother and then his wife, in a world where their virtue is under constant attack by powerful men and where marriage is a site of assault rather than protection, has shown him that survival does not lie in embracing that form of patriarchy or its false promise of domesticity. Living his life as a 'supernatural brain' (Leroux MCJ 1907: 121) may well marginalize him in social terms and define him as a thinking machine rather than as a sexual being, but it serves as a weapon against all that threatens to destroy 'civilized' society. Hence his immense popularity with the fictional 'gallery' and with the authentic reading public. Like Lupin, he is a superhero sent to expose the corruption and brutality of the belle époque and to refuse the false lure of scientific progress. His superpowers are derived from his intimate knowledge of, and stalwart resistance to, the beast within. His investigations, focused on the bedroom as the origin of crime, shine a light onto a society whose intellectual and technical prowess is reduced to naught by its repressive structures and murderous patriarchy.

Such conclusions are a far cry from the semantic simplicity and sense of resolution that are often said to characterize the locked-room mystery. The belle époque novels of Leblanc and Leroux stage the same kind of deep-seated fears that troubled society throughout the latter part of the nineteenth century: the threat posed by criminality, of course, but more especially by the anarchical tendencies and darker forces that lurk within us all, which social progress could not fully contain. Not only do these novels undermine the positivist spirit of the time, which they present as illusionary, they also (re)awaken and in many ways celebrate the very human characteristics that scientific progress had promised to quell: instinct, intuition, the 'primitive impulse'. And it is all the more ironic – and unsettling – that this subversion of the authority of science and of 'positive facts' should be played out through crime fiction, which is generally seen to be premised on the reliability of objective and material reality. For a reading public that had not yet rid itself of the anxieties of earlier times, the novels of Leblanc and Leroux were a reminder that there was still much to be feared behind the locked door.

Works Cited

Bielecki, Emma (2014). 'Arsène Lupin: Rewriting History', in Angela Kimyongür and Amy Wigelsworth (eds), *Rewriting Wrongs: Crime Fiction and the Palimpsest* (Newcastle-upon-Tyne: Cambridge Scholars), 47–61.

Colin, Jean-Paul (1999). *La Belle Époque du roman policier français. Aux origines d'un genre romanesque* (Paris: Delachaux and Niestlé).

Couegnas, Daniel (1981). 'Structures et thèmes de l'énigme dans "Les Aventures de Rouletabille"'. *Europe* 626: 113–27.

Deleuse, Robert (1991). *Les Maîtres du roman policier* (Paris: Bordas).

Dubois, Jacques (1992). *Le Roman policier ou la modernité* (Paris: Nathan).

Gaillard, Françoise (1986). 'Histoire de peur'. *Littérature* 64: 13–22.

Goulet, Andrea (2005). 'The Yellow Spot: Ocular Pathology and Empirical Method in Gaston Leroux's *Le Mystère de la chambre jaune*'. *SubStance: A Review of Theory and Literary Criticism* 34.2: 27–44.

Leblanc, Maurice (1963) [1908]. *Arsène Lupin contre Herlock Sholmès* (Paris: Livre de Poche).

— (1964) [1909]. *L'Aiguille creuse* (Paris: Livre de Poche).

— (1990) [1910]. *813* (Paris: Livre de Poche).

Leroux, Gaston (1988–2001). *Les Aventures extraordinaires de Rouletabille, reporter* (Paris: Editions Robert Laffont), 2 vols. Volume 1 includes the following novels:

  Le Mystère de la chambre jaune (cited as MCJ 1907);
  Le Parfum de la Dame en noir (cited as PDN 1908);
  Le Château noir (cited as CN 1914);
  Les Étranges Noces de Rouletabille (cited as ENR 1914).

— (1921). *Le Crime de Rouletabille* (cited as CR 1921). https://beq. ebooksgratuits.com/auteurs/Leroux/Leroux-crime-xpdf.pdf [accessed 15 November 2018].

Marill Albérès, Francine (1979). *Le Dernier des dandies, Arsène Lupin: étude de mythes* (Paris: Nizet).

Olivier-Martin, Yves (1979). 'Esthétique du gentleman-cambrioleur'. *Europe* 604–05: 35–42.

Platten, David (2001). 'Reading-glasses, Guns and Robots: A History of Science in French Crime Fiction'. *French Cultural Studies* 12: 253–70.

Robin, Christian (1976). 'Le "vrai" mystère de la chambre jaune', *Europe* 571–72: 71–91.

Ross, Gregory Thomas (2000). 'Crisis of Authority: Monarchy, Patriarchy and the Nineteenth-century French Detective Novel'. (University of Michigan, PhD dissertation).

Shuttleworth, Sally (2018). 'Fear, Phobia and the Victorian Psyche', in Daniel McCann and Claire McKechnie-Mason (eds), *Fear in the Medical and Literary Imagination, Medieval to Modern. Dreadful Passions* (London: Palgrave Macmillan), 177–202.

Thiesse, Anne-Marie (1985). 'Les Infortunes littéraires. Carrières des romanciers populaires à la Belle Époque'. *Actes de la recherche en sciences sociales* 60.1: 31–46.

Van Dine, S.S. (1928). 'Twenty Rules for Writing Detective Stories.' *The American Magazine* 106.3: 129–31.

Windish, Colette J. (2001). 'Arsène Lupin: une certaine idée de la France?' *French Cultural Studies* 12.35: 149–60.

Wolf, Nelly (1989). 'Le Voleur évalué', in Yves Reuter (ed.), *Le Roman policier et ses personnages* (Paris: Presses Universitaires de Vincennes), 11–24.

CHAPTER TWO

Moving Fergus Hume's *The Mystery of a Hansom Cab* and Breaking the Frame of Poe's 'The Murders in the Rue Morgue'

Alistair Rolls, University of Newcastle, Australia

In 2015 Australian crime fiction scholarship witnessed a double event. Two books, Stephen Knight's *Secrets of Crime Fiction Classics* and Lucy Sussex's *Blockbuster! Fergus Hume and the Mystery of a Hansom Cab*, were published with a common double motive: both wanted to give new voice to lesser-known, almost forgotten and, in some cases, underrated crime novels; and as a secondary aim, both aspired to harness this multiplicity of under-heard textual voices in order to drown out, or at least to Babelize, the dominant discourse of crime fiction's nineteenth-century origins, according to which the genre emerged in its recognizably modern form directly out of Edgar Allan Poe's self-styled tales of ratiocination, beginning with 'The Murders in the Rue Morgue'. Knight (2015: 4) is at pains to relegate Poe to a place among the later pioneers and, to this end, privileges the important early roles of both French and American authors, including Eugène Vidocq, William Godwin and Charles Brockden Brown; for her part, Lucy Sussex, in a passage redolent of Maurizio Ascari's 'refusal of any monogenetic account of the origin of literary genres' (2007: 8), cites individual pioneers but places her emphasis on a rich literary mix:

> Crime fiction has a creation myth: that it began with Poe, an immaculate genre conception with his 1841 short story 'The Murders in the Rue Morgue'. Mythic indeed: crime fiction's origins in the late eighteenth and early nineteenth century were more polygenetic, with DNA coming from various

sources, from legal reform to the development of policing and forensics. It arose from a stew of genres, where different forms of writing met and mingled promiscuously. (2015: 76)

At the heart of this myth of crime fiction's immaculate conception is the monolithic status of Poe's work itself. Against the Babelian promiscuity put forward by Sussex, Poe's tales of ratiocination seem to have spoken with one voice; indeed, the very term 'tales of ratiocination', despite the plural of the word 'tales', has come to embody the kind of univocity against which the Yale School of deconstruction simultaneously erected and pulled down its own (ivory *and* iconoclastic) Babelian towers (I am thinking especially here of Jacques Derrida's 'Des Tours de Babel' [cf. Derrida 1985: 209–48]). Rather than a receptacle or transmitter of diversity and miscegenation, Poe continues to be the rock on, and against, which crime fiction has grown up, reached out and become many. If we are to hear the voices of *The Mystery of a Hansom Cab* (1886), we shall need to balance out what might be considered an armchair analysis, 'distinctly distanced from the texts themselves' (Knight 2015: 3), with a more hands-on reading, one unobscured by the weight of received wisdom.

The discussion of *The Mystery of a Hansom Cab* that follows seeks to engage more closely with Poe's textual influence, focusing on, and between, the lines of Hume's novel, below the superficial mentions of its predecessor. To the transparent meanings of Poe and his texts (forefather of the armchair detective, inventor of the genre, and so on) will be preferred those that are to be furnished by the reader. Mobility of meaning here, therefore, is predicated on a mobile reading praxis. The direct references to Poe that dot the text (Mrs Sampson's 'Poe-like appreciation' of 'charnel-house horrors' and a reference to 'Poe's weird poems' with their haunted houses [Hume 2006: 66 and 210, respectively]) will be considered too superficial, too easy to spot, but by the same token also too easy to dismiss. Neither transparently meaningful clues, nor simple red herrings, clearly signposted intertextual references of this type – if not double agents as such – have double agency: on the one hand, they suggest the influence of another author, in this case Poe, or a hypotext (here Poe's poems are preferred to 'The Murders in the Rue Morgue'); on the other hand, they function fetishistically, symbolizing for readers what they know unquestioningly about the hypotext itself, which is to say the univocal or metaphysical text, while simultaneously disavowing a more extensive analysis of the dismembered hypotextual body. To spot such references is, to use Dupin's own critique of the Prefect of Paris, cunning, but only cunning (Poe 1986: 224); a profound intertextual reading has to move in closer and read between the texts, reading the body of the Other in place of the present text, and ultimately rereading the text, analyzing the way that it eschews self-coincidence. If this sounds like the way clues work in crime fiction, the simile is intended. By dropping Poe's name, Hume is not simply aligning himself with a literary tradition; rather, he is signalling the duplicity, the plurality, of his textual truth, and at the same time he is couching his clue as one of many potential intertextual lines of flight (we may think of Gaboriau, but also of Dickens, whose Mrs Harris rears her head [2006: 210]).

Let us begin our reading of Hume's text at the beginning, with its setting. As Simon Caterson records, '[t]he setting for the murder was inspired by a late-night journey taken in a hansom cab, a horse-drawn two-wheeled cabriolet for two passengers with the driver mounted behind'; he notes further that 'Hume realised that this vehicle was perfectly designed for murder, since the crime could be concealed from the driver, the only potential witness' (Hume 2006: vi–vii). The two points raised here – those of movement and concealment – are easily construed as the most striking features of the novel. And importantly, they are discussed literally. This appears logical enough, and it fits with Stephen Greenblatt's manifesto for cultural mobility, according to which any attempt to 'understand the metaphorical movements' between, for example, 'exteriority and interiority', must be secondary; for, and he is emphatic on this point, *'mobility must be taken in a highly literal sense'* (2010: 250, emphasis in the original). In textual terms, however, the fatal journey, the text of literal mobility, is completed in the first four pages of the novel; only a few lines are devoted to the trip itself, and none of those highlights the specific qualities of the hansom cab. Furthermore, neither victim nor murderer are described as being concealed from the cab driver; instead, not only does the driver see the victim, who is being propped up by the man who hails the cab, but he even gets down from his cab and helps him get in. The driver then turns around in order to 'remount his driving-seat', whereupon he sees a man dressed in the same way as the man who first hailed him, but who had left before he got down from his cab (Hume 2006: 3). The driver assumes the man to be the same person, thinking that he has changed his mind and has returned to accompany his friend home. In other words, a great show is made of revealing the victim, and the criminal, too, reveals himself, in order, we later learn, to make sure that the driver conflates the two men dressed in light coats as one single assassin. And there is much movement as well, but almost none of it is *of* or *in* the hansom cab; rather, the movement is to and from, and up and down, but always *around* the cab, which remains throughout this important initial phase quite stationary. Later, the cab stops twice – first to let out the man in the light coat, who again draws great attention to himself by talking to the driver, and second when the driver again gets down to open the cab door in order to find out where to take his fare. Clearly, for a supposedly mobile, secluded crime scene, the hansom cab struggles to move but is, in terms of ingress and egress, a hive of activity. The mystery of the hansom cab is from the outset all about movement, and literal movement at that, but so openly is it treated (and displaced) that it is difficult not to dismiss it as a red herring. As with suspects, the most literal of movements serve here to screen the metaphorical.

The first chapter, in which the movement of Hume's hansom cab is completed, is further delimited by a framing device, which, like the cab, simultaneously contains and fails to contain the mystery. On the opening page of the novel we read: 'Truth is said to be stranger than fiction, and certainly the extraordinary murder which took place in Melbourne on Thursday night, or rather Friday morning, goes a long way towards verifying this saying' (Hume 2006: 1). The chapter closes five pages later with the following:

> According to James Payne, the well-known novelist, fact is sometimes in the habit of poaching on the domain of fiction, and, curiously enough, this case is a proof of the truth of his saying. In one of Du Boisgobey's stories, entitled 'An Omnibus Mystery', a murder closely resembling this tragedy takes place in an omnibus, but we question if even that author would have been daring enough to have written about a crime being committed in such an unlikely place as a hansom cab. (Hume 2006: 6)

At either end of this opening chapter, then, the twin poles of reality and fiction are mobilized. In the first instance, reality ('truth', Hume calls it at this point) leaves fiction in its wake, but at the same time the essential value that is 'Truth' finds itself debased, prosaicized through comparison to a vulgar criminal act. In this way, extraordinariness appeals to the bringing into existence of an abstract concept. In the second instance, fact is guilty of 'poaching' from fiction, which suggests the opposite, upward movement – an aspiration of an everyday event towards the ethereal realm of the poetic, the literary. While Fortuné du Boisgobey may have been unable to compete with the strangeness of this real event, it is equally clear that fact is here again seeking the endorsement of fictional standards. Rather than a clear unidirectional movement, what is set up here is a double movement, which traces the comings and goings of the hansom *cabs*, as opposed to the single cab of the novel's title, between Melbourne and St Kilda. Intertextually, Hume's text draws here on Dupin's paradox of ratiocination, which, far from being a model of pure armchair reasoning, brings together under tension the twin poles of abstract thought and a visceral engagement with the scene of the crime. In terms of a poetics of detective fiction, the model recalls the oxymoronic prose poetry of Charles Baudelaire, Poe's French translator, which, unlike Poe's overly objective Prefect, 'has neither head nor tail, since, on the contrary, everything in it is both head and tail, alternately and reciprocally' (Baudelaire 1970: ix). If Poe can be said to be the inventor of modern crime fiction, I should argue that it is as a result of this paradox, which speaks to textuality as much as it does to investigation. For it is on this resistance to settling, this continuous double movement, that crime fiction is systematically predicated, which is to say, the insistent refusal on the part of crime novels to recognize themselves as such. Indeed, it is an accepted strategy for crime novels, typically received by the reader as a comic device, to oppose the reality of their own narrative to the extraordinary plot devices of the genre.[1] In short, crime fiction always establishes itself as other than it is.

In the framework of this paradox, the truth that is said (by novelists, like James Payn, it might be added)[2] must be called into question. For if the truth of the crime fiction text is stranger than fiction while being, nonetheless and at the same time, fiction, then the truths that it presents must necessarily be fictions, and quite reflexively so. This is perhaps the meta-textual clue, or the clue to the text's reflexivity, announced, but also disavowed under the wheels of passing cabs, by the final line of

---

1 *The Mystery of a Hansom Cab* makes liberal use of this device: Gorby dismisses love as a motive, noting that 'men in love don't go to such lengths in real life – they do in novels and plays, but I've never seen it occurring in my experience' (Hume 2006: 17), although he admits later that 'coincidences happen in real life as well as in novels' (28); Fitzgerald comments that murder in a cab is '[a] romance in real life' (57); and later, in an echo of the *Argus*, Calton remarks to Kilsip that 'truth is stranger than fiction' (231).

2 Knight and Sussex both detail Hume's misspellings. In light of the wilful contraposing of reality and fiction in this passage, the misspelling of Payn's name may be considered significant.

the opening chapter: 'Here is a great chance for some of our detectives to render themselves famous, and we feel sure that they will do their utmost to trace the author of this cowardly and daring murder' (Hume 2006: 6–7). The detectives in question are, it is natural to assume, those operating in Melbourne, because it is from the Melbourne-based *Argus* that the article that we are reading is purportedly sourced. And of course, the presentation of the case in the form of a newspaper article gives credence to the fictional by giving it the weight of fact (via the name of a real newspaper). But it also, for this is a commonly used ploy in fiction, functions as a self-parody and places us doubly as readers, that is, as readers reading what the *Argus*'s readers read – readers *en abyme*, then, or readers' doubles, double-readers. Thus, we too must recognize ourselves as the detectives summoned by the text, whose truths are to be traced, in both senses of the term: not only as facts to be read but also as fictions to be written.

In terms of the investigative narrative that follows, this initial chapter establishes a hermeneutics of self-alterity (crime fiction is/is not reality, and truth is/is not fiction) powerful enough for us to doubt from the outset whether the man in the light coat is indeed one man. The whole narrative turns around doubles: detective Gorby's case against Brian Fitzgerald is superseded by detective Kilsip's case against Roger Moreland, which, in turn, finds itself, once Brian is cleared of suspicion, opposed to the lawyer Calton's case against Mark Frettlby.[3] All this is predicated on that opening dyad of the man in the light coat who walks away and the one in the light coat who returns and gets into the hansom cab. Are they really two? In that case Brian Fitzgerald is justifiably acquitted. Or does Brian do, to borrow a phrase from Calton, 'what the fox often does' and 'double' (Hume 2006: 49)? If this is the case, then he is in fact guilty. And yet, it is not at all clear that the question is simply 'one or two men in light coats?', for the *Argus*, too, doubles its information: the 'additional evidence' reported in its issue of the Monday following the crime tells of a second (or double) hansom cab, which is hailed by 'a gentleman in a light coat' on St Kilda Road around the same time as the first cabman deposes his man in a light coat. Despite continual reminders that light coats are not uncommon (and are worn, we know, by Fitzgerald, by Frettlby and by the victim

3 It is noteworthy that Roger Moreland, who is (pen)ultimately unveiled as the guilty party, shares the same initials as Frettlby's first of two wives, Rosanna Moore, which makes him her double, or masculine alter ego.

Whyte, whose own coat is picked up by Moreland), the implication that the two travellers are one and the same man goes unchallenged in the text. In fact, only a small step is required for the fiction-poaching detective-reader to trace this evidence in reverse and to consider it proof not that this is the same man that alighted from the first hansom cab in St Kilda, but that it is instead a third man in a light coat: three light coats for three suspects, each championed by his own detective in the text. While at some point at least one man in a light coat is transported by a hansom cab, that is, at least one man in a light coat is the object of mobility *in the literal sense,* the man in the light coat is also mobilized *metaphorically.* And in the framework of the manifesto of crime fiction mobility proposed in this volume, mobility of meaning is metaphorical first, and literal second; all suspects must at least be considered to be virtual villains, and, detective criticism, in light of the pioneering work of Pierre Bayard,[4] can (and even *should* where possible) actualize new solutions, debunking fictional truths as, well, fiction.

Finally, the introduction's paradoxical framing device serves the twin, but contradictory, objectives of celebrating *The Mystery of a Hansom Cab*'s literary credentials (a novel that even the celebrated Fortuné du Boisgobey could not have written) while using the *Argus* newspaper to situate this fiction in the everyday experience of the Melbourne reading public. In this way, the possibilities of intertextual detective work are on the one hand enumerated as so many potential leads and, on the other, dismissed as just so much (inferior) fiction. One of the results is that the reference to 'The Murders in the Rue Morgue' is lost in the crowd of Gaboriau, Payn and others. And yet, quite famously, Dupin's investigation, like those of Gorby, Kilsip and Calton, begins with newspaper reports. Indeed, the extraordinariness of the rue Morgue and hansom cab murders is simultaneously made more commonplace and more extraordinary still by virtue of their both being characterized by this same adjective – 'extraordinary' (Poe 1986: 197; Hume 2006: 1). Furthermore, the framing device of the first chapter functions metonymically to echo a framing of the text at the level of the novel itself, for the twin revelation and concealment of 'The Murders in the Rue Morgue' proleptically signals the conclusion of the investigation in a scenario redolent of Dupin's Paris. In both texts, the

---

4 Bayard develops his notion of *la critique policière* throughout his three major studies (of Agatha Christie's *The Murder of Roger Ackroyd*, William Shakespeare's *Hamlet* and Arthur Conan Doyle's *The Hound of the Baskervilles*) but particularly in *L'Affaire du chien des Baskerville.*

detectives (Dupin and the narrator in Poe's case, Kilsip, Calton, Fitzgerald and Dr Chinston in Hume's) predict and await the arrival of the guilty party in a room that they will close upon him:

> At this moment we heard a step upon the stairs. [...] The front door of the house had been left open, and the visitor had entered, without ringing, and advanced several steps upon the staircase. Now, however, he seemed to hesitate. Presently we heard him descending. Dupin was moving quickly to the door, when we again heard him coming up. He did not turn back a second time, but stepped up with decision and rapped at the door of our chamber. (Poe 1986: 219)

> 'Hush!' said Calton, holding up his fingers as steps were heard echoing on the flags outside. [...] [T]here was a knock at the door, and, in response to Calton's invitation to enter, Thinton and Tarbit's clerk came in with Roger Moreland. The latter faltered a little on the threshold, when he saw Calton was not alone, and seemed half inclined to retreat. But, evidently, thinking there was no danger of his secret being discovered, he pulled himself together, and advanced into the room in an easy and confident manner. (Hume 2006: 301)

While the double liminal movement (upwards and downwards) of Poe's sailor is more marked than Hume's murderer's hesitation on the threshold, the stakes are higher in the latter case. The sailor confirms Dupin's analysis and is found innocent of the crime;[5] Moreland, on the other hand, walks uneasily, albeit with a final burst of bravado, to his conviction. The twist in Hume's tale is that the text escapes beyond the Parisian framing device: where 'The Murders in the Rue Morgue' ends with the release of the Prefect's prime suspect and Dupin's victory over his rival, Kilsip's victory over Gorby, but also over Calton, is followed by a final chapter that concludes with Fitzgerald's departure from Melbourne. He and Madge sail away beneath 'the flaring red light of the sinking sun' and, not inappropriately, 'through a sea of blood' (Hume 2006: 308).

---

5 The parallelism of the two scenes can be seen to be more interesting still if we take into account Loisa Nygaard's case against Dupin's final solution (1994). Nygaard contends that the sailor himself meets all the requirements of Dupin's killer (great strength and agility, and also the strangeness of voice associated with Maltese inflections). If the sailor is the killer, then Hume's scene is all the more similar to Poe's; if, on the other hand, we accept Poe's officially sanctioned simian solution, then the case against Moreland is necessarily destabilized by Hume's structural allusion.

The object of the remainder of this reading is not to take Bayard's detective criticism to its ultimate end, which is to say, to uncover literary murderers who have until now escaped justice; instead, I shall content myself with calling Hume's solution into question, restoring the full mobility of a text whose meaning is, it seems to me, unconvincingly locked in with the confession of the penultimate chapter. In its most basic terms, the investigation of *The Mystery of a Hansom Cab* is, to borrow Andrea Goulet's description of Dupin's investigation in 'The Murders in the Rue Morgue', 'hinged on the sites of access and communication between the inside and the outside, private and public, domestic and foreign' (2016: 9). And more specifically, it mobilizes these oppositions.

In terms of the inside *versus* the outside, after an initial inversion of reader expectations to do with the cab's furnishing of privacy in motion, the novel repeatedly exposes the brazen overtness of the crime. Gorby's first step in his investigation is to interview the victim's landlady, Mrs Hableton, at which point the opposition is first raised:

'He was murdered in a hansom cab on the St Kilda Road.'

'In the open street?' she asked, in a startled tone.

'Yes, in the open street.' (Hume 2006: 26)

And when afterwards Gorby goes over the interview in his head ('[t]he gentleman in the light coat had threatened to murder Whyte even in the open street'), these particular words seem to him 'especially significant' (Hume 2006: 30). At the most basic level of the choice of preposition, the idea of being 'in' the street is not without interest, suggesting as it does an enclosure that is opposed by the juxtaposition of the adjective 'open'. Furthermore, Hume's mystery, we should remember, is a mystery *of* a hansom cab, not *in* one.[6] The dynamics of the mystery – the tension between openness and enclosure – are the focus of the novel, far more so than the cab's role as scene of the crime. In 'The Murders *in* the Rue Morgue', on the other hand, the location as site (of enclosure) is stressed as early as the title, whereas the investigation text contraposes an official investigation, which gets stuck, along with all the principal witnesses, in the street, unable to penetrate the locked room of the crime scene, with

---

6 Goulet frames the tension between domestic violence and political violence that marks much of nineteenth-century French crime fiction in terms of the pull between crimes 'de la rue' and 'dans la rue'; dramas *of* the street, she notes, end up *in* the street (2016: 165, 172).

Dupin's unofficial investigation, which moves across space, engaging the inside and outside *of* the room and *of* the street.

Later, the idea of concealment is turned entirely on its head in a discussion between socialite Rolleston and lawyer Calton: Calton's suggestion, that 'the place [the murderer] chose for the committal of the crime was such a safe one', is rejected by Rolleston, who deems that 'a hansom cab in a public street would be very unsafe' (Hume 2006: 49). Rolleston's objection brings under tension the twin terms of enclosure and openness, as if it is from this tension that the unsafety derives. This confusion is further compounded when it transpires that Calton's words have been misgiven; his definition of safety defies the logic of the lay reader, since it is of the 'purloined-letter' variety: 'the more public the place', he explains, 'the less risk there is of detection' (Hume 2006: 49). Perverse as this appears, it is, of course, only to be expected by the detective fiction reader, since this is the dynamics of inversion upon which the whole genre is predicated: the culprit is the least obvious suspect, or the one who has been most clearly in view, and so on. Finally, the hermetic space of horse-drawn carriages as places of mortal danger is exploded, with some violence, when Frettlby's wife is the victim of a coach accident. While the others on board the coach survive, she alone is thrown out and, as a result, dies (Hume 2006: 42).

The opposition of the public and private spheres is well covered in Sussex's book, which gives an excellent account of the private misery lived inside the city represented to outsiders as Marvellous Melbourne. The nod in this term to a properly Baudelairean *merveilleux*, that uncanny, and non-synthesizing, co-presence of the Ideal (objective, or represented) and the real (subjective, or presented) is conveyed by Sussex, who makes the connection to the poet of modern Paris early in her text: 'Hume was a flâneur, a term defined by Baudelaire as "a person who walks the city in order to experience it". To stroll through Melbourne today is to experience both its present and its past, and Hume's experience of the city is accessible to us still' (2015: 2). A similar point is made by Ross Chambers in his remarkable account of what he dubs 'loiterature', except that for Chambers it happens to be Sydney and Brisbane that conjure sensations past, present and Baudelairean (1999: 217). All that is required for us to translate this understanding of urban double space (what Chambers calls a 'haunting') onto Hume's mobilization of spatial oppositions is to recall that the present (as city presented) and the past (as city represented) are already co-present, impossibly and yet manifestly, in Baudelaire's prose poems. Baudelairean *flânerie*, therefore, is an oxymoronic activity, one that brings together under tension voyeurism (*of* the street) with action (*in* the street).[7] Arguably, this palimpsestuous urban experience informs Sussex's use of Hume's text, which she reads within the broader framework of his œuvre, and notably his Melbourne trilogy, to shed light on his own historical voice (of which only fragments remain). Where, and Knight is the first to bemoan this,[8] crime fiction scholarship has been predominantly biographically oriented, Sussex's book bucks tradition, taking Hume's (public) writing as a pretext for writing his (private) biography.

The last of Goulet's oppositions is the domestic *versus* the foreign. While the most obvious binary in *Hansom Cab* is Australia's relationship to England, for which Hume uses the term 'topsy-turveydom' (Hume 2006: 186), Melbourne appeals continually to Paris in terms of its poetics of double movement. Consider the following description of Bourke Street by night: 'The restless crowd which jostles and pushes along the pavements is grimy in the main, but the grimyness is lightened in many places by the presence of the ladies of the *demi-monde*, who flaunt about in gorgeous robes of the brightest colours' (Hume 2006: 130). There is an evident aspiration here on the part of all that is grimy towards the poetic, while, on the contrary and *at the same time*, feminine beauty is reduced to walking the streets. One of the most striking aspects to arise from these counter-movements is the city's potential for cultural diversity. For it is not strictly diverse, nor is it strictly a melting pot; rather, it presents potential for diversity, both an adaptability to and an adaptation of otherness. Thus, the following scene, of a band playing a German waltz, does not suggest assimilation as much as aspiration through simile: '[s]ome writer has described Melbourne as Glasgow, with the sky of Alexandria; and certainly the beautiful climate of Australia, so Italian in its brightness, must have a great effect on the nature of such an adaptable race as the Anglo-Saxon' (Hume 2006: 131). Where Poe's adaptation of a microcosm of Parisian diversity produced a Babelian cacophony that forced the official investigator to choose one suspect from the crowd, or to look outside the crowd, Hume's Babel has the effect of seeing singularity in the plural, and vice versa.

---

7 Michel Covin (2000) conveys this twinning of presentation and representation by hyphenating them in the prose-poetic term 're-presentation'.

8 I am thinking specifically here of his plenary lecture at 'Why Crime Fiction Matters: The Italian Case' (La Trobe University, Melbourne, 21 November 2014).

In this scenario, pronouns reveal themselves to be treacherous. Following his arrest by Gorby, Brian paces in his cell, feverishly repeating the following words: 'It would kill her – it would kill her. [...] It would kill her, my darling' (Hume 2006: 87). The pronoun 'her' may designate his fiancée Madge, but he states repeatedly, freely and perversely that he has a secret that he cannot reveal. The repetition of the pronoun, coupled with the ambiguity of the referent, makes this third person singular decidedly, and even foundationally, plural. A few pages later this play on what we might consider a kind of pronominal *différance* is repeated, but also inverted. Here, Calton traps Brian with a pronoun:

'Then why did you take *them* [the valuable papers] from him?'

'What! Had he *it* with him?'

[...] 'Will you kindly tell me what "it" is?' (Hume 2006: 95, my emphasis)

The counter-movement, which sees the third person plural ensnare the third person singular, offers a mirror image of Brian's multiple assertions of singularity. Neatly framed, this eddying pronominal mobility stands *en abyme* for the investigation whose dyads and triads ultimately produce the one true culprit. The poetics of urban mobility, however, suggests a balancing act, which demands that plurality (what is implied, rejected or remains unsaid) be kept in play in the presence of, and alongside, abstracted Truth (what is ultimately, or in this case, penultimately, revealed). Thus, when the rivalry between Gorby and Kilsip is described in terms of 'an eternal conflict between uncongenial elements' (Hume 2006: 120), this tension can be mapped usefully onto the dynamics of the text as a whole.

The novel draws to a conclusion after Frettlby's death and the reading of his confession. The univocal truth of the written word is threatened, however, by the feverish state into which his daughter Madge falls immediately after his death. The sudden demise, while sleep-walking, of the patriarch with the guilty conscience, sees the daughter struck, not dumb, but febrile: the fall of her tower causes her to Babelize. While not strictly glossolalic, Madge's utterances are described as incoherent, for who could possibly understand her accusations *that her father killed Whyte*? Dr Chinston is so shocked by what he hears that he flees the scene and demands that the room in which she lies be sealed. He then moves into a parallel room to hear the more comforting lines of Frettlby's confession, whose text (carefully written by a man nearly driven out of his mind with worry and who, by his own account, begins as he writes to take pleasure in the crafting of his epitaph) is only coherent because it is both in written mode and composed by a well-respected man. Singularity and plurality pour forth at the same time, and only the locking of doors serves to privilege one reading over another. Far from *being* in an essential sense, the truth here is patently produced from those (competing) accounts that are available.

Ultimately, it is again Dr Chinston who serves as the agent of this truth. He refuses to listen to the debate that sees Calton's case against Frettlby opposed to Kilsip's against Moreland: 'I'm quite in the dark, and all your talk is Greek to me' (Hume 2006: 285). Babelizing is dangerous; knowledge is refocused on the written word: 'Read the confession,' Chinston demands, 'and we will soon know the truth without all this talk' (Hume 2006: 287). As it unfolds, however, Frettlby's confession reveals that falsified information can in fact arrive in the form of letters (the forged account of his first wife's death, for example, which is a transplanted newspaper account of another woman's fate), and it is difficult not to see this abuse of the written word reflected back onto the larger text, especially since the novel's key initial facts take the form of newspaper accounts. With this in mind, the true account that Frettlby bequeaths is quite possibly an attempt to settle a score, to punish a blackmailer. But if Moreland is a patsy, which, as I have already hinted, can be inferred from the bravado with which he accepts his fate, then it remains unclear which other wearer of light coats Moreland saw getting into the cab: Fitzgerald or Frettlby? The timelines that see Fitzgerald exonerated are thrown out if the third man to take a hansom cab (back to town) is simply an innocent third party; and it is certainly possible to explain Frettlby's sudden anger when his daughter notes the striking similarity to Fitzgerald that causes her to mistake him for her lover if her father is guilty of the murder (Hume 2006: 251). Indeed, both Fitzgerald and Frettlby shock Madge and become unrecognizable *as themselves* to her when she talks about the scene of the crime (Hume 2006: 77–78) or the possible interchangeability of men in light coats.

The last words on which we shall linger in our rereading of Frettlby and Moreland's double confession are two instances where sentences are cut short. First, detective Kilsip is interrupted by Calton: 'And what would Gorby say? – Gorby, who had laughed at all his ideas as foolish, and who had been quite wrong from the first. If only –' (Hume 2006: 301). The reader assumes that he is about to express his desire that Gorby should be present to witness his success ('if only he were here'); but he may equally be about to express doubt ('if only I am right'). Second, Kilsip himself prevents Moreland from diverting from his confession: 'having hidden the coat up a tree [...] I walked home – so I've done you all nicely, but –' (Hume 2006: 304). By this stage, Calton and Kilsip, and the other members of the locked room, are keen to bring the narrative to a close: '"You're caught at last," finished Kilsip, quietly' (Hume 2006: 304). And yet, structurally these twin unfinished sentences underscore the imperfect cadence of the locked-room conclusion. The truth is ushered in on a double instance of the unsaid.

The conclusion on which I wish to end is that the principal mobility of Hume's novel does not lie in the perspective of Melbourne seen from a hansom cab; instead, it is the mobility of textual meaning that is showcased. To read this novel it is not enough to let the story unfurl before your eyes or to faint before its complexities. Felix Rolleston suggests as much himself when he accuses those watching his tennis match of looking idly on *sub tegmine fagi* (Hume 2006: 304). Sussex notes how Hume plays more broadly in his œuvre on the etymology of the word detective, which refers to the lifting off of roofs (2015: 9). In this light, Rolleston's allusion can legitimately be interpreted as an appeal for readers to be more active participants in the text. Perhaps we are to peep like Madge through a narrow slit in the screen on the veranda (Hume 2006: 188), on the edge of the text, exchanging the locked room for the *camera obscura*, in which the world is seen in reverse – not just Australia as the climatic inversion of England, but singular truth as an eminently reversible proposition. Too many facts, too many words sit alongside the quest for truth, not necessarily leading to it therefore, nor even temporarily screening it, but forever haunting it, multiplying it.

It would be wrong, or at least inappropriately delimiting, of me then to conclude with Fitzgerald's parting thoughts in which he foresees Babel and remains nonetheless unaffected, sure at last of his own escape:

> His own name and that of Madge and her dead father would be on every tongue, yet he felt perfectly callous to whatever might be said on the subject. As long as Madge recovered, and they could go away to another part of the world, leaving Australia, with its bitter memories behind – he did not care. Moreland would suffer the bitter penalty of *his* crime, and then nothing more would ever be heard of the matter. It would be better for the whole story to be told, and momentary pain endured, than to go on striving to hide the infamy and shame which might be discovered at any moment. (Hume 2006: 306, my emphasis)

That the referent of 'his crime' is not necessarily Moreland but could just as easily be Fitzgerald himself, and that it is Fitzgerald who escapes the enclosure of the Rue Morgue framing device in the final chapter of departure are surely secondary factors when weighed against the boundlessly pluralizing effects of Babel. After all, readers can pick up whichever man in a light coat they wish, for no one knows for sure who, or how many, got in or out of the hansom cab.

Works Cited

Ascari, Maurizio (2007). *A Counter-History of Crime Fiction: Supernatural, Gothic, Sensational* (New York: Palgrave Macmillan).

Baudelaire, Charles (1970). *Paris Spleen, 1869*. Trans. Louise Varèse (New York: New Directions).

Bayard, Pierre (2008). *L'Affaire du chien des Baskerville* (Paris: Les Éditions de Minuit).

Caterson, Simon (2006). 'Fergus Hume's Startling Story', in Fergus Hume, *The Mystery of a Hansom Cab* (Melbourne: Text), v–xiv.

Chambers, Ross (1999). *Loiterature* (Lincoln and London: University of Nebraska Press).

Covin, Michel (2000). *L'Homme de la rue: Essai sur la poétique baudelairienne* (Paris: L'Harmattan).

Derrida, Jacques (1985). 'Des Tours de Babel', in Joseph F. Graham (ed.), *Difference in Translation* (Ithaca and London: Cornell University Press), 209–48.

Goulet, Andrea (2016). *Legacies of the Rue Morgue: Science, Space, and Crime Fiction in France* (Philadelphia: University of Pennsylvania Press).

Greenblatt, Stephen (ed.) (2010). *Cultural Mobility: A Manifesto* (Cambridge: Cambridge University Press).

Hume, Fergus (2006) [1886]. *The Mystery of a Hansom Cab* (Melbourne: Text).

Knight, Stephen. (2015). *Secrets of Crime Fiction Classics: Detecting the Delights of 21 Enduring Stories* (Jefferson, NC: McFarland).

Nygaard, Loisa (1994). 'Inductive Reasoning in Poe's "Murders in the Rue Morgue"'. *Studies in Romanticism* 33.2: 223–54.

Poe, Edgar Allan (1986) [1841]. 'The Murders in the Rue Morgue', in *The Fall of the House of Usher and Other Writings* (London: Penguin), 189–224.

Sussex, Lucy (2015). *Blockbuster! Fergus Hume and the Mystery of a Hansom Cab* (Melbourne: Text).

CHAPTER THREE

Reading Affects in Raymond Chandler's
The Big Sleep

Heta Pyrhönen, University of Helsinki

'I was neat, clean, shaved and sober, and I didn't care who knew it. I was everything the well-dressed private detective ought to be' (Chandler 1995: 589). Thus begins Philip Marlowe's first book-length investigation in Raymond Chandler's *The Big Sleep* (1939). The book's plot concerns a case of blackmail that changes into one of a sleazy porn business and then into multiple murders revolving around a missing man until all of these crimes are resolved in the end. The fast-paced events place Marlowe in life-threatening situations, thereby creating suspense as the dominant narrative interest. Dennis Porter characterizes detective narratives such as this as 'machine[s] for producing thrills', thanks to the careful calculation of their effects on readers (1981: 108). Readers go through states of curiosity, anxiety, and fear, until they reach a climax with a stunning twist. Porter depicts readers as pleasure-seekers who purposefully read to *feel* something. By immersing themselves in the recounted events, they become emotionally invested. They want to be moved so that they can experience the effects in their bodies. Emotions cause physiological changes: for example, curiosity sharpens readers' senses, whereas suspense makes their palms sweat. Reading detective fiction is comparable to a roller coaster ride, in which readers start from a position of safety, go through ups and downs, finally to be returned back to safety. According to Porter, readers crave the repetition of this experience (1981: 108). Martin Priestman claims that what strengthens such emotional reading is the genre's rejection of in-depth and symbolic explanations of its actions and any further interpretation of its themes than the detective's (1990: 50–51).

In spite of the current scholarly interest in literature and the emotions, research has been content to repeat the view that stock genres evoke stock emotions (Robinson 2005). It is useful to contrast this assertion with the ending of *The Big Sleep*. Although at first Marlowe brags about being 'everything' an investigator ought to be, the case closes on an altogether different note: 'I stopped at a bar and had a couple of double Scotches. They didn't do me any good. All they did was make me think of Silver-Wig, and I never saw her again' (Chandler 1995: 764). The investigation has changed the detective: brashness has turned into regret and resignation. In terms of the mobility of meaning, this change in emotions appears to run counter to the end-orientation typically associated with crime fiction, which takes the reader from the uncertainty of an unsolved crime to the certainty of resolution. In this case, Marlowe's change of mood invites readers to notice that while they are immersed in the suspenseful emotions the text evokes, and thus rushed along on the roller coaster of end-orientation, they also, and at the same time, process the characters' feelings, which do not necessarily move in the same direction or at the same pace. It is my contention here that the emotions displayed in crime fiction can be studied in order to mobilize crime fiction, to broaden its emotional range, as it were, and to challenge the authority of the final reveal.

In her impressive book *Deeper than Reason*, Jenefer Robinson explains that subjects respond automatically to events in their (internal or external) environment through affective appraisals that trigger physiological changes. They register these changes in their bodies, readying themselves to respond in an appropriate way. An emotional response thus begins in a non-cognitive affective appraisal, but it is invariably followed by cognitive monitoring and evaluation that enables subjects to review the nature, suitability and significance of their emotions (Robinson 2005: loc. 106, 796, 798, 1185–87, 1192). Hence, emotions occur neither in the mind nor the body, explains Robinson, but in a processual network that cannot be understood solely in terms of its corporeal or cognitive component parts. Instead, both parts need to be considered (Robinson 2005: loc. 787–89, 1017). Further, given that pre-cognitive affective appraisals do not discriminate between real and imagined scenarios, we respond automatically to fictive situations, as we would to real ones. It is cognitive monitoring that reminds us to adjust our reactions to the reading situation (Robinson 2005: loc. 1872–75).

Robinson emphasizes that many works of literature need to be experienced emotionally if we are to understand them properly. It is through emotional responses that readers gather important information about characters and plot. Experiencing literature helps us to 'become more perceptive and astute in our understanding of human motivation, human frailty, and human achievement' (Robinson 2005: loc. 1990). What makes emotions central in *The Big Sleep* is that from the start there is a disjunction between Marlowe's official assignment and the one he *feels* he has been asked to investigate. He begins to pursue a self-appointed agenda that deepens this rift, eventually inviting readers to question his motives and understanding of the case. Thus, readers need to reflect carefully on the novel's emotional realm. I examine the emotional responses *The Big Sleep* evokes from three different viewpoints. Firstly, that of the investigation, Marlowe's function as a narrator, and the overall emotional experience of reading this novel. As a detective, Marlowe must form a sense of the relationships between the causes and consequences of the crime case. This task requires a lot of gap-filling activities. Significantly, these activities draw not only on cognitive but also on emotional responses, if only because a detective needs to understand the emotional roots of the crime in order to solve it. In fact, he treats the suspects' emotions as clues while purposefully provoking them to react emotionally. But the case influences his emotions, too, guiding his actions and choices. I then consider Marlowe as a narrator who actively manipulates the emotional reactions of his narrative audience and the ends to which he does so. Finally, I ponder the whole reading experience, showing that the reader's emotional responses endow *The Big Sleep* with a depth and mobility of meaning amounting to the kind of polysemy that some scholars hold alien to the genre. In my analysis, I use the terms emotion and affect synonymously.

The Affective Method of Detection

The hard-boiled detective functions as a catalyst. Given the nature of his job, wherever he goes his presence makes people react. What Dashiell Hammett's Sam Spade says applies to this subgenre: 'my way of learning is to heave a wild and unpredictable monkey-wrench into the machinery' (86). This method of stirring things up aims to make others react emotionally. Because emotional responses begin automatically, they have value for detection. A suspect may, for example, blush, stammer or swoon in the grip of agitation. By observing emotional reactions, detectives may use them as clues.

In *The Big Sleep* Marlowe provokes suspects in order to get a better handle on his investigation. A look at a representative scene elucidates this strategy. Marlowe is with a small-time grafter, Joe Brody, who is embroiled in the case. Brody has Marlowe at gunpoint, while Marlowe threatens Brody with turning him in for a murder:

> [Brody's] brown face was as hard as a piece of carved wood. 'You take chances, mister. It's kind of goddamned lucky for you I *didn't* bop Geiger.' 'You can step off for it just the same,' I told him cheerfully. [...] Brody's voice went rough. 'Think you got me framed for it?' [...] 'There's somebody who'll tell it that way. I told you there was a witness.' [...] He exploded then. 'That goddamned little hot pants!' he shouted. [...] I leaned back and grinned at him. 'Swell. I thought you had those nude photos of her.' (Chandler 1995: 650)

Although Brody has the upper hand, Marlowe hides any fear he may feel beneath a cheery façade. Habitually, characters try to keep their emotional reactions in check so as not to give anything away. Controlling reactions is possible to a degree, as also is feigning them by, for example, altering one's facial expressions. Marlowe's strategy relies on up-ending attempts to mask emotions by throwing the opponent off-guard so that he can get a genuine reaction. In the present example, he achieves this by accusing Brody of murdering a man and lying about having a witness. He can measure his success by observing the other's bodily reactions. Thus, he sees how Brody's forced nonchalance changes into worry, until anger gets the better of him. Marlowe regards this heated response as proof that he has come to the correct conclusions about Brody's actions. Affective body language also demonstrates the power shift in this scene: Marlowe automatically relaxes, grinning to show that he is on top.

Body language can be used as a key to reading emotions that may then serve as clues. This explains why hard-boiled narratives dwell on tracing eye movements, facial expressions, gestures and other involuntary actions. Emotional reactions enable both detectives and readers to fill in narrative gaps by supplying them with information about the case. The scene with Brody illustrates how filling in these gaps is linked to suspense, for inciting emotions also leads to danger. For example, the power play shifts once again when the client's daughter busts in, touting and firing a gun. Here suspense is combined with surprise, as Marlowe could not have expected his earlier insinuations to have this effect on her. What is noteworthy is the seamless interplay the affective method of detection requires between body language and cognition:

the detective must keenly observe the suspects' emotional reactions and be able to name and appraise them fast if he is to master threatening situations. Given that the detective serves as a model reader, whose reading strategies readers both observe and emulate (Hühn 1987), readers too are engaged in a similar interplay. Immersed in the suspenseful and curiosity-provoking events, they are gripped by powerful emotions, but they must quickly reflect on those emotions if they are to keep up with the progress of the investigation. To be sure, detectives and readers are guided by generic conventions, which facilitates reflection on emotions: typically, they can be classified among the core emotions of anger, fear, disgust, contempt, surprise and sadness. Also, the predominant social emotions of shame, embarrassment, envy, hatred and guilt belong to this list (Keen 2011: 6, fn 5). Consequently, the genre relies heavily on what may be characterized as stock emotions.

The unforeseen consequences of this affective method include its possible effect on the detective. The murder of the small-time hustler Harry Jones in chapter 26 provides a good example. The unarmed Marlowe hears the encounter between a gangster's henchman and Jones through a door crack. His reactions are heightened by the fact that he can only listen to what is happening: his body is tense and he hardly dares to breathe. The realization that his casual question about Jones is the cause of this situation intensifies his remorse: he feels vulnerable, deeply frustrated, regretful and sad. This emotional reaction is heightened by Jones's protection of his girlfriend who, in Marlowe's estimation, does not deserve such chivalry. The scene ends with Marlowe out on the street: 'When one of [the rain drops] touched my tongue I knew that my mouth was open and the ache at the side of my jaws told me it was open wide and strained back, mimicking the rictus of death carved upon the face of Harry Jones' (Chandler 1995: 725). Marlowe empathizes with Jones to the point of identification, a fact that later influences his actions when he kills the henchman – in self-defence, but also to revenge Jones's death. This scene exemplifies the kind of sympathy and compassion that Robinson holds central to any reader's emotional understanding of characters and their situations. In a similar manner to Marlowe, readers dwell on Jones's condition, saddened by the perception of his predicament. As Robinson points out, readers do not necessarily identify with a character, but they imaginatively reconstruct what the other person is undergoing. In this particular scene, readers feel compassion for both Marlowe and Jones, actively involving themselves in their respective situations.

This affective and imaginative adoption of another's perspective as part of the investigative method has already been described by Edgar Allan Poe's C. Auguste Dupin, who explains that 'when I wish to find out how wise, or how stupid [...] is any one [...] I fashion the expression of my face, as accurately as possible, in accordance with the expression of his, as if to match or correspond with the expression' (1994: 347). The aim is to fathom what thoughts and feelings arise in the detective's mind and heart. This method relies on the detective's feeling into the opponent's mind and emotions by treating his own mind and emotions as other and probing into the ensuing reactions. It is thus based on the detective's cognitive and emotional doubling of the criminal. The approach postulates a basic likeness between the detective and the quarry as a condition for knowledge (Pyrhönen 1999: 31, 54). Thus, using emotions as an investigative tool involves the kind of transferential approach familiar from psychoanalysis, in which the detective gauges his own emotional reactions as clues to the suspects' emotions and their significance. What characterizes detective fiction, however, is that detectives frequently resort to what Karl Morrison calls malevolent sympathy, a condition and means of assimilation based on suspicion, strife and even hatred (1988: 70–71). Consequently, they may manipulate their emotional dexterity and their conclusions about suspects' emotions *against* these suspects, if it furthers the investigation – or a personal goal.

While detectives typically use the affective and imaginative method to identify with the criminal, Marlowe employs it in order to feel himself into the *victim*, a tactic that puts him in a vulnerable position. In *The Big Sleep* this strategy changes the detective's emotional investment in his job; it also affects readers' emotional investment in Marlowe, who, as the protagonist-narrator, enlists their empathy.

The Sternwood Case as Marlowe's Emotional Education

The significance of the affective method for Marlowe's investigation emerges as early as the first chapter, in which General Sternwood commissions him to sort out a blackmail attempt by A.G. Geiger based on his daughter Carmen's gambling debts. This assignment is perplexing, because it fits a lawyer better than a private detective. Paying attention not only to his client's speech but also to his comportment, gestures and tone of voice, Marlowe notices that the client is disappointed in his two daughters, but very fond of Rusty Regan, the son-in-law who has abruptly left his marriage. Afterwards Vivian Regan tries to find out whether Marlowe was hired to find her husband, thus reinforcing Marlowe's hunch that the client wants to ensure that Regan is not behind the blackmail. Thus, from the start there is a disjunction between what Marlowe is told about his assignment and what he feels he is asked to do. Deciphering the unspoken emotions of his client, he infers that the blackmail nests a more important missing person case. Although he investigates the blackmail, it is the case of the missing man that touches him emotionally, because he recognizes in the General and Regan characteristics of the chivalric ideal he cherishes: honour, bravery, commitment. This brand of chivalry adheres to a sentimental, paternalistic romanticism (Plain 2001: 60).

Marlowe's investigation in *The Big Sleep* has an ouroboric form, insofar as he is set the problem of the missing person in the Sternwood mansion and resolves it in the same place. The formal elegance of his narrative suggests that this case serves as a life-changer for Marlowe: it transforms his outlook on his profession. In Robinson's terms, it provides him with an emotional education, requiring of him that he reflect back on the whole emotional process of solving the case, including his physiological responses, affective appraisals and actions. This education targets his chivalric ideals as the basis of his job. On first entering the mansion, he sees a glass-window scene of a knight standing by a damsel in distress. The knight's ineptitude frustrates Marlowe, who thinks he should intervene to ensure the girl's rescue. Then Carmen accosts him, falling straight into his arms. On re-entering the mansion five days later, he observes that 'the knight in the stained-glass window still wasn't getting anywhere untying the naked damsel from the tree' (Chandler 1995: 747). Now he knows that Carmen, although in need of help, is no damsel; instead, she is an epileptic, a drug addict, a porn model, a nymphomaniac, and a killer to boot. Marlowe need not have looked further than at the girl in his arms for the answer.

Marlowe solves the blackmail early (chapter 18), and the case he was hired to handle is over. From this moment, his emotional investment in General Sternwood and Rusty Regan steers his actions, widening the discrepancy between his paid assignment and the self-imposed one. Marlowe's emotional education can be divided into three phases: clearing the blackmail case (chapters 1–19), tracing its links to the missing Regan case (chapters 20–29), and proving how these two cases intertwine, which serves as the solution (chapters 30–32). There is an emotional turning point halfway through: returning home, Marlowe finds Carmen lying naked in his bed (chapter 24). This scene is decisive and he immediately reflects on its meaning. At first he observes that '[t]here was a problem laid out on the [chess]board [...] I reached down and moved a knight'; but a little later on, he concedes that '[t]he move with the knight was wrong [...] Knights had no meaning in this game. It wasn't a game for knights' (Chandler 1995: 705, 707). Once he has thrown Carmen out, he tears 'the bed to pieces savagely' (1995: 709). His narrative attempts to come to terms with this forceful emotional realization that the values he cherishes do not apply in his world. Given Marlowe's character as 'a man of honor', and 'the best man in his world and a good enough man for any world' (Chandler 1972: 20), readers become emotionally invested in his dilemma of acting uprightly in a society that neither recognizes nor appreciates such conduct. Following Robinson, if readers do not perceive the emotional conflict of Marlowe's ethical quandary, they will neither fully understand his situation nor his attempts to navigate it. But simultaneously, the chivalric ideals and the emotions Marlowe invests in them generate room for reflection. Why does he commit himself emotionally to just these values? How does this commitment steer his actions and serve his wants, goals and interests? Are these values commendable in themselves and do they suit the context in which he is working? Although readers empathize with Marlowe, his emotional investment in chivalric values invites scrutiny and even disagreement.

Marlowe identifies with Regan to the point of taking the missing man's place as proxy; once he has inserted himself in Regan's place, he realizes that he is the same type of affective object for Carmen as the other man was. Given their supposedly shared values, Marlowe concludes that his disgust at Carmen's attempted seduction mirrors Regan's repulsion in a similar situation. Marlowe conjectures that Regan nevertheless acted in a chivalric manner toward Carmen, when she asked him to teach her to shoot. To prove this inference, he stages a replay of the events that ended Regan's life. Further, emotional identification helps Marlowe to access the backstory of the crime, consisting of a love triangle between Regan and the gangster Eddie Mars, both of whom are in love with the same woman, Mona. When Marlowe encounters Mona Mars, he too finds her charming. Consequently, affective identification guides Marlowe's assessment of who the villain is: not the deranged Carmen but the calculating Eddie Mars. What Marlowe sees as most damning about Mars is his businesslike approach to people and things. The gangster does not let emotions sway him; he even cooks up a story about Mona having run away with his rival, Regan, because it furthers his ends.

In their last meeting, the General voices displeasure at Marlowe's assumption of his ulterior motives (chapter 30). The General insists that he did not ask the detective to look for Regan, while Marlowe claims that that was exactly what the client wanted. This meeting consists of Marlowe's forceful attempts to persuade the General to accept his interpretation: he provides a long justification for his assessment of the General's intention. As he goes on, he observes the General's expressions, which change from stiffness and coldness to acceptance. These changes allow Marlowe to gauge the success of his persuasion. It appeals to the client's pride, honour, judgement of character and fondness of male camaraderie. He even interrupts the client, observing that he cares more about pride and male bonding than his daughters or money (Chandler 1995: 751). Thus, Marlowe identifies and names the General's emotions for him – especially the other's fears and wishes. This last meeting amounts to a replay of the affective relationship Marlowe thinks the client shared with Regan. When the General finally asks Marlowe to find Regan, he accepts the detective's interpretation.

As the case closes, Marlowe acts like a rescuer, unlike the knight who never saves the damsel: he demands that Carmen get treatment and frees the Sternwood sisters from Eddie Mars's clutches. Yet the mismatch between the blackmail story and the story of the missing man persists. Mars orchestrated the blackmail, but the climax – the confrontation between villain and detective – takes place in an unspecified future outside the narrative. The revelation about Regan's fate forms another let-down. Not only is Regan dead but his death is meaningless both for the killer, the detective and society. Carmen gets revenge but does not understand the gravity of her deed. Marlowe cannot idealize Regan's death, because falling victim to Carmen shows a lack of caution and misevaluation of character. Finally, this death has no social impact and will perhaps never be solved.

The denouement's inconclusiveness is compounded by clues that Marlowe has misconstrued the emotional dimension of the case. His assessment of the suspects' character, motives and goals appears inaccurate, even erroneous. Such misreading implies that what Pierre Bayard identifies as delusional thinking permeates Marlowe's understanding of the case. Delusional thinking constructs a falsified relation to reality, because the thinker does not see things for what they are; instead, he tries to impose his convictions on reality. Therefore, it involves both a distortion of reality and a psychological position in relation to this distortion (Bayard 2000: 85–87). Delusional thinking is apparent in Marlowe's bending of the facts and the way in which he connects them together so that they fit his formulation of the solution. It has the appearance of adhering to acceptable relations of causality and coherence, but is betrayed by its rigidity and its intimate ties with the unconscious. Delusional thinking rises from the unconscious, because it serves the thinker's psychic needs (Bayard 2000: 89–91) – and these needs are primarily emotional.

What alerts readers to Marlowe's delusional thinking is his presentation of affective relationships. Carmen is the hub of the case. He portrays her libidinal force as instinctual animality, beyond the ken of humanity. Further, the case involves impassioned relationships, leading to revenge murders: in love with Carmen, the Sternwood chauffeur, Owen Taylor, kills Geiger for taking advantage of her. Mistaking Brody for Geiger's murderer, Geiger's lover, Carol Lundgren, shoots Brody. Marlowe, however, holds these relationships to be perverted or self-serving. Further, Marlowe characterizes Mona's love for her gangster husband as inexplicable, when men such as Regan and he are available. He questions the genuineness of these characters' feelings, downplaying the emotional commitment they demonstrate. Hence, his chivalric ideals make him abhor actual love relationships, which are distasteful, as they involve complex and contradictory corporeal affects, making agents act irrationally.

Marlowe's delusional thinking becomes most apparent in his misevaluation of the two men he admires. Handling this case tarnishes him ethically and damages him emotionally, for he does not act according to chivalric ideals: he kills a man and his actions cause the death of another. Most importantly, he deems it charitable not to reveal to the General that Carmen killed Regan, because he wants to preserve the client's honour and pride. He reasons that were the General to learn the truth, he would report Carmen to the police and die deeply disappointed in his children. Yet nothing indicates that parenthood is meaningful for Sternwood. He is a callous businessman, and not even a soldier; it was his father who was. As for Regan, he is an ex-IRA soldier but the battles he fought have nothing to do with chivalry. He was also a bootlegger who fell in love with a nightclub singer, competing over her with a gangster. When he lost, he married on the rebound. The General and Regan are passionate, ruthless and reckless in love and other matters. Thus, it escapes Marlowe that they are more like Carmen than knights. They have vitality, fervour, and brutality to a degree that is alien to the detective. Therefore, it is uncertain whether the General sees his attachment to Regan in the same manner as Marlowe does. Yet Marlowe insists that his version is correct. Gill Plain characterizes his agenda as one of searching for an ideal man 'to set in the balance against the void of corruption and despair, and as a lover with whom he might form an idealized homosocial union, located not in the tarnished present' (2001: 65). This male double serves as the impossible object of the detective's desire (Plain 2001: 67). This emotional fixation thus explains why Marlowe separates chivalry from telling the truth – the elusive ideal would not survive its disclosure.

Handling the Sternwood case provides Marlowe with an emotional education that centres on death. The fact that Regan is dead and the General's death is imminent resonates with his concern that his cherished ideals will soon be obsolete. The emotional role chivalric values play and the decisions Marlowe makes on their basis invite readers to reflect on whether they are justified. Therefore, they are engaged in reflecting on complex emotions. Before discussing this fact, however, it is necessary to consider Marlowe as narrator, for it is in this role that he articulates the lessons he has learned.

Narrating Melancholia

Jonathan Flatley explains that it is the readers' projection of the narrator as a person that makes emotion emerge (2008: loc. 1249–54). Such projection creates the sense of communication that the silent text lacks as well as providing a space for shared emotions (2008: loc. 1263–67, 1252–56). Retrospective narration allows Marlowe to bring emotions into the conscious sphere. In reviewing past events, he relives them as if they were present, giving them verbal expression. Flatley claims that the first-person narrator relies on two kinds of memory in narrating emotions: a mimetic, repetitive kind and a conscious, narrative one. Their interplay enables the narrator's cognitive evaluation of his emotional experience. When dealing with gripping past events, the narrator constructs a mimetic relation to someone in the present. The presence of a real or a projected interlocutor strengthens the narrator's trust in the realness of affects; further, the narrator is able to relive emotions by projecting someone else as also experiencing them (Flatley 2008: loc. 763, 769, 776). This configuration opens a space for the narrative audience, that is, the recipient the narrator envisions as receiving his narrative in the optimal manner. The narrator's cognitive evaluation of emotions takes place whenever he recounts an affective experience he has had but that he is reviewing from a new vantage point. Although they use different terminology, Flatley (2008: loc. 1137) and Robinson (2005: loc. 2291–98, 3401) agree that during such instants the narrative audience learns about the role and significance of emotions for the narrator.

Marlowe's narration is framed by 'a look of hard wet rain' (Chandler 1995: 589); and indeed, it is mostly either raining or about to rain. Fredric Jameson claims that meteorological rhythms provide the mood for Marlowe's narration (Jameson 2016: loc. 1194). Such an evocation of mood signals a state of readiness for certain emotions. Flatley explains that moods provide narrators with ways of articulating their connections to their socio-historical context, because moods provide culturally accepted shapes and structures into which narrators may channel their emotions (2008: loc. 272–74, 289, 310). The constant evocation of (the threat of) rain in Marlowe's narration underlines the ominous and depressing mood in which his handling of the case takes place. It enables the narrative audience to catch on to the sense of mistrust, hostility, and fear of others impregnating this world. This mood refers to an all-pervading isolation in which there are no longer any forms of shared experience. As Jameson says, only Marlowe's narration fits characters together as parts of the same puzzle (2016: loc. 126, 190).

This dark mood frames Marlowe's narration of emotional episodes, that is, of events and experiences that evoked his affects. He repeatedly builds an episode by underlining its end as a transformation of its beginning. The scene in chapter 28 with Silver-Wig (aka Mona Mars) provides a representative example. It evokes the glass-window image of the knight and the damsel, but turns it upside down, for it begins with Marlowe 'trussed like a turkey ready for the oven' (Chandler 1995: 733). His narration records sound, sight and corporeal sensations, thus reflecting his utter helplessness. Such reporting is comparable to the portentous music of suspenseful film scenes: 'overhead the rain still pounded, with a remote sound, as if it was somebody else's rain'; Mona's voice has 'a tiny tinkle in it, like bells in a doll's house' (733), while the alarming sounds turn out to be 'only the rain drifting against the walls' (735). Against this ominous background, the narration lingers over Mona's attractiveness, which is expressed in a series of similes that provide the means for reflecting on the emotions she evokes. Mona has eyes like 'the blue of mountain lakes' (733) and breath 'as delicate as the eyes of a fawn', but is also characterized as 'tall rather than short, but no bean-pole', with a hand that is 'not the usual bony garden tool' (734). The narrator mixes idealizing similes with humorous ones, thus self-consciously pondering her charm. Reporting the sensations and similes underlines Marlowe's role as a hard-boiled detective, but it is 'the damsel' who frees him.

Going out, he pins her to the wall by pressing his body against hers:

'All this was arranged in advance, rehearsed to the last detail, timed to the split second. Just like a radio programme. No hurry at all. Kiss me, Silver-Wig.'

Her face under my mouth was like ice. [...] Her lips were like ice, too.

I went out through the door and it closed behind me, without sound, and the rain blew in under the porch, not as cold as her lips. (739)

Marlowe the narrator dramatizes what he felt. By referencing the script of a radio programme, he alludes to the typical situations in which an investigator lands. His narration portrays him as if he were a knight going to battle, kissing his lady for the last time. The repetition of the coldness of Mona's face and lips, related to the slanting rain, creates a self-conscious rhythm, the purpose of which is to convey his bodily response to, and heroic face-off with, danger. Yet this account contradicts what has actually taken place: he was in a highly vulnerable position and would have died without a woman's help. Despite self-mockery, the narrator's formulation of the emotional lesson of this scene highlights his bravery, toughness and chivalry. Narration enables him to foster delusional thinking, strengthening his falsified relation to reality. Consequently, narration serves as a further way for him to sustain an idealization of his role and performance.

In further reflecting on the emotional functions of Marlowe's narration, it pays to look at how he recounts his reactions after handling life-threatening situations. After shooting the henchman Canino, he reports that he began to 'laugh like a loon' (742); similarly, when Carmen fires at him, he relates that he laughed and grinned at her (755). There are no wise-cracking embellishments, but simple statements of facts. Not only does this reaction speak of relief but also of triumph: he has survived, while the missing man whose steps he has been tracing has perished. He is still here, among the living, while his double is there, among the dead. This realization forms the gist of his emotional education, one on which he muses at the conclusion of his narrative:

What did it matter where you lay once you were dead? [...] You just slept the big sleep, not caring about the nastiness of how you died or where you fell. Me, I was part of the nastiness now. Far more part of it than Rusty Regan was. But the old man didn't have to be.

On the way downtown I stopped at a bar and had a couple of double Scotches. They didn't do me any good. All they did was make me think of Silver-Wig, and I never saw her again. (763–64)

Marlowe's narrative ends in an elegiac tone. When relating the narrator's brash voice in the beginning to his resigned and chastened tone at the end, the narrative audience recognizes the narrator's mood as melancholic. He longs for lost ideals, broods over the tawdriness of the events and contemplates the irrationality of the persons involved – including himself. In interpreting this lesson, the narrative audience has to consider the whole narrative in order to capture its emotional impact. Given the compassion readers feel for the narrator, they perceive this plaint for the dead as also a plaint for the inevitability of the narrator's – and their own – death, saturated with feelings of impotence, inadequacy and spiritual emptiness. It is death as the radical annihilation of self that poses the narrator's greatest fear, and his narrative serves as an attempt to symbolize this dread (Pyrhönen 1999: 248–50).

The Narrator's Emotional Conclusion

I now return to the discrepancy between the official case and Marlowe's emotional entanglement that persists in the ending – and even beyond. This situation supports Bayard's claim that the solution provides textual closure signalling material closure but is not necessarily matched with subjective closure (2000: 104). The reason for this state of affairs is that Marlowe actually has two different cases to solve: the Sternwood case and an existential one. The former generates the latter, but the latter is what his narrative is really about. It is about a modern man's place in a world filled with violence and, given the nature of his job, this man's relationship to death and the dead.

As we have seen, the protagonist-narrator's delusional thinking reveals an obsession with his doubles. By replaying Regan's fate, Marlowe attempts to reinstate the kind of a personal, reciprocal and concrete bond between the living and the dead that existed in pre-modern societies. Modernity altered our relationship to death by turning what was formerly understood as a relation of symbolic exchange into one of biological and medical fact. Marlowe's effort centres on investing death with symbolic meaning, which is achieved through an exchange between parties. The living celebrate the dead with rituals, while the dead acknowledge that gift by their presence in the midst of life, thus suggesting a fluidity between life and death. Death is a continuation of life, not its definitive end (Baudrillard 1993: 131–32, 140–42). The detective's identification with the male victim, together with his elegiac, commemorative narrative, represents an attempt to establish such a bond of mutuality. Marlowe's narrative is his gift to his double, from whom he hopes to receive an understanding of what it means to be dead (Pyrhönen 1999: 252). Consequently, the narrator maps an affective experience of encountering death that alleviates the anxiety it causes. By insisting that death retains meaningfulness thanks to its vital links with life, the narrator enables the narrative audience to transform melancholia into hope Significantly, his narration constructs a pattern around this theme in all of his stories except *Playback*.

Thus, melancholia does not incapacitate Marlowe as he goes on to investigate and narrate six more cases. Flatley argues that melancholia may function as the emotional mechanism that enables one to be interested in the world (2008: loc. 34). As a practice, it produces emotional knowledge, expressed in what Flatley calls an affective map that converts depression into a strategy of engaging with the world. An affective map addresses the emotional values attached to the structures constituting our social worlds. Thus, analyzing affective maps shows how these structures shape our lives and our relationship to ourselves through emotions (2008: loc. 32–34, 65, 1107–11). In my understanding, as a narrator Marlowe summarizes his emotional education in an affective map that provides him with this new type of vital connection to the world. It helps him to be clear about the losses at the root of his grief as well as whom and what to blame for them: the fragmentation of society with people living in isolation, the objectification of human relationships, the dissolution of gender roles, and the corruption of social values. As a narrator he associates all these losses with death – the death of human connection and of ideals. Flatley states that an affective map allows a melancholic to recognize those with whom he shares this depressive condition (2008: loc. 64–67). In Marlowe's case, however, there is no such collective; instead, he attempts to turn his narrative audience into a community of melancholics for whom the depressive affective experience is converted – through his self-conscious wise-cracking, and stylized narration – into a source of connection, even pleasure. Marlowe's emotional education transforms his way of being in the world, and he narrates in order to impress this change on his narrative audience.

In reviewing the affective map that Marlowe's narration produces, the narrative audience may identify a concern with death as a key conflict of modernity. Familiar from anyone's life world, this issue calls for emotional reflection. This 'case', however, remains unsolvable. The closest Marlowe comes to experiencing death is during states of unconsciousness. Yet as he cannot remember anything from these states, he cannot narrate them. They are telling lacunae in his narrative, as being unconscious and being dead remain unnarratable mysteries. He nevertheless repeatedly returns to life from these states of unconsciousness. Thus, these lacunae serve as pointers to the narrator's delusional thinking, suggesting that ultimately *The Big Sleep* portrays its narrator's hopeful fantasy of death as the guarantor of life's meaning as well as a continuation of that life.

Detective criticism, according to Bayard, works out solutions that are more satisfying to the soul (2008: 57). In light of my examination, I would amend his formulation by saying that this approach works out problems that are more satisfactory and truer to what actually happens in the text than the problems the detective openly formulates. My analysis shows that within Marlowe's apparent problem of the missing Rusty Regan is nested the much more vexing one of death and being dead. Thus, as Bayard observes, detective criticism is interventionism: it intervenes in an active way, refusing to go along. It boldly looks for the true problem (2008: 59).

Textual closure is material closure, but not necessarily subjective closure. Every reader fills in textual gaps. All literary worlds are incomplete (Bayard 2000: 105). Readers complete texts in differing ways. As I have shown, reading *The Big Sleep* provides readers with a suspenseful experience, making their palms sweat and stomach contract. But this experience exceeds mere thrills, thanks to the complex manner in which the hard-boiled narrative investigates the emotions its true problem evokes. Further, these emotions cannot be expressed in folk psychological or stock emotional terms. This novel thus provides readers with a demanding emotional challenge, one that genuinely contributes to their becoming more perceptive and astute in their understanding of human affairs.

Works Cited

Baudrillard, Jean (1993). *Symbolic Exchanges with Death*. Trans. Iain Hamilton Grant (London: Sage).

Bayard, Pierre (2000). *Who Killed Roger Ackroyd?* Trans. Carol Cosman (New York: The New Press).

— (2008). *Sherlock Holmes Was Wrong: Reopening the Case of the Hound of the Baskervilles*. Trans. Charlotte Mandel (New York: Bloomsbury).

Chandler, Raymond (1972). *The Simple Art of Murder* (New York: Ballantine).

— (1995). *The Big Sleep*, in *Stories and Early Novels* (New York: The Library of America).

Flatley, Jonathan (2008). *Affective Mapping: Melancholia and the Politics of Modernism* (Cambridge, MA: Harvard University Press E-book).

Hammett, Dashiell (n.d.). *The Maltese Falcon* (New York: Vintage Crime/ Black Lizard; Random House E-book).

Hühn, Peter (1987). 'The Detective as Reader: Narrativity and Reading Concepts in Detective Fiction'. *Modern Fiction Studies* 33.3: 451–66.

Jameson, Fredric (2016). *Raymond Chandler: The Detections of Totality* (London: Verso E-book).

Keen, Suzanne (2011). 'Introduction: Narrative and the Emotions'. *Poetics Today* 32.1: 1–53.

Morrison, Karl F. (1988). *I Am You: The Hermeneutics of Empathy in Western Literature, Art, and Theology* (Princeton: Princeton University Press).

Plain, Gill (2001). *Twentieth-Century Crime Fiction: Gender, Sexuality and the Body* (Edinburgh: Edinburgh University Press).

Poe, Edgar Allan (1994). 'The Purloined Letter', in *Selected Tales* (London: Penguin).

Porter, Dennis (1981). *The Pursuit of Crime: Art and Ideology in Detective Fiction* (New Haven: Yale University Press).

Priestman, Martin (1990). *Detective Fiction and Literature: The Figure on the Carpet* (London: MacMillan).

Pyrhönen, Heta (1999). *Mayhem and Murder: Narrative and Moral Problems in the Detective Story* (Toronto: Toronto University Press).

Robinson, Jenefer (2005). *Deeper than Reason: Emotion and its Role in Literature, Music, and Art* (Oxford: Clarendon E-book).

CHAPTER FOUR

Contradicting the Golden Age

Reading Agatha Christie in the Twenty-First Century

Merja Makinen, Middlesex University London

Agatha Christie is synonymous in the popular imaginary with country houses and conservative middle-class complacency (its ruffling and then its restoration). Accordingly, Christie has been positioned as the epitome of the Golden Age whodunnit, the cosy puzzle plot whose crime is resolved and dispelled by the brilliant if eccentric private detective upholding law and order and thus a cultural status quo. This is a familiar critical interpretation from Raymond Chandler (1950) to Franco Moretti (2005). A conservative writer with cardboard cut-out characters, according to P.D. James (Maslin 2009), but also one with a genius for plotting that typically leaves her readers unable to guess the identity of the villain. Earl F. Bargainnier argues that it 'accounts for a large part of her success in the genre' (1980: 166), and Edmund Wilson agrees: 'Her supreme skill was in the construction of plot, and she has never been excelled as the creator of detective puzzles' (2002: 77). However, millennial criticism has begun to break down this monolithic view of Christie's work. As literary criticism infects and subsumes the limitations of 'genre criticism' with its focus on antecedents, influences and developments, crime fiction is opened up to a multiplicity of readings. Christie's work is open to analysis that constructs such a mobility of meanings for a contemporary readership. Small surprise, perhaps, that her texts quietly explore and critique a number of conventions within the Golden Age she is supposed to epitomize, particularly in relation to identity, metafictional textuality, cultural relevance and social intervention. Liberating Christie's texts from the forced compression of Golden Age formatting not only exposes the mobility of meanings within individual texts but also unhinges the subgenre's (theoretically) static identity. Contemporary crime fiction is dynamic and evolving, but so too are our readings of earlier examples, informed by twenty-first-century analysis.

Identity

Re-claiming Christie means challenging the description of her novels as 'cosy' conservative reassurances of a fixed status quo and to argue instead that they chart, for example, cultural traumas of betrayal (Knight 2004: 91) and 'epistemological anxiety' (Klapscik 2012: 43). Christie's plots are successful precisely because she upheld that murder was not the regime of one aberrant individual who could be excised, because everyone in her novels is a potential murderer. John Curran's examination of her notebooks demonstrates that in the planning of the novels, every character is drafted as the murderer before she decides who will finally be singled out as the villain (Curran 2010). In consequence, disturbingly, every one of her characters continues to perform a masquerade and can be neither known nor trusted. Characters' performativities are garnered from cultural expectations and stereotypes to mask much more dangerous and mendacious identities, and these remain unresolved by the identification of the specific murderer(s). Christie's novels demonstrate the lack of surety and the inability to know and feel safe with anyone. In *Ordeal by Innocence* (1958) a returning traveller gives the convicted murderer an alibi, and expects his family to be relieved that he has been exonerated. However, since this is a closed-community crime, the rest of the household are distressed because they now come under suspicion again. One daughter voices her family's miasma of masquerade: 'Sometimes [...] I think one does not know anybody' (Christie 1961: 173); another elaborates the fear this encompasses:

> I just don't know, I'm – it's an awful thing to say – but I'm frightened by everybody. It's as though behind each face there was another face. A – sinister sort of a face that I don't know. (148)

The chilling aspect is underlined by the fact that she is discussing her own father and her siblings, people she has spent her life among, trusting in their love and knowableness. The husband of the third sister develops the fractured, intangible nature of identity, and hence an inability to know anyone, even those as intimate as a spouse:

That was his Polly. But there was another Mary – a Mary who was hard as steel [...] And that Mary he did not love. Behind the cold blue eyes of that Mary was a stranger – a stranger he did not know. (168)

Identity as both a fractured multiplicity and continuous masquerade of competing cultural impositions is a Butlerian concept of performativity that postmodern criticism has embraced (Butler 1993; 1999), but of course modernism too questions the slippery, unfixed nature of the self in the era in which Christie starts writing. Christie's own writerly performativity did not position her as either modernist or literary, but her texts display ideas of identity, and of gender, shared with this cultural movement.

A Murder is Announced (1950) unsettles the question of identity further, with the introduction of twin sisters. This same device has since been employed with great success by Angela Carter in the postmodern *Wise Children* (1991) in which Dora Chance masquerades as her twin Nora, exchanging her clothes, make-up and perfume. What is the self, when it shares a history and an appearance with your other, and the accoutrements of femininity make these interchangeable? The close of Carter's novel complicates identity further when an ex-wife transforms herself through plastic surgery to 'become' Dora and win her husband back, taking Dora's place in the marriage ceremony, a true simulacrum that reinforces Butler's thesis that 'the doer' is constructed in and through 'the deed' (Butler 1999: 181). Identity becomes a practice, an act of continuous repetition or variance.

Forty-one years earlier, Christie's text has one twin masquerading as the other with the same interchangeable clothing and hairstyles, the accoutrements of femininity that construct the self in praxis. Charlotte Blacklock dons Letitia's identity with the notable pearl choker: 'As Charlotte she had played second fiddle. She now assumed the airs of command [...] They were not really so unlike mentally' (Christie 2002: 349). Christie's take on the crime genre ensures that the repetition of performativity encompasses the dangerous, as Charlotte murders three people and is apprehended while attempting the fourth. Christie's version of the self in process proves both precarious and perilous, and, as such, anything but cosy. Charlotte may well be arrested and removed from society, but the masquerade infects all the suspects: the novel concludes with the unmasking of Pip and Emma who had also assumed other identities. Christie employs the device of assuming other identities through make-up and clothing and hairstyles for the interchanged young murdered girls in *Body in the Library* (1942) to more bathetic effect, reminding the reader of the pathos and horrors of life alongside its instability.

Textuality

Christie's novels contain much more of value than just the plotting; their generic confrontation and intertextuality point to a questioning and playful metafictionality that is easier to note now that postmodern literary criticism vaunts them in later novels, such as Paul Auster's *New York Trilogy* (1987). A major indication of this instability comes in Christie's thwarting of the safe conventions of the Detection Club; indeed, she tears up the rule book over the course of her fifty-year oeuvre. Her early novels in particular comment on their own genre and their relationship to the modern medium of cinema. Christie returns to commenting on writing and writerliness much later with the introduction of the crime writer Ariadne Oliver assisting Poirot. In the 1966 *Third Girl*, Poirot writes his own critique of the crime genre, his magnum opus, in true Detection Club judgement:

> He had dared to speak scathingly of Edgar Allen Poe, he had complained of the lack of method or order in the romantic outpourings of Wilkie Collins, had lauded to the skies two American authors who were practically unknown. (1988: 5)

In the novels written at the beginning of her career, during the six years between the publication of *The Mysterious Affair at Styles* (1920) and her assuming the role of a professional writer, perhaps the most notable aspect of the texts, generically, is their metafictional playfulness. Alongside the radical representations of the new femininities (Makinen 2006), these novels hold a playful self-referentiality and intertexuality that we are more accustomed to finding in postmodern texts. More than at any other time, the real pleasures of creativity erupt in a meta-textual playfulness that also belies conformity. An amateur buoyancy, since while it was obviously important that the texts were good, novel writing did not yet constitute a crucial part of her self-definition. In the second novel, *The Secret Adversary* (1922), Tommy and Tuppence self-consciously converse in both literary and cinematic syntax:

> if Mr Brown is all he is reported to be, it's a wonder he has not ere now done us to death. That's a good sentence, quite a literary flavour to it.

… it is certainly queer that Mr Brown has not yet wreaked vengeance upon us. (You see, I can do it too.) We pass on our way unscathed. (2001c: 83)

The dialogic plurality of the two separate discourses, one 'real', the other 'fictional', within a novel's context, are called to our attention by the focalizers' comments, creating an ironic metanarrative for the readers, potentially flaunting the Beresfords' own lack of literariness self-consciously.

Tuppence further engages young Albert's interest by referencing the threepenny detective novel's diction and syntax: '"Ready Rita," repeated Albert deliriously. "Oh ain' it just like the pictures!" It was. Tuppence was a great frequenter of the cinema' (2001c: 115). This latter conversation encompasses three pages of American hard-boiled dialogue (predating Chandler's reaction to Golden Age texts) and reappears with Albert through the novel. The self-conscious intertextual pastiche plays with the variant narrative modes of the crime genre for the fun of it, bending the reader's dissociation of particular frames of narration while simultaneously re-engaging them with its humour. The next novel, *The Murder on the Links* (1923), opens with Hastings's self-reflexive and rather ponderous view of how novels begin:

> I believe that a well-known anecdote exists to the effect that a young writer, determined to make the commencement of his story forcible and original enough to catch and rivet the attention of the most blasé of editors, penned the following sentence: '"Hell!" said the Duchess.' Strangely enough, this tale of mine opens in much the same fashion. Only the lady who gave the exclamation was not a duchess. (1977: 5)

This is a particularly trickster narrative, since Hastings positions himself as an already published narrator, without the same exigencies, while clearly still trying to engage and rivet the reader through his simultaneous same and not same opening – the confessed lack of similarity which humorously further undercuts his own attempt. Indeed, it is not even the opening by the time he gets to it, his own fictional profanity coming in the second paragraph. The playfulness of this utterance ostensibly striving to be original while characterizing his painfully laborious pedantry also calls attention to the authorial difficulties of starting any narrative, to effectively inscribe the infamous blank page. The main comic pastiche again develops from a filmic thread, with Poirot suggesting Hastings's solution would make a good film plot, since it bears no resemblance to reality (151), and Hastings acting on a further misconception in his clichéd heroism:

With a bound I reached him and pinioned his arms to his side [...] in a grip of iron.

'Mon ami,' observed the latter mildly, 'you do this sort of thing very well. The strong man holds me in his grasp and I am helpless as a child. But this is uncomfortable and slightly ridiculous'. (173–74)

The unreality of the cinematic syntax, allied to Hastings's folly for thinking in such hackneyed tropes, contrasts to Poirot's humoured, intelligent recourse to the same semantics, before the detective rejects it as inappropriate for the real narrative. This dialogic of alternative utterances playfully risks calling the reader's attention to the fictionality of the 'real' as well as the cinematic 'unreal', a daring narrative tightrope walk as the author both risks and hopes to contain the reader's engagement.

With *The Man in the Brown Suit* in 1924, the narrative excess develops into a full-blown pastiche of dislocating proportions. This too, like the previous novel, opens on a self-conscious account of narration, with everyone asking Anne to tell the story because it is 'just like the pictures', then beginning: 'So here goes. Anne Beddingfield starts to narrate her adventures' (1989: 11). One major strand of this metanarrative self-consciousness is the analogy to the cinematic 'Perils of Pamela', which sees Anne remake herself textually as 'Anna the Adventuress', creating a more appropriate appearance in the mirror, and introducing the various adventures as episodes I, II and III. Decoyed by the enemy and captured, Anne references Episode III of Perils of Pamela watched in the safety of the cinema 'eating a tuppenny bar of chocolate' but complains it is less fun in 'textual real life':

It's all very well on the screen – you have the comfortable knowledge that there's bound to be an Episode IV. But in real life there was absolutely no guarantee that Anna the Adventuress might not terminate abruptly at the end of any Episode. (1989: 118)

The narrative irony comes in the readers' knowledge that they are at the beginning of chapter 19 of a 26-chapter novel. Holding the physical object of the book tells them this, if not Anne's dramatic self-creation. Here the competing semantics have tripled, with the hackneyed cinema-ese of Pamela, the naïve younger self, the 'Anna' trying to invest real life with the glamour of contemporary media, and finally the narrating older, experienced Anne. However, Anne herself needs rescuing when she falls off the cliff and Rayburn rescues her from the ambush and crocodile-infested waters, finally carrying her into Livingston on his shoulders. In an example of self-irony, the text appears to make Anne complicit in the rejected femininities of both Pamela and the self-created adventuress Anna. Since Anna and Pamela also conform to cinematic tropes in this particular sequence, the real Anne collapses into their rejected inauthenticity. Her unusual passivity is explained by her illness and gives an authentic explanation to this conflation of the three viewpoints into a momentary unreality. But the tightrope continues as the enunciation plays with the novel's readers, with a dizzying élan. The polyphony of reduplications means telling has become bound up in a questioning reworking of how one writes an adventure thriller, through parody, displacement and adaptation. In its own small way, *The Man in a Brown Suit* is 'a critical deconstruction of the tradition', to quote Hal Foster on postmodern pastiche (1983: x), a site of contention and revision of the discourse of earlier adventures, while tackling its conservative ideologies of the role of women.

Of course, the second strand of polyphony in this amazing novel is Christie's first outing of the extended unreliable narrator, the alternating first-person narrative of the villain Sir Eustace, with its opening warning to the reader: 'I may commit indiscretions, but I do not write them down in black and white' (1989: 79). This first use of the charming but unreliable narrator is not yet as well-crafted as the endeavour two novels later, but it does perhaps result in the text's inability quite to condemn him, as villain, since we have shared his viewpoint, however deceptive and restrictive it has finally proved to be.

This slightly unworked use of the unreliable narrator is, of course, brought to fruition in 1926 in *The Murder of Roger Ackroyd* with its countless quiet omissions and carefully planted red herrings. Dr Sheppard points out self-consciously in his final revelation how it gave him a shock to encounter Parker on leaving the murder room. Within the order of the narrative, however, the idea of a lurking Parker, perhaps listening at the door and hence being the blackmailer, sends the reader off after a potential suspect, displacing our attention from the text's judicious wording until Sheppard finally, self-referentially calls our attention back to it:

> I am rather pleased with myself as a writer. What could be neater for instance, than the following: 'The letters were brought in at twenty minutes to nine. It was just on ten minutes to nine when I left him, the letter still unread. I hesitated with my hand on the door handle, looking back and wondering if there was anything I had left undone.' All true, you see. But suppose I

had put a row of stars after the first sentence! Would somebody then have wondered what exactly happened in that blank ten minutes? (2011: 236)

This special pleading for having enacted the Golden Age 'fair play' is of course a double bluff on the part of the author, who hides behind the self-proclaimed writer/narrator and strives to avert cries of foul from the reading public, a textual self-justification which we know to have been only partially successful. But as a narrative that gives us all the facts, while averting the reader's gaze to them by dangling brighter baubles in front of our eyes, it is superbly effective unreliable narration, working as it does with that most conventionally trustworthy of personages, the village doctor (a double if not triple bluff).

The stories that will become *Partners in Crime* were being penned for the magazine market, during this period. Published in 1929, this collection consists of fifteen stories where the Beresford couple assume the detective identities of contemporary fictional sleuths, thereby pastiching Arthur Conan Doyle's Sherlock Holmes, R. Austin Freeman's Thorndyke, Valentine Williams's Okewood Brothers, 'Sapper' H.C. McNeile's Bull-dog Drummond, Isabel Ostrander's McCarty, Clinton H. Stagg's Thornley Colton, G.K. Chesterton's Father Brown, one of Baroness Orczy's cases, the 'Old Man in the Corner', Freeman Wills Crofts's Inspector French, Anthony Berkeley's Roger Sheringham, H.C. Bailey's Dr Fortune and finally, Hercule Poirot. In this way, *Partners* displays Christie's knowledge of her contemporary crime writers and offers a playful challenge to their individual habits of detection. The self-referential metafictionality of her critique of the crime genre relies simply on the knowingness of the Beresfords and the recognition of the reader for most of its pleasures. The scenarios soon become repetitive, for the most part, though the final Poirot story sparkles as Tuppence suggests it should have Hastings triumph and Tommy rejects this, as Christie fictionally critiques her own creation: 'It isn't done. Once the idiot friend, always the idiot friend. There is an etiquette in these matters' (2001b: 329). However, since such a pairing belies Tuppence's flair and intelligence, the young helper, Albert, becomes the idiot friend in her place. Christie's self-pastiche takes the textual referentiality to a new level of self-consciousness. *Partners in Crime* exhibits a belief in textual pastiche of her crime genre as a way of writing crime fiction.

In the 1920s, when modernist novels were questioning the conventions of narration and creating new and self-conscious tropes, these early crime texts similarly celebrate writing a narrative situated within a specific genre and allying it to other similar media, especially contemporary cinema. The meta-narrativities exhibited in these amateur novels are more usually expected in what are termed 'literary' modernist and postmodernist works.

The Golden Age Detection Club

The Detection Club was set up by Anthony Berkeley in 1930, with twenty-eight members and G.K. Chesterton as its first President (as seen above, *Partners in Crime* had pastiched both writers). Two years before, Ronald Knox had created his light-hearted ten rules with their insistence on fair play, no inscrutable Chinamen or poisons unknown to science, no more than one set of twins and then only if properly introduced into the narrative, and the exclusion of narrator or detective from being the murderer. Christie was not the only writer to experiment with breaking these rules. However, as Martin Edwards explains, the club was serious about supporting the literary value of detective fiction, and of its twenty-three rules, the first insists 'that it is a demerit in a detective novel if the author does not "play fair" with the reader' (2015: 343).

Christie's novels broke almost all of the gentlemanly Detection Club 'rules', deliberately teasing the genre out of all recognition while ostensibly secure within its confines. In this sense, her novels encapsulate generic mobility as defined in the editors' introduction to the present volume, according to which crime fiction displays a 'transgressive impulse' thereby proclaiming and challenging its own limitations. The most acclaimed and publicly successful novels were precisely the ones that confounded generic expectations, becoming intangibly impenetrable if playing by the Golden Age rules. The 1934 novel, *Murder on the Orient Express*, published four years after she joined the club, is iconic for precisely these reasons: out of the twelve suspects everyone has done it and, as Poirot reveals, everyone is masquerading behind false personae. It is an illegal denouement if playing by the generic rules, and virtually impossible to guess. Raymond Chandler furiously commented: 'only a halfwit could guess it' (Chandler 1995: 984). Even more outrageously, the victim is transposed into the villain and the deliberate, calculating murderers are white-washed as piteous, grieving victims and allowed to go scot free, while the brilliant detective duplicitously creates two contradictory solutions and lies to the Yugoslavian police. Despite its reputation as a classic example of the Golden Age whodunnit, when we strip away our familiarity, it is an extraordinarily transgressive narrative.

As noted above, the most famous furore came in 1926, with the publication of *The Murder of Roger Ackroyd*, the novel that really made her name. It embodies the crime novel's betrayal of the reader's trust: the first-person narrator, the Hastings/Watson sidekick character, gives us the information of the case while quietly withholding the crucial point that he is the murderer. As Bayard suggests, this is 'a violation of the tacit pact between the author of a detective novel, and her public' (2001: vii). It is also a fictional trope that Christie revisits forty years later in *Endless Night* (1967). *In Murder is Easy* (1939) the sidekick again proves to be the villain, a duplicitous serial killer made even more unlikely by being a little old spinster in the mould of Miss Marple.

If the rules say that not everyone should have done it, and that neither the narrator nor the sidekick should, they also, and most definitely, say that the detective should not. Darkest of all, the detective himself masquerades as the trusted character while plotting the murder in *Curtain: Poirot's Last Case*, which was written in the forties and kept unpublished until the year before Christie's own death. Using a similar justification to *Murder on the Orient Express*, that the real villain cannot be brought to justice but endangers numerous lives, in this case through his psychological persuasiveness in encouraging others to murder, Poirot shoots the perpetrator and confesses posthumously to Hastings, having engineered his own death as punishment. Poirot is, at times, a particularly amoral detective. Yet, it needs to be said, given the magnitude of Christie's oeuvre, he is, at other times, intensely conservative in upholding law and order: he lets perpetrators go free; he often allows them the 'honourable suicide', thereby allowing them to escape the ignominy of the justice system and the gallows; and finally, he becomes the murderer. As Bayard questions,

> What faith can we grant the testimony of a man who boasts of murdering someone who has not committed a crime? [...] It makes any narrative impossible, since a narrative implies, as a guarantee of its authenticity, a position external to the crime where the law [...] might be spoken. (2001: 116)

Thus, when *Curtain* was finally published in 1975, the construct of the detective narrative was radically ruptured. (Consider, too, the effect of Christie knowing, for thirty-five further years of her writing, that Poirot has murdered.) For a body of work that is often held up as the epitome of Golden Age fiction, Christie's texts on closer inspection prove remarkably transgressive and duplicitous.

Social Intervention

The traditional view of Christie is of a writer incarcerated within the Golden Age genre of escapist puzzling and uninterested in politics. While there is no mileage in trying to claim Christie was a consistently political writer, there were two clear periods where the texts reached outside of their engagement with the readers' detection of whodunnit, to discuss what she saw as political crises. The first period was the Second World War. Other critics, including Stephen Knight (1995), Virginia Nicholson (1997), Gill Plain (2001) and Kristine Miller (2009), have argued for the context of the war permeating some of her writing of the forties. *One, Two Buckle My Shoe, Taken at the Flood, Sad Cypress* and *The Moving Finger* all increase their body count, for example. Knight suggests 'a radical displacement, not recognizing the war as itself but representing its effects in terms of disruptions to the normal balance of power, of gender and social power' (1995: 163), making powerful figures the villains, to condemn the abuse of power. For her part, Miller argues that novels such as these 'expose cultural tensions about class and gender hierarchies under siege [...] on the [...] homefront' (2009: 128). The thriller *N or M?* writes about the war directly, for propaganda purposes, but it is usually seen as an exception. It is certainly true that Christie's most overt bid for political intervention comes in her few thrillers (a genre where political views are customary) or her Westmacott novel *The Rose and the Yew Tree* (1948), which comments on Labour's first sweep to power in the 1945 Khaki election. And yet, a number of her detective texts also embrace cultural relevance in ways we are so familiar with in twenty-first-century crime, but which is usually denied the Golden Age.

Appointment with Death (1938), published a year earlier than *N or M?*, examines the power of dictators from a medical and psychological viewpoint. Written before Britain's declaration of war, it contains both anxiety and urgency. Mrs Boynton epitomizes the monstrous tyrant, the Hitler or Mussolini figure in a personal and familial form, to allow the novel to interrogate on a private scale why the ordinary person might not be able to resist tyranny. On the eve of world war, Christie elucidates both the power and the immorality of fascism through the form of a dominating mother. Mrs Boynton's sadistic delight in dominating her stepfamily and denying them personal freedom is observed by the psychologist Dr Gerard, who names it a will to power. Boynton is deliberately monstrous: 'a gross spider', sadistic and 'evil' (2001a: 426), born with an ambition to dominate and impress her personality on other people. Invoking the fairy-tale figure of the wicked stepmother, her preying on her own daughter shifts the fairy tale into horror, crossing the bounds of the 'natural' to the mythic ogress. The text deliberately raises the question of why her stepchildren allow themselves to be driven into such cowed submission: Gerard explains Mrs Boynton's incarceration of the family away from the outside world, her indoctrination of them in their youth and the way that she hypnotized them into believing they had no choice but to obey her. Where the discerning reader might link this to Hitler's creation of the Nazi youth movement, Gerard overtly connects her malevolent tyranny to the European political context:

> We see it all round us today – in political creeds, in the conduct of nations. A reaction from humanitarianism – from pity – from brotherly good-will. The creeds sound well sometimes – a wise regime – a beneficent government – but imposed by force – resting on a basis of cruelty and fear. They are opening the door, these apostles of violence, they are letting up the old savagery, the old delight in cruelty for its own sake. (2001a: 446)

For the 1938 British reader, the references are clearly to the totalitarian regimes of Hitler, Franco, Mussolini and also Oswald Moseley's rallies in Britain. The text opens with the question of whether it is justifiable to assassinate tyranny in the name of the freedom of the many, suggesting that it isn't 'wrong', to kill 'something that is doing harm in the world and must be stopped' (2001a: 423). Poirot, of course, cannot concur; he 'always' abhors murder (although, of course, a few years later, in 1940, Christie was composing *Curtain*, in which Poirot himself carries out a judicious assassination for the benefit of the world), but his denunciation of it is as muted as his character will allow. Boynton's murder does free her cowed followers. The assassin is a female politician in the Nancy Astor mould, domineering but no dictator. A Liberal MP, she shifts the portrayal from the personal into the political sphere as a character who stands for democracy, able to voice views that are both different and disagreeable in the House. Her feminism is one part of this dissent. Lady Westholme is a complex figure, a successful public woman, self-opinionated, standing for British democracy and the engine of freedom from tyranny via assassination, even while she advocates wrong-headed Liberal appeasement and dominates her social intercourse. Following the expected generic conventions, the murder is made personal not political, but Poirot allows her to escape public opprobrium by honourable suicide. The text ends not on the culpability of the crime, but on the restitution of normality and happiness to the

Boynton family, leaving the reader to question just how 'wrong' such an assassination of an evil dictator actually was – the very question that the text opened with.

The second period of cultural relevance and social intervention in Christie's oeuvre comes in the late 1960s and early '70s, during the cultural revolution of the swinging sixties and the political unrest fuelled by the student uprisings of Paris 1968 and the increasingly violent anti-Vietnam marches in Britain and the United States. As with Dr Gerard's opinion in *Appointment with Death*, Christie voices a fear that the young are being led astray in embracing anti-humanitarianism. While the thriller *Passenger to Frankfurt* links this directly to a Hitler conspiracy, her detective fiction explores the dangers for, and corruption of, the ordinary British youth. *Third Girl* (1966) is concerned with the welfare of young women freed from parental confines and exposed to the bohemian lifestyles and illicit drug taking of the swinging sixties. *Endless Night* (1967) turns its fears to young men's social liberation, which sees them freed from familial control to drift through life bereft of humanitarian mores to anchor their behaviour. Christie's comments during this period of youthful cultural revolution and civil unrest that her 'interest was aroused by the youth attitude of rebellion and anarchy, chronicled in news all over the world' (Thompson 2007: 468–69). In *Third Girl* the generation gap is voiced by both Norma Restarick and Poirot, but the detective is sure that '[s]he needs help', that '[s]he is not competent', a victim in waiting (1988: 13, 14). The text's urgency about protecting the young living alone in London is of course proved necessary. Behind the careful plotting of villains usurping the family fortune, this concern for the newly vulnerable young women powers the tension. The novel takes elaborate care with the sixties style, the women with their lank hair, sloppy joe jumpers and short skirts with 'high leather boots, white open work woollen stockings' (1988: 7), the men more flamboyant with long hair, tight trousers and velvet waistcoats. Placing the styles and the drug taking correctly ('purple hearts, and dream bombs, and probably L.S.D.' [1988: 99]), the novel simultaneously alienates the younger generation through the knowledgeable eyes of Poirot and Mrs Oliver. Who looks after young girls now that they leave home to live alone, 'helpless as a fly in treacle' (1988: 220)? For Norma Restarick, the answer is the young psychiatrist Dr Stillingfleet, who, under Poirot's guidance, is a hard-working professional of the old school. Unfortunately, there is no such psychiatric help for Michael Roberts, the drifting youth in *Endless Night*, whose lack of fixed morals leads to his downfall. Initially introduced as a restless youth unable to settle ('I never stuck to anything. Why should I?' [1972: 14]), with a succession of easy jobs (chauffeur, groom, fruit picker, garage mechanic, washer-up), Michael Roberts rejects his mother's wish that he would settle down to a steady job and a nice girl in favour of the easy life and an unspecified desire for wealth and glamour. Sex, something Christie had accepted as important for her female protagonists in the 1920s through to the 1950s, as part of a loving, fulfilling relationship, in the sixties becomes divided from love as she contemplates the 'free love' mantra of the swinging sixties: 'I didn't know at that time anything about love. All I knew about was sex. That was all anybody of my generation seemed to know about' (1972: 23).

Michael takes the wrong path, choosing sex with Greta over love with Ellie, to get the wealthy lifestyle he has envied since a child: 'Greta was the woman I belonged to. She was sex personified' (1972: 178). He has previously murdered one friend to steal a coveted gold watch and later stabbed another for his winnings; both murders are opportunistic and are positioned as passive enactments: 'I still had that queer feeling in me of waiting for something, for something to be offered to me, or to happen to me' (1972: 23). He takes no responsibility for killing and has no compunction as to how he gets what he wants. When he chooses 'the wrong girl', his amoral, unfocused ambition creates a psychopath condemned to the depths of 'endless night'. Alongside the careful plotting and the contemporary reinventing of the unreliable narrator, the text explores the dangers for disaffected working-class young men in the sixties, rebelling against the older generation's certainties, desiring of a good lifestyle and easy money, with no serious possibility of effecting it: 'I suppose the trouble with me was that I wanted things too much, always. Wanted them too, the easy way, the greedy way' (1972: 190). The real character under threat in *Endless Night* is not the old-fashioned Ellie, victim of the murderous new breed of callous, inhumane sixties me-generation, but the apathetic Michael.

In the late 1960s Christie's detective fiction shifts away from the traditional Golden Age to make a bid for cultural relevancy as, in her eighties, she comments on what she sees as the inveterate egoism of the young and the lack of moral support being offered to them. The old hidebound values of her generation were being overturned and, in her eyes, nothing of value was being put in their place. These late crime novels represent an urgent plea in the face of a feckless new world.

Millennial criticism, willing to embrace crime fiction as worthy of the serious critical tools of literary analysis, can reclaim Christie's detective fiction for the twenty-first century. To this end, it argues for her continuing relevancy by recognizing anew her complex, fractured conceptions of identity; it highlights the wealth of textual challenge presented by her writing, and its playfulness; and it acknowledges the serious attempts that she made to intervene culturally at two specific periods in her crime fiction. Christie's sole value can no longer be considered to reside in her mastery of the cosy puzzle plot and the conventions of Golden Age fiction, but in the mobility of meanings in her texts. And a mobilized Christie paves the way for the re-examination, and re-mobilization, of the subgenre as a whole.

Works Cited

Bargainnier, Earl F. (1980). *The Gentle Art of Murder: The Detective Fiction of Agatha Christie* (Bowling Green, OH: Popular Press).

Bayard, Pierre (2001). *Who Killed Roger Ackroyd?* Trans. Carol Cosman (London: Fourth Estate).

Butler, Judith (1993). *Bodies That Matter: On the Discursive Limits of Sex* (New York: Routledge).

— (1999). *Gender Trouble: Feminism and the Subversion of Identity*, 2nd edition (New York: Routledge).

Carter, Angela (1991). *Wise Children* (London: Chatto).

Chandler, Raymond (1995) [1944]. 'The Simple Art of Murder', in *Later Novels & Other Writings* (New York: The Library of America), 977–92.

Christie, Agatha (1961) [1958]. *Ordeal by Innocence* (London: Fontana).

— (1972) [1967]. *Endless Night* (London: Fontana).

— (1977) [1923]. *The Murder on the Links* (London: Pan).

— (1988) [1966]. *Third Girl*. (London: Fontana).

— (1989) [1924]. *The Man in the Brown Suit* (London: Fontana).

— (2001a) [1938]. *Appointment with Death: Poirot in the Orient* (London: HarperCollins).

— (2001b) [1929]. *Partners in Crime* (London: HarperCollins).

— (2001c) [1922]. *The Secret Adversary* (London: HarperCollins).

— (2002) [1950]. *A Murder is Announced* (London: HarperCollins).

— (2011) [1926]. *The Murder of Roger Ackroyd* (London: HarperCollins).

Curran, John (2010). *Agatha Christie's Secret Notebooks* (London: HarperCollins).

Edwards, Martin (2015). *The Golden Age of Murder* (London: HarperCollins).

Foster, Hal (1983). *Postmodern Culture* (London: Pluto).

Klapscik, Sandor (2012). *Liminality in Fantastic Fiction* (Jefferson, NC: McFarland).

Knight, Stephen (1995). 'Murder in Wartime', in Pat Kirkham and David Thoms (eds), *War Culture: Social Change and Changing Experience in World War* (London: Lawrence and Wishart), 161–72.

— (2004). *Crime Fiction 1800–2000* (London: Palgrave).

Makinen, Merja (2006). *Agatha Christie: Investigating Femininity* (London and New York: Palgrave Macmillan).

Maslin, Janet (2009). 'Mysteries of Crime Fiction? P.D. James is on the Case'. *New York Times*, 6 December. https://www.nytimes.com/2009/12/07/books/07book.html [accessed 2 September 2015].

Miller, Kristine A (2009). *British Literature of the Blitz* (London: Palgrave).

Moretti, Franco (2005). *Signs Taken for Wonders* (London: Verso).

Nicholson, Virginia (1997). *Millions Like Us: Women's Lives During the Second World War* (London: Virago).

Plain, Gill (2001). *Twentieth Century Crime Fiction: Gender, Sexuality and the Body* (Edinburgh: Edinburgh University Press).

Thompson, Laura (2007). *Agatha Christie: An English Mystery* (London: Headline).

Wilson, Edmund (2002). 'Foreword: A Portrait of Agatha Christie', in Harold Bloom (ed.), *Modern Critical Views: Agatha Christie* (Broomhall: Chelsea House), 73–78.

Part II

Mobility of Genre

CHAPTER FIVE

Criminal Minds

Reassessing the Origins of the Psycho-Thriller

Maurizio Ascari, Università di Bologna

While this volume pivots around three main axes of mobility – meaning, genre and transnationality – the present chapter privileges the first two perspectives in its reassessment of the origins of one particular genre, or subgenre, of crime writing. Rather than crossing language borders, it explores British and Anglo-American literatures and cultures in the attempt to trace the development of early psycho-thrillers from the eighteenth century to the mid-twentieth, when this subgenre was recognized as such. The aim of this critical enquiry is to highlight key factors such as the impact of pseudo-scientific theories of the mind on the representation of the criminal, the use of first-person narratives that make readers experience warped perceptions and worldviews, and the thematization of amnesia as a device engendering suspense.

Despite its success, the psycho-thriller is still under-theorized, probably because it typifies the mobility of the crime fiction galaxy, whose complexity and volatility resist systematization. Even the critical term is, as Sharon Packer argues (2007: 86), still mobile since the shortening of *psychological thriller* to *psycho thriller* is in itself revealing of the increasing relevance of madness within this subgenre. Here I will hyphenate the term to clarify that I intend psycho as a prefix, meaning 'relating to the mind', rather than as an abbreviation for psychopath.

The identity of this subgenre is also elusive in other respects. Tracing borders between the psycho-thriller and neighbouring territories is not easy, as recognized by Philip Simpson (2010: 188), who reminds us that

Robert Bloch's *Psycho* (1959) is not only 'often designated as the origin of the fictional psycho thriller' but also, and as often, 'labelled "horror"'; nor is it easy to trace the inception of this literary phenomenon. Without questioning the received idea that the psycho-thriller originated in the mid-twentieth century, Simpson claims that it derived 'its mood and atmosphere' from noir (2010: 188). Focusing on these intermedial exchanges is certainly important, but this should not divert our attention from the much deeper roots this subgenre has in previous literature.

The development of the psycho-thriller has arguably escaped closer critical scrutiny precisely because it is at the crossroads between literature and cinema. Significantly, it is in the field of film criticism that most recent studies of the genre have appeared. Simpson is therefore right to direct our attention to the cinema and to the aftermath of the Second World War, for it was at that time that Alfred Hitchcock's *Psycho* popularized this formula. It was also in those years that literary psycho-thrillers such as Margaret Millar's *Wall of Eyes* (1943), Jim Thompson's *The Killer Inside Me* (1952), Patricia Highsmith's *The Talented Mr. Ripley* (1955), John D. MacDonald's *The Executioners* (1957) and Ross MacDonald's (aka Kenneth Millar) *The Galton Case* (1959) were published.

Rather than focusing on the 1950s, however, I will move back in time to investigate the prehistory of the psycho-thriller, following in the footsteps of scholars such as Kristopher Mecholsky. After describing this genre as self-conflicting, Mecholsky claims not only that 'it confronts the modern anxiety about the nature of the mind and self through the Enlightenment struggle to subjugate myth and superstition', but also that it 'simultaneously seeks to reveal the limits of knowledge of the individual self' (2014: 51). Mentioning both Gothic and Sensation novels as conduits to what he labels the psychological thriller, Mecholsky considers writers like Edgar Allan Poe and Henry James as prefiguring the twentieth-century development of this form, which he explores, starting from practitioners such as Daphne du Maurier, William Faulkner and James M. Cain.

The hybrid nature of twentieth-century psycho-thrillers, which combine the scientific investigation of psychoanalysis with the shady labyrinths of Gothic minds and settings, invites an archaeological approach. Gothic and Sensation fiction paved the way for the development of Freudian psycho-thrillers thanks to the ambivalence of first-person narratives, the protagonist's misperceptions of reality, and the biased mental constructions they engender, leading to a 'rewriting' of the external world and to forms of deviant/criminal behaviour. Psychoanalysis was not the first attempt to develop a theory of the mind, and previous philosophical/

scientific systematizations had likewise engendered a literary response in the field of crime fiction, which has always been concerned with the origin of evil.

The prehistory of the modern crime story is often considered to lie in Sophocles' *Oedipus the King*. There is also a distinct *psychomachia* apparent in medieval morality plays, where virtues and vices battled for the possession of the soul within a religious framework. The early modern incipient secularization of society inevitably impacted on the conceptualization of the criminal mind, as shown by Shakespeare's tragedies, where evil is no longer unproblematically presented as stemming from a supernatural conflict. The mind becomes a dark site of mystery, but also an object of philosophical and medical investigation, an invisible 'stage prop' that contributes to the theatrical appeal of stories that are meant to entertain.

Shakespeare is a master of introspection whose plays often pivot on the friction between different explanatory paradigms of the human. The torments of guilt and madness that Macbeth shares with his resolute wife certainly straddle the border between natural and supernatural, as shown by the uncertain status of Banquo's ghost or Macbeth's 'dagger of the mind' (2.1.38–39). When Lady Macbeth shows signs of mental derangement, it is a doctor – a professional – who is called to assess her mental health, although he soon interprets her symptoms as clues to her guilt, concluding that 'More needs she the divine than the physician' (5.1.81).

Between Gothic and Sensation Fiction

Despite the advent of the Enlightenment, this ambivalence between the religious and the secular is still at the core of Gothic fiction, whose appeal to the emotions is rooted in early modern drama, as Horace Walpole acknowledged in his preface to the second edition of *The Castle of Otranto* (1764). A philosopher as well as a novelist, William Godwin is an exception to this rule, as shown by his politically inflected *Things as They Are, or The Adventures of Caleb Williams* (1794), where plot and characterization resulted from a highly rational project. Reassessing the composition of the book in 1832, Godwin provided valuable insights into its structure, describing his choice of a first-person confessional narrative as the most expedient way to analyse 'the private and internal operations of the mind, employing my metaphysical dissecting knife in tracing and laying bare the involutions of motive' (1970: 339).

Godwin conceived his philosophical novel in support of the ideas he had expounded in his *Enquiry Concerning Political Justice* (1793), where a complex 'theory of the human mind' is developed (1976: 360). Convinced that 'mind is a topic of science' (1976: 340), Godwin defined his deterministic 'doctrine of moral necessity' as follows:

> He who affirms that all actions are necessary means that the man who is acquainted with all the circumstances under which a living or intelligent being is placed upon any given occasion is qualified to predict the conduct he will hold, with as much certainty as he can predict any of the phenomena of inanimate nature. (1976: 336–37)

The psychological paradigm Godwin articulated in this study and subsequently popularized in the novel marked the beginning of a new brand of Gothic, in which the study of power combines with that of the psyche, under the aegis of the Sublime, as shown by Charles Brockden Brown's *Wieland, or The Transformation* (1798) and Mary Shelley's *Frankenstein* (1818).

As Stephen Knight remarks of *Edgar Huntly* (1799), most of Brown's novels 'deal with interpersonal dramas – including some psychic conflicts within a single personality' – and can also be read as commentaries on 'the state of the nation' (2015: 23). *Wieland*, a complex novel that evokes the religious and political turmoil of the late eighteenth century, also explores the psychological views of the time, especially the sensory- and perception-centred theories of eighteenth-century empiricist philosophy. The unreliable nature of perceptions – and the danger of drawing uncritical or superstitious inferences – is at the core of Brown's novel, where a biloquist, whose motives remain unclear, engenders a series of misunderstandings, climaxing in multiple murders. The mysterious voices that the novel's characters hear resonate with Theodore Wieland's inner voices, prompting him to kill his wife and children. Further killing is prevented by the biloquist's intervention and the suicide of Theodore, a name that means God-given and has clear ideological implications. In his advertisement, Brown felt the need to clarify that despite relating extraordinary incidents, the book aims at psychological verisimilitude: 'Some readers may think the conduct of the younger Wieland impossible. In support of its possibility the Writer must appeal to Physicians and to men conversant with the latent springs and occasional perversions of the human mind' (1991: 3–4). This is the study of an aberrant mind, the portrait of a multiple murderer whose motivation is a misplaced religious fervour. What we are reading is an early psycho-thriller.

Even *Frankenstein* can be related to this category insofar as it depicts the increasing psychological awareness and ensuing despair of a creature whose otherness condemns him to solitude, ultimately turning him into a Romantic outcast, a superhuman criminal who is ready to plot, harm and kill in order to pursue his revenge against his improvident creator, Victor Frankenstein. Although it is tempting to regard this as a book about persecution, the creature's psyche is actually centre stage. Far from being congenitally evil, the creature is perverted by his interactions with humans, echoing Godwin's idea that 'the actions and dispositions of mankind are the offspring of circumstances and events, and not of any original determination they bring into the world' (1976: 97). The creature himself confirms this when he remembers his early days, in which 'I looked upon crime as a distant evil; benevolence and generosity were ever present before me' (Shelley 1969: 127). We might also think of James Hogg's *The Private Memoirs and Confessions of a Justified Sinner* (1824), which is not only marked by the double but is also told twice, first through a more objective 'Editor's Narrative', then through a private memoir that introduces us to the increasingly deranged mind of the sinner. The story tells of the ambivalent relation between the protagonist and his mysterious companion, Gil-Martin, whom we are led to consider either as the devil or as a projection of the protagonist's mind. Although the text never dissipates this hesitation, towards the end we are offered clues in favour of a psychological interpretation, pointing to a split personality, as shown by these words Gil-Martin addresses to his friend: 'I am wedded to you so closely that I feel as if I were the same person' (1990: 229).

In the same period, another writer revelled in the exploration of altered states of consciousness. Soon after publishing his *Confessions of an English Opium-Eater* in 1821, Thomas De Quincey planned to write a book entitled *Confessions of a Murderer*, which never saw the light. This interest in the homicidal mind resurfaced in the essay 'On the Knocking at the gate in Macbeth' (1823), where De Quincey invited his contemporaries to follow Shakespeare's example by shedding light on the psyche of the perpetrator: 'in the murderer, such a murderer as a poet will condescend to, there must be raging some great storm of passion, – jealousy, ambition, vengeance, hatred, – which will create a hell within him; and into this hell we are to look' (2006: 5). These words resonate with the aesthetics of murder De Quincey would later articulate in 'On Murder Considered as One of the Fine Arts', which appeared in *Blackwood's Magazine* in 1827. Founded in 1817, this magazine hosted a large number of first-person narratives about extreme experiences such as being buried alive. Verging on the grotesque, these sensational stories exerted a major influence on Poe, as shown by his parodic 'How to Write a Blackwood Article' and 'A Predicament' (both originally published in 1838, respectively as 'The Psyche Zenobia' and 'The Scythe of Time'). Poe's interest in the criminal mind is evident in stories such as 'The Tell-Tale Heart' and 'The Black Cat', two first-person narratives pivoting on murder and guilt, both published in 1843. The former opens with these words:

> True! – nervous – very, very dreadfully nervous I had been and am; but why *will* you say that I am mad? The disease had sharpened my senses – not destroyed – not dulled them. Above all was the sense of hearing acute. I heard all things in the heaven and in the earth. I heard many things in hell. How, then, am I mad? Hearken! and observe how healthily – how calmly I can tell you the whole story. (Poe 1984: 313)

While rejecting the accusation of madness, the narrator is actually betraying his own perturbed mental state, which is evidenced by his abnormal sensitivity to sounds. The strange things he can hear gesture back towards Brown's story, although the obsession that will actually lead him to murder stems from the 'Evil Eye' of an old man with whom he lives and of whom he needs to rid himself (Poe 1984: 314). It is after this monomaniac has killed the old man that a strange sound manifests itself, a sound he believes to be the old man's heart, although readers rather associate it with the madman's own pounding heartbeat.

While in this story the exploration of a deranged criminal mind is divorced from supernatural connotations, a few years later, and on the other side of the Atlantic, the rise of Sensation fiction would revive this tradition, complicating it through new pseudo-scientific explanatory paradigms. It is in the work of William Wilkie Collins that the sensational exploration of the psyche produces the most interesting results. As Jenny Bourne Taylor argues, Collins's novels combine

> [d]iscourses about consciousness and identity, about the social formation of the self, about the workings of the unconscious and the interlinking of the mind and the body, about the problematic boundaries between sanity and madness – the concerns of nineteenth-century psychology. (1988: 2)

Rather than in *The Woman in White* (1860), whose persecuted heroine is confined to an asylum, Collins's interest in the criminal mind comes across in texts such as *Armadale* (1866). In this highly melodramatic novel, the aptly named Miss Lydia Gwilt, a fascinating villainess, is torn between love and greed, not to mention revenge, as readers learn through long introspective excerpts from her diary.

However, it is in *The Moonstone* (1868) that the psyche of the 'criminal' is finally at the core of an innovative psychological investigation. Having stolen a diamond while in a state of trance, Franklin Blake discovers his 'guilt', but he is unable to prove his innocence. Thanks to Ezra Jennings, the assistant of the doctor who gave Blake opium without his consent, he later succeeds in clearing his reputation. Jennings, who has spent years writing 'a book on the intricate and delicate subject of the brain and the nervous system', unlocks the mind of the doctor, who has lost his memory, by noting down the broken sentences he repeats in his delirium (Collins 1982: 414). After obtaining this testimony, Jennings helps Blake set up an experiment. The circumstances that accompanied the theft will be recreated, in the hope of locating the valuable object, which may still be concealed in the house. Collins took great pains to ground this experiment as solidly as possible. The novel is set in 1848–49, and to prove his point Jennings refers to recent studies such as John Elliotson's *Human Physiology* (1840) and William Benjamin Carpenter's *Principles of Human Physiology* (1844), from which he quotes this passage:

> There seems much ground for the belief, that *every* sensory impression which has once been recognised by the perceptive consciousness, is registered (so to speak) in the brain, and may be reproduced at some subsequent time, although there may be no consciousness of its existence in the mind during the whole intermediate period. (1982: 433)

As we can see, contemporary research on the physiology of the brain and the phenomenon of consciousness filtered into Sensation fiction, where it coexists with superstitious references to the supernatural. The complexity of this conceptual scenario should not obscure the fact that nineteenth-century crime novelists, as Stephen Kern argues, 'typically crafted clear and strong deterministic causal factors' (2004: 4), such as the biological paradigm of heredity that Collins explored in *The Legacy of Cain* (1888).

The *fin de siècle* was also marked by a new interest in the criminal, under the aegis of Cesare Lombroso. Havelock Ellis's *The Criminal* (1890) includes chapters on both physical and psychical criminal anthropology. The impact of this new science was so powerful that in Bram Stoker's *Dracula* (1897) the vampire is described by Van Helsing as 'a criminal and of criminal type'; he continues, adding that 'Nordau and Lombroso would so classify him, and *qua* criminal he is of imperfectly formed mind' (1993: 439). Dracula's mind is attentively studied by Van Helsing in order to anticipate his strategy, and the regressive nature of the vampire-as-criminal is rendered as follows: 'The criminal has not full man-brain. He is clever and cunning and resourceful; but he be not of man-stature as to brain. He be of child-brain in much' (Stoker 1993: 439). These words call our attention to the overlap between crime fiction and Victorian Gothic, which is also evidenced by Robert Louis Stevenson's *Dr. Jekyll and Mr. Hyde* (1886) and Oscar Wilde's *The Picture of Dorian Gray* (1891), two stories about divided selves. Stevenson's *Markheim* (1885) also testifies to this renewed appeal of the criminal psyche, possibly revealing the influence of Fyodor Dostoevsky's *Crime and Punishment* (1866).

Positivism and Syncretism

In the age of Positivism, human beings felt ready to appropriate the divine attribute of omniscience, as famously articulated by Sherlock Holmes when he claims in *A Study in Scarlet* (1887) that 'all life is a great chain, the nature of which is known whenever we are shown a single link of it' (Doyle 2003: 16). Science offered the key to see through the mystery of a world that had progressively been deprived of its supernatural aura, and this led many scientists to explore phenomena or beliefs that had been previously ascribed to superstition and religion, thus engendering a new form of syncretism. In order to render the mobility of late-nineteenth-century crime fiction, often stemming from experimental cross-pollinations, I will contrast two texts which both connect the exploration of the psyche with crime, respectively gesturing towards the clue puzzle and the Gothic.

Grant Allen's *Recalled to Life* (1891) may be regarded as the first fully-fledged psycho-thriller, a novel that rests on Allen's in-depth knowledge of contemporary psychology, of which full proof is offered by his early *Physiological Æsthetics* (1877). Dedicated to Herbert Spencer, this study straddles the border between the body and the psyche, as acknowledged by the author, in whose eyes the essay 'might with equal propriety be called either *physiological* or *psychological*' (1877: viii). The book teems with references to scientific studies, ranging from Spencer's *Principles of Psychology* (1855) to Alexander Bain's *The Senses and the Intellect* (1855) and *The Emotions and the Will* (1859), not to mention works by Hermann von Helmholtz, Julius Bernstein and others.

In line with this scientific background, and in obedience to the laws of the market, *Recalled to Life* sheds lurid light on the mind right from the opening of its thrilling first-person narrative, focused on shock-induced amnesia:

> It may sound odd to say so, but the very earliest fact that impressed itself on my memory was a scene that took place – so I was told – when I was eighteen years old, in my father's house, The Grange, at Woodbury.
>
> My babyhood, my childhood, my girlhood, my school-days were all utterly blotted out by that one strange shock of horror. My past life became exactly as though it had never been. I forgot my own name. I forgot my mother-tongue. I forgot everything I had ever done or known or thought about. Except for the power to walk and stand and perform simple actions of every-day use, I became a baby in arms again, with a nurse to take care of me. The doctors told me, later, I had fallen into what they were pleased to call 'a Second State.' I was examined and reported upon as a Psychological Curiosity. But at the time, I knew nothing of all this. A thunderbolt, as it were, destroyed at one blow every relic, every trace of my previous existence; and I began life all over again, with that terrible scene of blood as my first birthday. (1891: 1–2)

What causes Una Callingham to fall into this Second State is the murder of her father, a traumatic event she witnesses, although she subsequently proves unable to remember any details preceding the fatal shot. Her first memory, which she describes as a 'strange mental photograph', includes a vision of a man jumping out of a window, a man she believes to be the murderer (1891: 4). Una's horrifying and obsessively recurring memory of the event – 'No sensitive-plate could have photographed it more instantaneously, as by an electric spark, than did my retina that evening' – resonates with the favourite pastime of Una's father, taking pictures of moving objects (1891: 5). (We might think here of the case of pioneering photographer Eadweard Muybridge who in 1874 famously murdered his wife's lover but was acquitted by the jury on the grounds of justifiable homicide.) As we can see, this novel is topical in many respects. The murder scene itself is repeatedly photographed by Una's father's apparatus, which is accidentally set in motion during the confrontation that leads to the fatal shot. The plates, however, are missing – all but one, which coincides with Una's visual impression, and which will play a role in Una's brave investigation, aimed at both finding the culprit and retrieving her own identity.

While *Recalled to Life* exploits and popularizes state-of-the-art science and technology, Henry James's *The Turn of the Screw* (1898) has been regarded by Tzvetan Todorov as a pure example of the fantastic due to its inherent ambiguity, which makes it impossible to choose between a natural and a supernatural account of events (1975: 43). This undecidable text is indeed the product of a syncretic cultural background that the author experienced, among other things, via his brother William James, who not only authored *Principles of Psychology* in 1890, but who had also contributed to the foundation of the American branch of the Society for Psychical Research as early as 1884.

The Turn of the Screw can be regarded as a psycho-thriller if we embrace the so-called Freudian reading, which was first propounded by Edna Kenton (1924). From this perspective, the ghosts of Peter Quint and Miss Jessel exist only in the mind of the neurotic young governess, who is invested with too great a responsibility, who is prevented by her employer from communicating with him if anything goes wrong, and who is moreover in love with him. The governess's attempts to protect her young wards, Flora and Miles, from demonic possession are thus utterly misguided and result in the unnecessary death of Miles, whose heart fails under mounting psychological pressure to confess to connivance with the ghosts.

James renders the governess's psychological instability by enmeshing his readers in a set of undecidable oppositions, as shown by the opening of her narrative: 'I remember the whole beginning as a succession of flights and drops, a little see-saw of the right throbs and the wrong' (2011: 11). The governess's excitability, her sleepless nights and her anxiety concerning her task result in a fretful mental state: 'It wasn't so much yet that I was more nervous than I could bear to be as that I was remarkably afraid of becoming so' (28). This emotional crescendo makes the heroine subject to delusions and reminds us of Poe's deranged protagonists, whose hyper-sensitivity she shares: 'The shock I had suffered must have sharpened all my senses' (28).

Considering the governess as an unreliable narrator whose course of action produces 'criminal' results typifies the text as a psycho-thriller, while its inherent ambiguity exemplifies the overlap between the psycho-thriller and the ghost story. Literature revels in complexity and we should be wary of creating critical pigeonholes. While certain texts deliberately exploit a formula, others can be profitably studied in relation to various genres, the conventions of which they combine. As a result of this textual mobility the atlas of genres is unceasingly reconfigured by writers, although critical investigations sometimes obliterate this complexity in the attempt to offer easy-to-use guidebooks to past literature.

Let us remember that Sherlock Holmes coexisted at the turn of the century with detectives of the occult like Flaxman Low and John Silence, who used their pseudo-scientific knowledge to combat, like Van Helsing, a variety of supernatural opponents. In his first adventure – 'A Psychical Invasion' (1908) – Silence presents himself as a 'psychic Doctor' and deals with the case of a man whose drug-taking has put him into contact with a dangerous discarnate entity (Blackwood 1997: 2). As we can see, while the scientific exploration of the human psyche was advancing, alternative avenues were also being explored both in literature and in real life, as shown by the spectacular split between Sigmund Freud and Carl Gustav Jung in 1913.

Psychoanalysis and Film Adaptation

We have now reached a Freudian stage in the development of the psycho-thriller in which psychoanalysis provides a paradigm for both the conceptualization of the mind and its investigation, but the genre is not yet recognizable in the eyes of the public. It is my contention that its popularization coincides with Hitchcock's mid-twentieth-century film adaptations. This testifies once again to the mobility of genres, the development of which is not restricted to a single medium, but is effected through ceaseless metamorphoses. A transdisciplinary critical approach is therefore needed.

The disparate British novels Hitchcock domesticated into Hollywood cinematic products provide the missing link between post-Second World War (film and literary) psycho-thrillers and the antecedents previously mentioned. Of course, calling attention to these texts should not make us oblivious to the relevance American noir had on the development of the psycho-thriller, thanks to its emphasis on the criminal mind and the bitterly retrospective gaze that marks first-person narratives like Horace McCoy's *They Shoot Horses, Don't They?* (1935), James M. Cain's *The Postman Always Rings Twice* (1934) and *Double Indemnity* (1943). Hard-boiled narratives are fraught with domestic and social tensions that pave the way for the development of aberrant anti-heroes.

Let us now focus on Hitchcock's early psycho-thrillers, which came well before his 1960 adaptation of Robert Bloch's *Psycho*, and date back to the first half of the 1940s, when he moved to Hollywood after signing a seven-year contract with producer David O. Selznick. Not all of these psycho-thrillers stem from previously published works. *Shadow of a Doubt* (1943), for instance, is based on a story outline by Gordon McDonell entitled 'Uncle Charlie', which Hitchcock was sent in May 1942. In other cases, Hitchcock and Selznick were inspired by printed novels. *Rebecca* (1940) is based on the eponymous best-seller Daphne du Maurier authored in 1938; *Suspicion* (1941) is an adaptation of Francis Iles's (aka Anthony Berkeley Cox) *Before the Fact* (1932); while *Spellbound* (1945) rewrites *The House of Dr. Edwardes*, published in 1927 by John Palmer and Hilary A. Saunders under the pseudonym of Francis Beeding.

Hitchcock believed he owed his success to his '"ruthlessness" in adapting stories for the screen' (Leff 1987: 39), and it was through this transformative process that the psycho-thriller formula came into being, for the three novels I have just listed are very different. Since the chronology of their adaptation does not coincide with that of their publication, I shall begin with Francis Iles's *Before the Fact*, which is a case apart. One of the founding fathers of the London Detection Club, Cox pursued a parallel career, signing as Francis Iles a series of stories – starting from *Malice Aforethought* (1931) – in which the identity of the criminal is known from the outset and the focus is on his modus operandi. The impersonal narration of *Before the Fact* combines an uncannily ironic tone with the perspective of the victim, as shown by its opening lines: 'Some women give birth to murderers, some go to bed with them, and some marry them. Lina Aysgarth had lived with her husband for nearly eight years before she realized that she was married to a murderer' (Iles 2011: 5). In both avatars of this story, suspense stems from Lina's difficulty in reading the motives behind her husband's behaviour, her harrowing suspicion, although the dark conclusion of the book is turned into a happy ending by Hitchcock.

Unlike *Suspicion*, both *Rebecca* and *Spellbound* revisit the Gothic in the light of psychoanalysis, although the relation between these two films and the novels on which they are based is different. It was Selznick who had chosen to work on du Maurier's old-fashioned story, which moreover demanded a rather faithful adaptation, being too famous to take liberties with. Despite Hitchcock's qualms about this late-Gothic narrative, *Rebecca* introduces a number of elements that are central to the psycho-thriller, starting with the dream sequence that opens both novel and film: 'Last night I dreamt I went to Manderley again' (du Maurier 1943: 1).

The plot hinges on the survival of a malevolent past in the present, while exorcism takes the form of the fire that destroys Manderley itself. The emblem of Maximilian de Winter's aristocratic pride, which prompted him to compromise with his corrupt first wife to save appearances, the country house is imbued with the spirit of Rebecca, a revenant who is kept alive through the mediumistic agency of Mrs Danvers. Doubles abound in this story, climaxing in the costume the second Mrs de Winter wears to the fancy dress ball, not knowing that she is mimicking Rebecca. The novel itself can be regarded as a parodic double of the Gothic, starting from its conventional set of characters – the second Mrs de Winter, insecure and awkward; her apparently Bluebeardish husband, actually a traumatized, vulnerable man; the villainess, whose madly unconditional love for her former mistress and hatred for her successor result in tragedy. The aberrant mind at the core of the narrative is hers, but it is through the eyes of the heroine that we experience this suspenseful story.

While du Maurier's *Rebecca* provided Selznick and Hitchcock with ready-made ingredients for a cinematic psycho-thriller, *Spellbound* retains very few elements of the adapted novel. Marked by excess, *The House of Dr. Edwardes* is predicated on the tension between a scientific investigation of the psyche and its uncanny power as a Gothic site of darkness. The book is imbued with Satanism, which indelibly tinges its Alpine setting, starting from the opening scene, set in the Gorge du Diable. It is at this time that Doctor Murchison – who has just arrived from England to take the place of Dr Edwardes as the director of a nearby asylum – is introduced. We learn through his testimony that a few moments earlier the patient he was driving to the asylum had hurled the chauffeur down the gorge and attacked the doctor himself, although the latter had managed to strike the madman unconscious. A different interpretation of events is possible, notably in view of the fact that the supposed madman is immediately taken to the asylum – housed in a Gothic castle – and immured, in his unconscious state, in a former dungeon.

We become acquainted with these preliminaries in a prologue narrated through the letters of a casual witness, an Englishwoman on her honeymoon. The heroine – young psychoanalyst Constance Sedgwick – is introduced from chapter 1 and starts relating events in her own voice. Arriving at the asylum, she promptly falls in love with the charmingly clever Dr Murchison, only to discover him at the head of a conspiracy that will increasingly turn the castle into a site of confinement.

This story of madness and Satanism will be sanitized in the process of adaptation, also with an eye to the notorious Hays Code, which pre-emptively censored both profanity and sex perversion. The result is a film that retains only some basic aspects of the novel, notably a young female psychoanalyst who falls in love with a suitably handsome young gentleman who has assumed the identity of a presumably dead doctor. Selznick was interested in 'a picture about psychotherapy, not psychopaths', as Leonard J. Leff argues (1987: 117), reminding us that Selznick had been treated for depression by May E. Romm, who is mentioned in the credits as psychiatric advisor for the film. Due to the producer's influence, the film insists on psychoanalysis with educational clarity, right from the opening screen statements. Against the backdrop of what will soon be revealed to be a lunatic asylum, viewers can read this sentence: 'The fault... is not in our stars, but in ourselves... – Shakespeare' (Hitchcock 1945). It is through the mediation of the Bard – the authoritative figure par excellence in the humanities – that the scientific import of Freud's theories is then introduced:

> Our story deals with psychoanalysis, the method by which modern science treats the emotional problems of the sane. The analyst seeks only to induce the patient to talk about his hidden problems, to open the locked doors of his mind. Once the complexes that have been disturbing the patient are uncovered and interpreted, the illness and confusion disappear... and the devils of unreason are driven from the human soul. (Hitchcock 1945)

Although these lines may raise a smile, they effectively detail the minimal knowledge original viewers needed to master in order to understand a film focusing on a psychoanalyst's investigation into trauma-induced amnesia.

This broadly sketched scientific background takes on sensational undertones thanks both to the amnesiac hero's violent reaction to a specific trigger (a set of parallel lines drawn on a white background) and to a dream sequence that was famously designed by Salvador Dalí. These aspects of the film were influenced by German expressionist cinema, notably by Georg Wilhelm Pabst's *Secrets of a Soul* (*Geheimnisse einer Seele*, 1926), the story of a scientist who suffers from nightmares and an irrational fear of knives, feeling driven to kill his wife. According to Gary Giddins (2010: 207), 'Hitchcock had to have seen this film. Probably more than once'. Pabst's early psycho-thriller includes not only a specific trigger, but a long dream sequence that is painstakingly decoded by a specialist. The film is even preceded – like *Spellbound* – by a concise introduction to psychoanalysis:

> Inside every person there are desires and passions which remain unknown to 'consciousness'. In the dark hours of psychological conflict, these 'unconscious' drives attempt to assert themselves. Mysterious illnesses arise from such struggles, the resolution and cure of which form the field of psychoanalysis. (Pabst 1926)

Hitchcock may have also had Robert Wiene's *The Cabinet of Dr. Caligari* (*Das Cabinet des Dr. Caligari*, 1920) in mind, due to the film's representation of a madman's ravings through a non-naturalistic visual style and against the backdrop of an asylum. Madness and asylums famously feature also in the Dr Mabuse series Fritz Lang filmed from 1922, based on Norbert Jacques's novel *Dr. Mabuse, der Spieler* (1921). Clearly, *Spellbound* resulted from the hybridization of literary and cinematic sources, not to mention a variety of genres. Dr Petersen's (Ingrid Bergman) inquiry even recalls those nineteenth-century female detectives whose investigations were motivated by their desire to save the man they loved, as in Collins's *The Law and the Lady* (1875).

Conclusions

As shown by this critical itinerary, which stops before *Psycho* had been either written or filmed, the psycho-thriller has a long history, antedating psychoanalysis, since one may claim that this form ripened already in Godwin's *Caleb Williams*, a narrative that is informed by the philosopher's theory of the mind. Having said this, I am more interested in tracing connections rather than in marking beginnings, which are after all a matter of convention. Far from aiming to identify the precise origin of the psycho-thriller, this essay has investigated the period in which this form was not yet recognizable by the public, and no critical term had been coined to define it, a stage of incubation in which conventions such as trauma- or drug-induced amnesia were already experimented with.

There is another lesson this case study teaches us, concerning the mobility not only of genres but also of criticism. Stories focusing on the criminal mind were marginalized by critics in the early twentieth century, when an increasing body of essays concurred in the definition of what was newly perceived as a literary genre under headings such as detective or mystery story. The Golden Age focus on the investigation obscured any fictional explorations of the criminal mind. In Carolyn Wells's seminal *The Technique of the Mystery Story* (1913: 238), for instance, the 'ideal criminal' is portrayed as 'sane, respectable and well-educated' in order to 'escape the reader's suspicion'. In 1931 H. Douglas Thomson even voiced his hostility to any attempt to delve into the criminal mind: 'The recent tendency to make of the detective story a psychological study of criminal "types" and "complexes," though in a sense legitimate, cannot but be distasteful to the true lover of detective fiction' (24).

A notable exception is provided by Dorothy Sayers's *Great Short Stories of Detection, Mystery and Horror* (1928), an anthology that embraces a 'new kind of terror' stemming from the study of the psyche: 'the nightmare country between sanity and madness; the pressure of mind upon living mind, and the lonely horror of the dark places of the soul' (45). Sayers's acknowledgement of this formula, however, failed to inspire contemporary critics. One would have to wait until the publication of Julian Symons's *Bloody Murder. From the Detective Story to the Crime Novel: A History* (1972) to see this critical tendency reversed, in relation to a changed literary landscape, a highly diversified spectrum of crime writing that demanded to be investigated regardless of artificial boundaries.

Symons's book is ironically introduced by a nonsensical question and a curt reply: 'Is it a detective crime psychological analytical suspense police story? No, it's a hybrid' (1985: 13). Far from being waterproof containers, subgenres are permeable, and we are now ready to recognize the situated quality of criticism itself. We theorize and historicize cultural phenomena within frameworks that make sense to us, but that may prove less meaningful to future readers. Crime criticism is as mobile as crime fiction, and we need to maintain its flexibility in order to mediate our ever-changing relation with both our present and past.

Works Cited

Allen, Grant (1877). *Physiological Æsthetics* (London: Henry S. King).
— (1891). *Recalled to Life* (New York: Henry Holt).
Blackwood, Algernon (1997). 'A Psychical Invasion', in S.T. Joshi (ed.), *The Complete John Silence Stories* (Mineola, NY: Dover), 1–43.
Brown, Charles Brockden (1991) [1798]. *Wieland; or, the Transformation*, in Jay Fliegelman (ed.), *Wieland and Memoirs of Carwin the Biloquist* (Harmondsworth: Penguin), 1–278.
Collins, William Wilkie (1982) [1868]. *The Moonstone* (Oxford and New York: Oxford University Press).
De Quincey, Thomas (2006) [1823]. 'On the Knocking at the gate in Macbeth', in Robert Morrison (ed.), *On Murder* (Oxford: Oxford University Press), 3–7.
Doyle, Arthur Conan (2003) [1887]. *A Study in Scarlet* (New York: The Modern Library).
Du Maurier, Daphne (1943). *Rebecca* (New York: The Modern Library).
Giddins, Gary (2010). *Warning Shadows: Home Alone with Classic Cinema* (New York and London: Norton).

Godwin, William (1970) [1794]. *Caleb Williams*, David McCracken (ed.), (Oxford and New York: Oxford University Press).

— (1976) [1793]. *Enquiry Concerning Political Justice and Its Influence on Modern Morals and Happiness*, Isaac Kramnick (ed.), (Harmondsworth: Penguin).

Hitchcock, Alfred (1945). *Spellbound* (United Artists).

Hogg, James (1990) [1824]. *The Private Memoirs and Confessions of a Justified Sinner* (Oxford and New York: Oxford University Press).

Iles, Francis (2011) [1932]. *Before the Fact* (London: Arcturus).

James, Henry (2011) [1898]. *The Turn of the Screw* (Harmondsworth: Penguin).

Kenton, Edna (1924). 'Henry James to the Ruminant Reader: *The Turn of the Screw*'. *The Arts* 11: 245–55.

Kern, Stephen (2004). *A Cultural History of Causality: Science, Murder Novels, and Systems of Thought* (Princeton and Oxford: Princeton University Press).

Knight, Stephen (2015). *Secrets of Crime Fiction Classics: Detecting the Delights of 21 Enduring Stories* (Jefferson, NC: McFarland).

Leff, Leonard J. (1987). *Hitchcock and Selznick: The Rich and Strange Collaboration of Alfred Hitchcock and David O. Selznick in Hollywood* (Berkeley and London: University of California Press).

Mecholsky, Kristopher (2014). 'The Psychological Thriller in Context', in Gary Hoppenstand (ed.), *The American Thriller* (Lansing, MI: Michigan State University), 48–70.

Pabst, Georg Wilhelm (1926). *Secrets of a Soul* (Geheimnisse einer Seele) (UFA).

Packer, Sharon (2007). *Movies and the Modern Psyche* (Westport, CN and London: Praeger).

Poe, Edgar Allan (1984) [1843]. 'The Tell-Tale Heart', in *Tales of Mystery and the Imagination* (London: Dent).

Sayers, Dorothy (ed.) (1928). *Great Short Stories of Detection, Mystery and Horror* (London: Gollancz).

Shelley, Mary (1969) [1818]. *Frankenstein; or, The Modern Prometheus* (Oxford and New York: Oxford University Press).

Simpson, Philip (2010). 'Noir and the Psycho-Thriller', in Charles Rzepka and Lee Horsley (eds), *A Companion to Crime Fiction* (Malden, MA: Wiley-Blackwell), 187–97.

Stoker, Bram (1993) [1897]. *Dracula* (Harmondsworth: Penguin).

Symons, Julian (1985) [1972]. *Bloody Murder. From the Detective Story to the Crime Novel: A History* (Harmondsworth: Viking).

Taylor, Jenny Bourne (1988). *In the Secret Theatre of Home: Wilkie Collins, Sensation Narrative, and Nineteenth-Century Psychology* (London and New York: Routledge).

Thomson, H. Douglas (1931). *Masters of Mystery: A Study of the Detective Story* (London: Collins).

Todorov, Tzvetan (1975). *The Fantastic: A Structural Approach to a Literary Genre*. Trans. Richard Howard (Ithaca and New York: Cornell University Press).

Wells, Carolyn (1913). *The Technique of the Mystery Story* (Springfield, MA: The Home Correspondence School).

CHAPTER SIX

Foggy Muddle

Narrative, Contingency and Genre Mobility in Dashiell Hammett's *The Dain Curse*

Jesper Gulddal, University of Newcastle, Australia

In a little-noted episode in Dashiell Hammett's *The Dain Curse* (1928/29), the anonymous detective (the 'Op'), the ill-starred Gabrielle Leggett and Eric Collinson, her fiancé, are involved in a dramatic, although ultimately harmless, car accident. Having rescued the young woman, a drug addict, from the eerie Temple of the Holy Grail, the Op wants to take her home in Collinson's Chrysler. The fiancé, however, in a state of near panic, has misgiving about returning Ms Leggett to her father and stepmother, preferring to have her examined by a doctor. When the detective insists, trying first to grab the wheel and then proceeding to curse the young man 'bitterly, fairly thoroughly, and from the heart' (Hammett 1999: 230), Collinson speeds up the vehicle and eventually loses control when swerving to avoid a sedan at an intersection:

> Collinson did what he could, giving the roadster its head, going with the skid, but the corner curb wouldn't co-operate. It stood stiff and hard where it was. We hit it sidewise and rolled over on the lamp-post behind it. The lamp-post snapped, crashed down on the sidewalk. The roadster, over on its side, spilled us out around the lamp-post. Gas from the broken post roared up at our feet. (231)

In an insightful study, Inka Mülder-Bach has positioned the traffic accident as 'a key scene of modernity', connecting the modernist interest in accidents to contemporary discourses of risk and trauma while also reading it as a means of representing the modern world from the point of view of its discontinuities and contingences (2000: 198–99). The scene in *The Dain Curse* – one of two car crashes in this novel – exemplifies this logic. A critic looking for meaning and purpose might suggest that the brief account of the accident, apart from adding another piece of action, highlights the contrast between the two aspiring protectors of Miss Leggett, that is, between Collinson's timidity and the Op's uncouth but capable masculinity. In strictly narrative terms, though, the car crash has no discernible function and could have been edited out without materially affecting the overall plot. Unconnected in this manner, it instead takes on emblematic significance. On the one hand, the high-speed getaway indexes a preoccupation with mobility in Hammett's novel, not simply in the sense of actual movement, but more generally as an abhorrence of stasis – a desire to carve out new potentials by breaking free, even violently, from any form of rootedness that has become restrictive. On the other hand, it points towards a corresponding preoccupation with contingency, both in the sense of a moment of suddenness that interrupts the flows of continuity and predictability and, narratively, as an episode that is not integrated into the plot in a logical and motivated way. Bringing together these emblematic meanings, the strange car crash is suggestive of what I propose is a defining feature of both *The Dain Curse* and of Hammett's crime fiction in general: the urge to disrupt all generic scripts and thereby transform detective fiction from a narrative of necessity into one of contingency.

In this chapter I read *The Dain Curse* as a paradigmatic manifestation of the 'genre mobility' discussed in the introduction to the present collection. The critical shift outlined here from a conception of detective fiction as a static form characterized by close adherence to established formulae to one that instead emphasizes the non-conforming and experimental dimensions of the genre, in short, its mobility, offers an attractive model of understanding what is at stake in this highly idiosyncratic work. Hammett's second novel can in fact be read as an all-out attack on the very notion of 'genre fiction' as a form of literature defined by its performance of a generic template. As I aim to show, it continuously evokes the norms and conventions of the contemporary pulp genres in ways that deliberately 'crash' them by violating the narrative constraints that they embody. The result is a novel that is anything but conventional, but also one whose essence lies in the negation of pre-existing tropes. If *The Dain Curse*, as is often suggested, is a flawed novel, its flaws are due not so much to its alleged incoherence, but rather to the fact that its negativity keeps referring it back to the genre norms it wants to overcome.

As a way of turning these theoretical reflections into analytical method, the chapter focuses on the mobile textual practices that define the novel and that ultimately lead it to challenge the very foundations of the detective genre. The aim, in short, is to observe the novel as it escapes from genre rules and constraints.

* * *

In *Gumshoe America*, Sean McCann offers a detailed analysis of Hammett's unusual position within the literary field of the 1920s. Showing how Hammett was active across several emerging subfields while at the same time straddling the more and more rigorously policed divide between popular and elite literature, McCann reads the author as defined by a productive 'combination of attitudes' – a flexible stance epitomized by the fact that he found his material in the world of pulp and aspired to turn it into art, yet remained equally resentful of pulp's lack of literary ambition and the pretentiousness of the literary establishment (2000: 95; see also 91–102). Building on McCann's characterization, I want to suggest that it is this eccentricity in relation to the dominant literary groupings of the day that makes Hammett an eminently mobile writer, and in particular a writer with a mobile take on the established conventions of his chosen genre.

Perhaps the strongest testimony to Hammett's commitment to literary mobility is the fact that each of his five published novels in a radical sense represents a new beginning. They share a certain 'hard-boiled' attitude but are different across most other parameters. The raw violence of *Red Harvest* (1927/28), a novel often regarded as a reimagined western (González 2016), is fundamentally different from the light-hearted urbaneness of *The Thin Man* (1933), while *The Maltese Falcon* (1929/30), with its adventure plot involving the intercontinental pursuit of a precious historical artefact, is far removed from the complex political intrigues of *The Glass Key* (1930). *The Dain Curse*, for its part, is not only at odds with every other novel in the corpus, but also with itself. Moreover, Hammett appears to have been oddly uninterested in what had long been the genre's principal marketing device, namely the detective series. The Op is the only one of his protagonists to appear in more than one novel, yet lacks name, biography, family, an existence beyond the job and indeed all the individual traits and idiosyncrasies that make for a successful serial detective. A highly changeable character, he retains a certain physical identity as a 'middle-aged fat man' (Hammett 1999: 291), but at the same time morphs from a cynical *agent provocateur* in *Red Harvest* to something of a chivalric hero in *The Dain Curse*, prefiguring Chandler's Marlowe.

The latter work replicates this restlessness internally. Stuart Burrows remarks that Hammett's novels 'escape strict genre classification' and specifically suggests that *The Dain Curse* is 'as much horror as noir' (2016: 56). While this is an apt characterization, the novel in fact displays a more generalized discomfort with genre and goes much further in combining and disaggregating established formats. Rather than embodying one genre, or forging a two-element hybrid, it offers a compendium of popular forms, incorporating aspects not only of noir and horror, but also of mystery, gothic, adventure, weird and romance as well as the sex story and the drug narrative, both topical formats in the late 1920s (Panek 2004: 154–58). Yet, the novel never simply executes these genre blueprints, but subverts them, baiting readerly expectations only to disappoint them while at the same time consistently preventing generic scripts from running their full course from the beginning to the more or less preordained end. Part One is a case in point. With its manor house-like setting, its locked room narrative, its cast of eccentric characters with secretive pasts and, most strikingly, its dramatic reveal scene in Leggett's laboratory, this part clearly references the clue puzzle format, which by the 1920s had become dominant in both British and American detective fiction. However, the narrative repeatedly veers off course, incorporating, for example, a somewhat disconnected story of a small-time black hustler, an outrageous adventure subplot focusing on Leggett's escape from Devil's Island and an ending full of genre-defying gore and violence; moreover, the story presented in Part 1 is reframed in the subsequent parts, thereby largely invalidating the detective's concluding interpretation of events, another stock feature of the clue puzzle genre. As Brooks E. Hefner notes, Part 2 of the novel, which focuses on Gabrielle Leggett's involvement with the cult of the Temple of the Holy Grail, is indebted to the weird horror fiction of H.P. Lovecraft. Yet, while drawing on weird tropes and sharing, as Hefner convincingly demonstrates, the latent racism of this genre, *The Dain Curse* breaks from the script by repeatedly demystifying weird events – as, for example, when the Op learns that his bizarre altercation with 'God' in Minnie Hershey's temple cell was a scam involving hallucinogenic drugs and intricate visual effects.

The novel's plethora of genre references should not be mistaken for genre hybridity in the sense of a combining and intermixing of genre elements to produce new formats. No real blending occurs. The peculiar alternation of styles and scripts, which is such a prominent feature of this novel, should be seen instead as a specific form of genre mobility whereby the novel, rather than settling within one pre-existing framework, successively tries on different genre vestments, each time outgrowing them and ripping them up from within. Genre, as a result, becomes something provisional: a territory that the novel passes through rather than occupies.

Mobility of a comparable kind, effecting a similar provisionality, manifests itself in the novel's overall narrative structure. The distinctive feature of this structure is its segmentation into three seemingly self-contained parts. Each part sees the Op take on a new case involving Gabrielle Leggett, yet each constitutes a separate investigative problem: Part 1 revolves around a set of diamonds stolen from the Leggett residence; Part 2 on the rescue of the drug-addled Gabrielle from a religious cult; and Part 3 on a series of killings beginning with the murder of Gabrielle's now-husband, Collinson, on their honeymoon. While the two first parts end with what, superficially considered, are conventional revelation scenes where the riddles find their solutions, the second and third parts retrospectively cast doubt on the previous solutions and gesture instead towards a larger and more intricate mystery. It is only at the very end of the final part that the novel's individual episodes are revealed by the Op to form a coherent whole with a criminal mastermind as the organizing centre – although not, as I will show, without raising further questions.

Understanding this idiosyncratic structure has been a major concern in the critical literature. A widespread view maintains that the novel's storyline is flawed, resulting in a disjointed collection of episodes rather than a coherent plot. Robert L. Gale, in *A Dashiell Hammett Companion*, ascribes the novel's 'manifest lack of unity' (2000: 54) to the fact that it was first published across four issues of *The Black Mask*; however, four of Hammett's five completed novels first appeared in serial form, and none of the others appears similarly affected. LeRoy Lad Panek explains the incoherence of *The Dain Curse* as a result of Hammett having packed more action into the novel than its structure and scope could sustain, leaving some of its episodes 'muddy and confused' (2004: 164), while Hefner describes what he calls 'Hammett's messiest long-form work' as a novel pushed to the limit by its spatiotemporal jolts and its 'exceedingly pulpy' agglomeration of episodes (2014: 652–53). Other critics, most prominently Sinda Gregory and Bruce Gatenby, have put a more positive spin on the novel's fragmented structure, the former arguing that the novel's circular, self-reflexive form amounts to a scepticism regarding our ability to 'uncover any final solutions to life's mysteries' (1994: 35), whereas the latter makes the similar point that *The Dain Curse* 'disrupts traditional literary notions of completeness, of a revelatory interpretive truth or final solution' (1994: 57).

Critics lamenting the incoherence of the plot are sometimes implicitly subscribing to a traditionalist understanding of the detective genre as defined by narrative linearity and 'end-orientation' (Gulddal 2016a), that is, by a unidirectional progression towards an endpoint where mystery is dispersed and the full truth of the crime revealed. This account already represents an unwarranted interpretative constraint in the context of the subgenre with which it is most commonly associated, namely detective fiction of the Golden Age, which is often less streamlined and more complex than commonly assumed. Applied to Hammett, it completely misses its mark. The narrative mess of *The Dain Curse* is not due to the author somehow failing to achieve the full structural integration expected of the detective novel. Far from aspiring to this ideal, the novel self-reflexively and programmatically departs from it. This departure can be seen from two different aspects. From the point of view of an aesthetics of mobility, it amounts to a narrative car crash designed to break free from the categories that, in their most rigid application, make detective fiction a particularly uncompromising realization of some of the basic dispositions of narrative: necessity, integration, balance, motivation, finality, sensemaking. The result is not failure, but rather the emergence of a different set of aesthetic categories characteristic of Hammett's fiction as well as, to a lesser degree, hard-boiled detective fiction in general: mess, contingency, excess, contamination, absence of final and authoritative meanings. From the point of view of epistemology, the departure from established detective fiction conventions leads to scepticism concerning the decodability of crime. The revelation scenes at the end of the first two parts seem to suggest a traditional linear plot culminating in the detective's authoritative solution. Yet, the novel's macrostructure – its repeated reopening of the case – disrupts this teleology and thereby also challenges its correlates: meaning, truth, closure. Isabelle Boof-Vermesse has usefully theorized this structure as a 'feedback loop' (2003: 164–65) where the output of one part becomes the input for the following, and where each subsequent part undoes any closure achieved up to that point. This circularity inevitably raises the question of how the novel can be brought to a definitive and authoritative conclusion.

Before turning to the novel's ending, however, I want to highlight another example of how Hammett's novel plays on reader expectations only to thwart them in ways that also challenge the authority of the narration. Referred to by Gregory as 'Hammett's most brilliant strategic success in the novel' (1994: 49), the interactions between the Op and his acquaintance, novelist Owen Fitzstephan, offer a mobile take on the classic partnership between the detective and his sidekick. In its canonized form, this partnership is functionally tied to the representation of an exceptional mind; the presence of a moderately gifted assistant provides a foil for the incomparable brilliance of the detective while at the same time offering readers a point of identification within the text. However, this partnership is also about authority. The sidekick figure is precisely someone who underwrites the authority of the detective, not only by being mediocre, but above all by assuming a passive and deferential stance towards him – that is, by observing, listening, not understanding, learning, admiring and agreeing, and ultimately committing the detective's final truth to paper and signing it with his own authorial name.

This authoritative dimension of the detective/sidekick duality gets short shrift in Hammett's novels. *Red Harvest* ignores the trope altogether, and in *The Maltese Falcon*, Spade's unloved partner, Miles Archer, is killed off between the first and second chapter, thus clearing the way for a private investigator who professionally and existentially is wholly on his own. *The Dain Curse* takes a different course. In a strict formal sense, the relationship between the Op and Fitzstephan is in fact that of a detective/sidekick team, and their recurring conversations reference and transform the convention of the final post-mortem where the detective explains the mystery to his obtuse partner. In tone and content, however, these conversations go far beyond the classic version of this trope. Further, the novel's twist ending, which sees Fitzstephan confess to numerous murders, is an all-out attack on the sidekick convention and hence a move that in its sheer counter-formulaic boldness bears comparison to Agatha Christie's fingering of the narrator as the guilty party in the *The Murder of Roger Ackroyd* (1926).

Rather than undertaking a full analysis of the relationship between the Op and Fitzstephan, I want to highlight how this relationship is closely connected to narration and the authority of the narrative. It is worth recalling that the detective/sidekick structure is inherently self-referential because it is tied to the narrative articulation of the case; it is precisely a function of the Watson character to turn the detective's insights into a clear, orderly and often publishable storyline. The interactions between the Op and Fitzstephan reference this convention, yet the two men's views on truth and narrative never converge. In the discussions that conclude Parts 1 and 2, Fitzstephan, following a professional inclination while potentially also trying to manipulate the Op, is a consistent advocate for narrative simplicity, representing the view that a coherent story, which explains the elements of the case, must by definition also be true. The Op, on the other hand, acts in the role of an anti-narrative sceptic who is wary of reducing the complexities of the case to a straightforward storyline. From the point of view of Fitzstephan, this approach overcomplicates matters, and the writer therefore urges the detective to present the story coherently and with a definitive ending: '[A]fter you've finished the story, you can attach your ifs and buts to it, distorting and twisting it, making it as cloudy and confusing and generally hopeless as you like. But first please finish it, so I'll see it at least once in its original state' (Hammett 1999: 285). For the Op, however, Fitzstephan's insistence on meaning and coherence is naïve, akin to taking at face value the story 'about the wolf that went to the little girl's grandmother's house' (285).

The contrast between the Op and Fitzstephan is rich in philosophical implications and highlights – as Stephen Marcus was the first to point out (1974: xxi–ii) – a central theme of Hammett's fiction: the chasm between our rational or narrative thinking about the world and the world as it really is. The Flitcraft parable in *The Maltese Falcon*, the most famous figuration of this theme, uses a randomly falling beam to shock a car salesman into recognizing that the certitudes on which he has based his middle-class existence – the conviction that life is a 'clean orderly sane responsible affair' (Hammett 1999: 444) – is simply a veil hiding the uncertainty and contingency of life. In *The Dain Curse*, the Op articulates this duality explicitly in conversation with Gabrielle:

> Thinking's a dizzy business, a matter of catching as many of those foggy glimpses as you can and fitting them together the best you can. That's why people hang on so tight to their beliefs and opinions; because, compared to the haphazard way in which they're arrived at, even the goofiest opinion seems wonderfully clear, sane, and self-evident. And if you let it get away from you, then you've got to dive back into that foggy muddle to wangle yourself out another to take its place. (342)

In this passage, the Op is voicing an epistemological scepticism that runs counter to everything the detective story was and to some degree still is. The key idea is that all discursive practices that people deploy to make sense of their world – beliefs, opinions, causes, judgements – are in fact narratives whose coherence and seeming meaningfulness allow us to forget that the world itself is defined by entirely opposite characteristics: insanity, contingency and irreducible mystery. Whereas Fitzstephan, possibly with the aim of leading the Op astray, recommends putting one's faith in simple and neatly rounded narratives, the Op is repeatedly outing narrative as a discursive form designed to offer solace and reprieve, casting himself as someone steely enough to stare into the abyss or, in Hammett's version of this Nietzschean metaphor, take a dive into the 'foggy muddle'. However, as early as in Part 1, Fitzstephan unsettles the conventional divide between the logical analysis of the detective and the imaginative synthesis of the storyteller by suggesting that the two professions are more similar than commonly assumed: while the former aims to '[put] people in jail', the latter, Fitzstephan's own, aims to '[put] people in books', yet in both cases this happens by weaving an explanatory narrative that makes their motivations and actions legible (210). The novel as a whole bears out this claim by highlighting the many competing narratives that the various characters deploy either defensively or offensively with the aim of influencing the investigation; the narratives offered by Mr, Mrs and Miss Leggett and, finally, by Fitzstephan are prominent cases in point, each exhibiting a certain formal perfection in the way in which they cover and connect the facts of the case. The sheer volume of conflicting accounts suggests that the plausibility of a narrative, whether exonerating or accusatory, depends more on its internal coherence than its truthfulness and the Op is accordingly cast as a particularly suspicious literary critic who pokes holes in seemingly unassailable narratives, his own as well as those of others.

Yet, even though the novel offers ample evidence of the need to be sceptical of narrative closure (and hence also of the truth claims of detective fiction), and even though such scepticism is integral to the protagonist's investigative attitude, the Op appears to reverse course in the novel's third part when he accepts the suspiciously neat confessional narrative offered by Fitzstephan. This volte-face should give us pause and make us consider whether the solution provided is in fact as authoritative as it seems. Having carefully cultivated a distrust of narratives and lectured on the need to recognize that 'foggy muddle' and 'dizzy business' form the epistemological basis of detective work, and indeed of knowledge in general, it seems strange indeed that the Op should proceed to accept a story that is more obviously flawed than any of the narrative strands encountered in the first two parts of the novel.

While several critics have commented on how *The Dain Curse* espouses a condition of epistemological uncertainty, most shy away from the most radical consequences of this uncertainty. Carl D. Malmgren, for instance, calls attention to the novel's 'floating signifiers', yet concludes his chapter on Hammett by anchoring these signifiers on what he calls the novel's 'commitment to the truth of narration'; according to Malmgren, 'the narrator of detective fiction cannot and does not break faith with the reader because his narration is the last, best, and only ground' (2001: 89–90), a point that seems to ignore the fact that detective fiction narrators, like all other narrators, can be ignorant, lazy, unreliable and many other things that weaken their claims on truth. Similarly, Gregory offers an insightful discussion of the conversations between the Op and Fitzstephan, arguing that they 'suggest the arbitrary basis of final truths' (1994: 42) and even going so far as to consider in a footnote an alternative solution where Gabrielle Leggett's confession turns out to be true (55); nevertheless, and somewhat paradoxically, the main part of her chapter does not question the 'fact' that Fitzstephan is the 'actual murderer' (50). Only Gatenby draws the logical conclusion by proposing that the Op's solution is 'only one more little narrative in a series of little narratives which never add up to a metanarrative of legitimation' (1994: 64), yet as the wording suggests, this point is based more on postmodern philosophy than on the actual textual logic of the novel's ending.

The solution to the Dain curse mystery eventuates in two stages. In the novel's penultimate chapter, following the bomb attack that almost kills Fitzstephan, the Op confronts the writer in the hospital, accusing him of being the 'one mind behind all Gabrielle's troubles' (Hammett 1999: 375). The heavily bandaged writer responds in his 'usual lazily amused manner' (376–77), first dismissing the allegations with overbearing irony, stating that he always suspected the Op of 'secretly nursing some exceptionally idiotic theory', and then startling the detective by revealing himself to be Gabrielle Leggett's second cousin and hence a carrier of the Dain curse (375). Without ever directly admitting to any of the crimes laid at his feet, Fitzstephan concludes by previewing his legal defence strategy, which is to confess to as many crimes as possible on the assumption that the jury will find him to be insane. The final chapter sees the implementation of this strategy. Tried only for the murder of Mrs Cotton, which, importantly, is the only crime for which any kind of witness or evidence can be produced, Fitzstephan succeeds in putting on the 'splendid circus' he promised the Op (375). He is ultimately committed to an asylum, yet is discharged after only one year, partly due to his severe physical impairment after the explosion.

This ending, like the ending in detective novels generally, is tasked with achieving investigative and narrative closure. The problem in this case, however, is that the two forms of closure, far from being each other's necessary correlate, are in fact incompatible and cannot be realized simultaneously. When the Op accuses Fitzstephan of being the only character 'whose connection with each episode can be traced' (375), he is assuming that connecting the various subplots and incidents – that is, establishing narrative order – is the same as arriving at the truth. This assumption is borne out, not only in the genre's classics, but arguably in most mainstream detective fiction to the present day; although it is a rule with many exceptions, the detective story ending is conventionally understood to the be the point where epistemological disambiguation and narrative denouement coincide in what Christie's Poirot memorably calls 'beautiful shining order' (Christie 2007: 338). Breaking with this convention, Fitzstephan's response brutally dissociates narrative from truth. The story he offers is a grotesquely caricatured version of the Op's own desire for narrative closure. It purports to be a comprehensive explanatory framework and does in fact fulfil this role insofar as it convinces the jury. Yet, what it ultimately shows is that the perfectly ordered narrative has no epistemological valency and might as well be a lie.

A full 'counterinvestigation' in the style of Pierre Bayard may not be a promising approach to *The Dain Curse*, given that the novel seems to move beyond the ideas of clues and final interpretations, but Bayard's discussion of the liar's paradox as a key device in Agatha Christie's detective fiction is nevertheless helpful as a means of understanding the logical problems raised by Fitzstephan's confession. For Bayard, this paradox is primarily linked to first-person narration. Although detective novels work hard to make readers forget this fact, a first-person narrator never simply embodies an authoritative perspective; on the contrary, this narrator 'is also a character, therefore a possible liar, and therefore a possible murderer' (Bayard 2000: 53). The narrative logic of Hammett's novel is different insofar as the solution is not pronounced by the Op as the detective-narrator, but by Fitzstephan whose courtroom confession is positioned as authoritative and final. Yet, this structure is even less immune to the destabilizing effects of the liar's paradox. In fact, this paradox manifests itself in three different forms in the novel's final chapters, each of which undermines the authority of the ending.

Most obviously, the all-encompassing nature of the guilty plea begs the question whether Fitzstephan is a rational individual or a delusional lunatic. In the final chapter, the Op explicitly reflects on this conundrum, and although he seemingly opts for the latter option and mainly thinks of this problem in terms of the author's personal pride, the paradoxical consequences are inescapable:

> As a sane man who, by pretending to be a lunatic, had done as he pleased and escaped punishment, he had a joke – if you wanted to call it that – on the world. But if he was a lunatic who, ignorant of his craziness, thought he was pretending to be a lunatic, then the joke – if you wanted to call it that – was on him. (Hammett 1999: 379)

The paradox is only heightened when considering, secondly, the legal as opposed to psychological dimension of Fitzstephan's confession. As the writer indicates himself in the penultimate chapter, he has an objective interest in committing perjury in order to secure an insanity verdict. Not long before, the Op has similarly threatened Gabrielle Leggett's attorney by stating that 'there's not necessarily any connection between what's true and what you go into court with' (362), indicating in this way that he is willing to perjure himself to engineer the attorney's downfall. The implication is that Fitzstephan's testimony would have been *exactly the same* regardless of whether he is guilty of all murders, guilty only of some of them or wholly innocent but feeling threatened by the narrative that the detective is constructing around him. While it seems likely that he was involved at least in the murder of Mrs Cotton, it is distinctly *un*likely that his confession to 'crimes and crimes, dating from the cradle' (376) is true. Thus, the novel provides no certain means of determining the extent of his culpability. Fitzstephan's profession offers further support of this reading and generates a third version of the liar's paradox. We need not subscribe to Plato's view of writers as liars to recognize that the inclusion of authors as characters in detective fiction (cf. Grauby 2016) inevitably troubles the neat distinction between fact and fiction and, as is evidently the case in *The Dain Curse*, effects a rapprochement between the author and the detective as storytellers with an equal talent for stringing together places, characters, actions and objects to form narrative sequences. This uneasy relationship between authors and the truth is commented upon explicitly. In Part 1, the Op withholds information from Fitzstephan on the grounds that he is a 'story-writer' who cannot be trusted 'not to build up on' what he tells him (207). Similarly, in Part 3, Fitzstephan himself argues that his literary works will help him in court because they bear 'all the better known indications of authorial degeneracy' (376). The reliability of his testimony is, in other words, undermined both by his professional association with fictionality and his personal penchant for everything unconventional and outrageous. In a final manifestation of the liar's paradox, these attributes make it impossible to determine whether or not he is telling the truth.

These three versions of the liar's paradox restrict the ending's ability to provide narrative closure. Fitzstephan's confession ostensibly succeeds in establishing the missing connections between the novel's three parts, the three separate settings and the lengthy list of murders, yet in reality it falls short of the classic detective fiction requirement that the solution must not only be internally coherent, but also *true* in the sense of capturing events as they really happened. Instead of tying up all loose ends, the ending produces new uncertainties. Most importantly, when Fitzstephan reveals that he is a Dain, just as the Op has confidently announced the end of 'the Great Dain Curse' (375), he not only disrupts a classic mystery script based on the rational elucidation of superstitions (think of *The Hound of the Baskervilles*), but also reactivates, by way of ending the novel, an entirely different explanation, which the Op has consistently sought to discredit. By the same token, the undue faith he invests in Fitzstephan's confession at the end of the novel compels us to question whether the Op was not too quick to dismiss Miss Leggett's earlier, similarly comprehensive confession on the assumption that she was simply desperate for drugs. The ending accordingly raises more questions than it answers, and if the Op neglects to engage with these new questions, it is arguably for the pragmatic reason that he offers on the final pages, namely that Gabrielle Leggett is safe and 'happy enough with what had already been dug up' (386).

The finale thereby produces a double paradox. Firstly, as the point of investigative closure the ending is meant to be final, rationally argued and authoritative, yet is in fact underwritten by a self-serving insanity plea, put forward by a person who straddles the divide between lucidity and lunacy as well as that between fact and fiction. Secondly, as the point of narrative closure the ending is tasked with healing the body of the text, yet does so incompletely and unconvincingly, metaphorically undermining any claims to coherence via the references to the dismembered body of the author.

* * *

This chapter's discussion of genre mobility in *The Dain Curse* began with a brief analysis of one of its two car crashes, which presented this narratively gratuitous episode as a figuration of the principle of genre mobility itself. The violent interruption of the car's road-bound, rule-ridden and goal-oriented mobility is suggestive of a transition from a world of necessity to one of open-ended contingency and in that sense a fitting metaphor for the novel itself as it swerves from the established paths of its genre. The explosion that reduces Fitzstephan to a 'mangled pile of flesh and clothing' (333) has a similar valence. It is important to note that the bomb attack is not only insufficiently explained by the Op's solution, but also is an event not foreseen by the alleged criminal mastermind; as such, it sits uneasily within the novel's narrative order as an intrusion of contingency. Furthermore, Fitzstephan is represented in the conversations with the Op as a defender of straightforward narratives defined by neat causalities and perfect closure. This position is gradually exposed as either simplistic or, if we accept the logic of Fitzstephan's confession, as an attempt to manipulate the Op. His mutilation by the explosion completes the discrediting of his narratological position, leaving him 'really cracked' (377) even as he claims to make the novel whole.

What stands out about these events as figurations of genre mobility is their violence. As argued across the contributions to the present volume, crime fiction, far from being the static and formulaic construct it is often taken to be, is in fact inherently mobile in the sense of constantly questioning and transgressing against its own boundaries. In the specific context of genre, this mobility sometimes takes relatively affirmative forms that extend the genre, selectively break its conventions, or subject it to parody; the works of Agatha Christie are exemplary in this regard, exhibiting a keen awareness of the genre's norms coupled with a willingness to suspend them in favour of playful innovation. While it is important to recognize such playfulness as a genuine form of genre mobility, *The Dain Curse* engages in a more fundamental criticism of the detective genre. As I have shown, the novel systematically attacks some of the core structural constituents of the classic detective novel, replacing linearity with circularity, closure with open-endedness and authority with ambiguity. At the same time, it disrupts the genre's ontological basis, above all by positing that the world is a 'foggy muddle' of contingency and incomprehension, and by resisting the idea that detective fiction is based on stable and decodable correlations linking motivations to actions and actions to evidence.

Hammett famously hoped to 'make "literature"' of the detective story (qtd in McCann 2000: 97). If we assume that the category of 'popular fiction' consists of works that more or less perfectly embody the genre while 'literature' is conversely linked to textual singularity, we might argue that it is Hammett's undermining of the detective genre's established tropes that makes this novel a work of literature. Yet, this would be misguided on several levels. I want to suggest instead that *The Dain Curse* incarnates a specific mode of genre mobility that unsettles the neat dichotomy of embodiment and transgression. This mode, which I have previously labelled 'genre negation' (Gulddal 2016b: 55), is a creative process that calls attention to the established tropes of the genre in order to critique and ultimately undo them, yet by doing so remains bound, like any negation, to that which it endeavours to overcome. The effect of this critical impetus is an unmooring of the genre, enabling the launch, successful or not, of a new form of detective fiction.

Works Cited

Bayard, Pierre (2000). *Who Killed Roger Ackroyd?* Trans. Carol Cosman (New York: The New Press).

Boof-Vermesse, Isabelle (2003). 'Secret Passage to Chaos. Dashiell Hammett's *The Dain Curse'. Polysèmes* 6: 163–86.

Burrows, Stuart (2016). 'Noir's Private "I"'. *American Literary History* 29.1: 50–71.

Christie, Agatha (2007) [1934]. *Murder on the Orient Express* (London: Harper).

Gale, Robert L. (2000). *A Dashiell Hammett Companion* (Westport, CT: Greenwood).

Gatenby, Bruce (1994). '"A Long and Laughable Story". Hammett's *The Dain Curse* and the Postmodern Condition', in Christopher Metress (ed.), *The Critical Response to Dashiell Hammett* (Westport, CT: Greenwood), 56–67.

González, Jesús Ángel (2016). '"Going Blood Simple". *Red Harvest* in Film', in Lee Broughton (ed.), *Critical Perspectives on the Western. From A Fist Full of Dollars to Django Unchained* (London: Rowman and Littlefield), 103–18.

Grauby, Françoise (2016). '"This Isn't a Detective Story, Mrs Oliver". The Case of the Fictitious Author'. *Clues: Journal of Detection* 34.1: 116–25.

Gregory, Sinda (1994). '*The Dain Curse*. The Epistemology of the Detective Story', in Christopher Metress (ed.), *The Critical Response to Dashiell Hammett* (Westport: Greenwood), 34–56.

Gulddal, Jesper (2016a). '"Beautiful Shining Order". Detective Authority in Agatha Christie's *Murder on the Orient Express*'. *Clues* 34.1: 11–21.

— (2016b) 'Clueless. Genre, Realism and Narrative Form in Ed McBain's Early 87th Precinct Novels'. *Clues* 34.2: 54–62.

Hammett, Dashiell (1999) [1928/29]. *The Dain Curse Complete Novels* (New York: Library of America), 189–386.

Hefner, Brooks E. (2014). 'Weird Investigations and Nativist Semiotics in H.P. Lovecraft and Dashiell Hammett', *Modern Fiction Studies* 60:4. 651–76.

McCann, Sean (2000). *Gumshoe America. Hard-Boiled Crime Fiction and the Rise and Fall of New Deal Liberalism* (Durham and London: Duke University Press).

Malmgren, Carl D. (2001). *Anatomy of Murder. Mystery, Detective, and Crime Fiction* (Bowling Green: Bowling Green State University Popular Press).

Marcus, Steven (1974). 'Introduction', in Dashiell Hammett, *The Continental Op* (New York: Random House), ix–xiv.

Mülder-Bach, Inka (2002). 'Poetik des Unfalls'. *Poetica* 34: 193–221.

Panek, LeRoy Lad (2004). *Reading Early Hammett. A Critical Study of the Fiction prior to* The Maltese Falcon (Jefferson, NC and London: McFarland).

CHAPTER SEVEN

Burma's *Bagnoles*

Urban Modernity and the Automotive Saccadism of Léo Malet's *Nouveaux mystères de Paris* (1954–1959)

Andrea Goulet, University of Pennsylvania

'Je roulais [...]. Je stoppai.'

Malet, *Les Eaux troubles de Javel*

Léo Malet's œuvre stands at multiple generic, temporal and spatial crossroads. Eschewing the formulaic stasis of detective fiction in favour of surrealist surprise mixed with hard-boiled cynicism, Malet always drew outside the lines. The hybridity of his fiction was already visible in *120, rue de la Gare* (1943), which criss-crossed the Occupied Zone of Second World War France with American noir tropes and proto-Oulipian linguistic play and punning (Goulet 2015; Gorrara 2001). And while his arrondissement-bound *Nouveaux mystères de Paris* of the 1950s might seem to narrow his scope to the French capital's city-space, its very title alludes to a tradition that refused to stay within national limits: as recent critical work has explored, Eugène Sue's 1842 *Mystères de Paris* was 'always already' transnational (Kalifa and Thérenty 2015). In addition to this transnational mobility, Malet's unfinished *Nouveaux mystères* are also generically mobile; indeed, they represent the intersection of multiple generic referents that include not only the global urban mystery, but also Poe's Dupin stories and the American wartime noir – each with its own unstable formal conventions. Any generic instability, moreover, maps onto a fictional space in Malet that grapples in surprisingly literal ways with the central tension between mobility and constraint.

It is hard, in fact, to think of a writer whose prose rhythm is more stop-and-go than Malet's. In his *Nouveaux mystères de Paris*, a scene of stillness (quiet as a corpse) will suddenly burst into a volley of frenetic violence: shots and motion appear out of nowhere; the narrative pace quickens to the sound of rat-a-tat gunfire or screeching tyres; and the chaotic momentum builds until it hits the abrupt wall of a 'k.o.', or knockout, for detective Nestor Burma. When a pistol butt or slab of concrete invariably hits Burma's head, the frenetic paragraph ends and the reader is given a breather, indicated by a break in the text and corresponding to Burma's temporary loss of consciousness. Then it starts all over again...

Inertia and mobility, spatial stasis and explosive entropy: these are the poles that determine the saccadic, alternating rhythms of Malet's unfinished series of arrondissement mysteries. From the 'open closure' of the *Nouveaux mystères*' first story, *Le Soleil naît derrière le Louvre* of 1954 (Goulet 2014), to the paradoxical title of its last, *L'Envahissant cadavre de la plaine Monceau* of 1959, the instalments thrust Burma and the reader into an urban space characterized by jerky jolts rather than harmonious continuity. The past and the present butt heads with violence, leaving scars and open wounds on the capital city in the form of demolition/ construction sites, these *chantiers* that show up so often on Burma's urban terrain. Transportation infrastructure – Métro rails and taxi stands, tight-curved roads and broad boulevards, bustling intersections and fountain squares – plays a role, not only as background ambiance, but also as an active determinant of Burma's movement in around the changing city of Paris.

Perhaps most importantly, Burma's city is a city of cars. The 1950s were, as Kristin Ross notes, a time of 'accelerated transition into Fordism' for France (1995: 4); and the centrality of the automobile to the mid-century French cultural imaginary was directly connected to similarly accelerated – though uneven – urbanization: '[I]t was above all the unevenness of the built environment of the city, its surroundings, and its social geography that came to crystallize, for Lefebvre, the contra-dictions of postwar life. [...] Paris, the city itself, became the new site for a generalized exploitation of the daily life of its inhabitants through the management of space' (1995: 8). That management of space necessarily takes different forms for the rich and the poor, citizens and immigrants – or, in the case of Nestor Burma, detectives whose entire identity is based on the ability to blend in while remaining apart. For Peter Schulman, that peripheralized man-of-the-crowd status makes Burma a car-driving *flâneur*, one whose circulation through urban space is mythic and ludic, while also being marked by the shock of postwar modernity during the *Trente Glorieuses*, a time of tension between nostalgia for 'good old Paris' and a thrust for renewal through high consumption (Schulman 2000: 1160). Malet and his investigative anti-hero do indeed inhabit this in-between zone between old Paris and new; and like some other writers mentioned by Claire Gorrara in her essay on French crime fiction and the reconstruction of France (André Héléna, Serge Arcouët and Jean Meckert), Malet reveals through his writing a 'profound unease over the costs and conditions' of modernization as he grapples with its accelerated pace (2009: 122). More specifically, *Les Nouveaux mystères de Paris* register the 'shock' of modernity rather literally, through Burma's automotive jolts and the narrative's own stop-and-go rhythm.

Indeed, if we look at the mid-century *Nouveaux mystères* through the lens of the 'automobile revolution' (Flonneau 2009) and a social sciences 'mobility turn' emphasizing uneven access to the freedoms of car culture (Kauffmann 2011), we find that Nestor Burma's own automotive peregrinations and personal relationship to cars crystallizes a number of aesthetic and political ambivalences – or unresolved antimonies – that render Malet a key figure of in-between-ness: between *fin de siècle* French urban mysteries and post-Second World War American noir (Gorrara 2009; Bridgeman 1998), between conservative nostalgia and revolutionary restlessness, between the *roman policier*'s apparent closure and the open-ended *saccades* of surrealism (Walz 1997: 122), between the inertia of death and the excitement of sex, between order and bombs, local and global, stasis and change (Rolls 2014: 146).

In this essay, I explore these co-existing antimonies in Malet through the prism of transportation in mid-century France. A focus on four novels in the *Nouveaux mystères* affords us a glimpse into the overlapping ways in which urban automotive culture might be seen as the hidden 'crime' of this age's crime fiction: as American import of glamour and violence; as indicator of troubled class crossings; as hope and failure in the realm of industrial production; and as the ultimate site of precarity, or uneven access. Taking mobility in its literal sense, I propose the following thesis: Malet's bumpy ride gives us a particularly visceral street-level view of entry into the 'time-space compression' that David Harvey identifies as the condition of postmodernity (1990).

1. Cut! Action!: *Corrida aux Champs-Élysées* (1956)

Fast cars and Hollywood-style cinema, both mid-century transplants of American culture into Paris, typify the eighth arrondissement in Malet's seventh *Nouveaux mystères* adventure. At the story's start, Nestor Burma has been staying at the 'Cosmopolitan-Palace', aptly named as the transatlantic stopover for American starlets and movie directors, but the real action is on the road: 'The June sun bathed the Champs-Elysées, causing the sumptuous cars [*bagnoles*] to sparkle as they glided by in an uninterrupted flow' (1985, vol. 2: 3).[1] The cars signal luxury and leisure, of course, but also the animation of the *quartier*, its sense of being perpetually 'on the go'. Movers and shakers don't bother with public transportation – and even less with the plebian *pédibus* pedestrianism that first motivated Malet to write *Les Nouveaux Mystères de Paris*. No, in this chi-chi world, even the short hop from the Cosmopolitan-Palace hotel to Fouquet's brasserie, where movie heartthrobs like to lounge, warrants displacement by private vehicle: when the journalist Marc Covet instructs Burma to bring his car for the jaunt, the detective responds, 'To go 200 metres? Did you suddenly get paralyzed, or what?' (1985, vol. 2: 18). Despite his sarcasm, Burma buys into the local car culture and takes the wheel throughout the story, which includes dozens of references to *bagnoles*, including of course the speedy car chase of the titular 'corrida'. After all, Burma likes to be where the action is. Bored with the 'sleepy' Fiat Lux agency, our detective decides to stay in the Champs-Elysées because he believes the area will be 'sparkling' with animation (1985, vol. 2: 4, 6), but is quickly disenchanted when a stifling inertia sets in (1985, vol. 2: 11). So, to keep things going, Burma moves his vague investigation to various locales, including the Crazy-Horse cabaret and a movie production studio on the rue Marbeuf, each time sussing things out until the action can kick into the high gear of gunfights and car chases. The whole novel, in fact, seems to connect the 'Cut! Action!' logic of movie-making to the red-light/green-light rhythm of the eighth arrondissement's car traffic by organizing Burma's investigation around alternating scenes of stasis and movement, inertia and action.

From the start, that staccato rhythm is linked to the capital city's own built environment in an age of accelerating urban renewal: 'Right in front of the Cosmopolitan-Hôtel, some kind of worksite had just gone up, in accordance with that well-known custom by which Paris has to

1 All translations mine.

be constantly turned upside down [*bouleversé*] by some construction or maintenance project or other, and even the labourers lugging sacks of sand seemed to join in the general enjoyment' (1985, vol. 2: 3). The slightly negative irony of the phrase's start is balanced by the apparent positivity of its end, resulting in an ambivalent tone vis-à-vis the constant *bouleversement* of Paris and its streets. Is it a good thing that the capital city is on the move? Certainly, Burma seems here to be a far less grouchy observer than Malet himself, who expressed a strong distaste for the capital city's constant upheaval and its so-called progress at the hands of 'the gang of scoundrels known as urban planners who decided to destroy Paris' (Alfu 1996: 74; Gudin de Valerin and Bouchard 2007: 209). But when Burma's own desire for movement is impeded by urban construction in *Corrida*, his narrative joins Malet's critique by undercutting any official narrative of urbanistic progress:

> A large car [...] charged at me like a speedster with bad intentions. I swerved desperately, but – wouldn't you know it? – it kept coming right at me. For years now, Alma square has been transformed into a construction site [*chantier*]. And for years now, I've grumbled about it every time I pass through. Turns out I was right to grouse and groan about these public works. In order to avoid the nutcase trying to ram into me, I smashed through the barrier, sending this shady place's [*mauvais lieu*] red warning lights flying, and in a loud racket of broken glass I plunged into a dank and foul-smelling pit. (1985, vol. 2: 87)

This is one of those moments when a fast-paced chase screeches to a sudden stop – but rather than a pistol butt to the face, it's the *chantier* itself, this '*mauvais lieu*' against which Burma (like Malet) had been railing for years, that provides an open tomb for his fleeing car, stopping it mid-flight. Construction site has become site of destruction. And any progressivist myth of state-sponsored urbanism is stopped in its tracks.[2]

The wider plot of *Corrida* itself turns on various aspects of modern car culture: 1) the name Melganno sparks Burma's delayed comprehension through its homophony with '*mécano*'; 2) automobiles become metonymies for the film industry; 3) American-style '*gangsters motorisés*'

---

2 The Place de l'Alma had been renovated and expanded during the Second Empire *travaux*. See my *Legacies of the Rue Morgue* (2015) on the ways in which the gashes of construction sites undercut progressivist ideology in the Hausmannian projects. In *Paris and the Fetish*, Alistair Rolls traces a line between Baudelaire's splenetic reaction to Haussmannization and Malet's urbanistic ambivalence a century later (2014: 145).

turn out to be accomplices to the crime (1985, vol. 2: 90); and 4) the crime itself plays on the combined meaning of the word *'circulation'*, denoting both drug trafficking and car traffic. Indeed, the illegal international network of drug trafficking depends in the story on open borders, so that stopped car traffic means an interruption of the free circulation of the criminals' stock: 'Trafficker stopped at the border, huh?' (1985, vol. 2: 90). What's at stake here is not just the alternating fixity and porousness of city/nation boundaries, but the mobility of both criminals and their foils – whether official police or, in Burma's case, an independent agent. Burma's automotive ability to speed up, swerve, zigzag and sudden-stop his vehicle allows him to match the accelerated pace of these Hollywood-style gangsters in order to interrupt their flow. And like the gangsters, he also depends on continuous access to his car in order to guarantee his ability to move freely within the city space: 'If they find a corpse in my car, the cops will take me out of circulation for a while' (1985, vol. 2: 98). A body in the trunk means an end to movement (and not only for the dead guy). Cadavers, car thefts and high-speed chases – these are the narrative 'motors' of Malet's plot. In the end, then, it's no surprise to learn that Burma's car has taken on the feature role in this whole cinematic spectacle: when an admirer of Burma's investigative success tells him they could make a movie about it, he responds 'Yeah, a movie with a role set aside for my *bagnole*' (1985, vol. 2: 103). The car is the star.

2. Cars and Sex, Cars and Death: *Pas de bavards à la Muette* (1956)

In Malet's eighth *Mystère*, Burma uncovers a ring of chauffeurs who steal jewels and sleep with their wealthy female clients in the sixteenth arrondissement. Chauffeurs: that is, automobile drivers *par procuration*, those lower-class and mechanically minded men who are paid to take the place of rich absent husbands at the wheel, not (officially) in the bed. When seduction crosses the line – as in the case of Célestin, a chauffeur who runs off with Mme Ailot's twenty-year-old niece Suzanne – things turn south: Célestin is found shot dead, next to his drugged and confused young lover. Burma has been brought in by the moneyed Mme Ailot ostensibly to investigate the theft of her precious jewels, but it turns out that she herself had orchestrated the framing of Suzanne in order to divert attention from her son and from a complicated backstory involving Nazi treasure and her own sordid amorous past.

The sexual charge that subtends *Pas de bavards* connects the upper and lower classes in this story where chauffeurs are pimped to *grandes dames* and even the female prostitutes drive cars. In a gender reversal of the usual pick-up scene, Burma watches lady hookers drive by the Ranelagh gardens in order to find their johns. His description of the scene fuses ladies of the evening with their mode of transport in a cheekily poetic manner: 'These motorized hookers, these perfumed amazons at the edge of the lake. The cars that roll slowly by, supple and shiny, gracious and discreet' (1985, vol. 2: 178). With all these adjectives in the feminine in Malet's original French, we might well ask whether it is the cars or their female drivers who are supple and shiny, gracious and discreet. The attributes are deliberately metonymic, of course, and Burma continues with his lyrical evocation of the motorized drag scene by describing its effect on a '*promeneur solitaire*' (one whose urban strollings situate him far from rustic, Rousseauistic innocence): 'And when you lean in to the driver's side window, you notice, nestled into the deliciously shaded interior, a pair of half-clad gams emerging from the stuff of soft stockings, or an impertinent tit that jumps out at you like a burglar pup [*un jeune chien cambrioleur*]' (1985, vol. 2: 178). Here, the synecdoche of female parts – gams and tits, yes, but seductively wrapped in elegant prose – tilts into the realm of crime ('cambrioleur') in order to remind us that these 'hookers on wheels [*Vénus à roulettes*]' are caught up in the same circulating network as the male chauffeurs: the traffic of sex and money, all negotiated at the wheel of a car (1985, vol. 2: 206).

This is certainly not the only time that cars are eroticized in the *Nouveaux mystères*. In *Boulevards... Ossements* (1957), Malet again uses poetic language – in this case, alliteration – to displace a woman's sensuality onto the car she's driving: 'A *bagnole* slides sleekly [*glisse en souplesse*] along the sidewalk. It's my car and Hélène is at the wheel' (1985, vol. 2: 454). This story, too, features the international circulation of prostitutes; and when Burma's secretary Hélène goes undercover as a lingerie model, she is pulled out of her comfort zone by the car-driving hooker Natacha, who speeds her away from the city's ninth arrondissement in a 'luxury six-seater convertible' (1985, vol. 2: 488). But perhaps most telling is the fact that this sex-and-cars nexus is presented under a title whose homophonic pun – *Boulevard...Ossements*/Boulevard Haussmann – reminds the reader of the violence (*ossements* means 'bones') underlying apparent urbanistic progress.

Indeed, if we return to *Pas de bavards à la Muette*, we find that the eroticized class crossings made possible by automobile circulation rely on an urban setting of uneven development – even in the heart of the supposedly cushy and well-protected sixteenth. The run-down façade of the hotel in which Burma is staying makes him wonder what distinguishes these 'so-called nicer districts' from the others in the city and he's somewhat surprised to find the area containing 'vacant lots [*terrains vagues*], a cemetery', i.e. spaces associated with crime and death rather than luxury living (1985, vol. 2: 120). The place is teeming, moreover, with those confounded construction sites:

> As for construction sites, there's no shortage of those, between Trocadero and Saint-Cloud. I wonder what Abbé Pierre was complaining about. Soon, in this sector once known for its adorable private residences, there will be nothing but skyscrapers. [...] Even the *terrains vagues* will be busy [*boulottées*]. Finally! Not that I give a damn anyway! (1985, vol. 2: 121)

Under the thin cover of protesting that he doesn't care, Burma bemoans the urban renewal that threatens to replace picturesque homes with skyscrapers; the allusion to Abbé Pierre, whose first Emmaus house for the homeless was based in wealthy Neuilly-Plaisance, indicates the social repercussions of modernization's effacement of class distinction.

Suggestively, these urban changes are connected not only to mobility but also to morbidity, figured through the circulation of cars. Near the Métro station of Passy, trash-covered *terrains vagues* abound and the rhythm of automobile traffic in the area intersects with that of construction sites: 'The circulating cars went by in a quick swish [*froissement*]. At irregular intervals, a metallic groan [*grincement*] arose from the deserted construction site' (1985, vol. 2: 128). As Burma approaches the Chaussée de la Muette, he muses:

> It was right at the start of this main road, and the commercial animation of the rue de Passy died [*venait mourir*] at the feet of the café tables on its stylish and sunny terrace. Cars crossing the Ranelagh gardens [...] passed by silently. There aren't a lot of noisy cars in the 16th *arrondissement*. (1985, vol. 2: 124)

The car culture matches the *quartier*: silent, moribund. One of the running jokes in *Pas de bavards* is the repeated pronouncement of the sixteenth's tranquillity. This is given its full irony as a screen for the crimes that punctuate, discreetly, the tony area: 'Sure, people kill each other here, but no-one would steal a car' (1985, vol. 2: 151). Upper-crust discretion trumps low-class felonies, so that even brutal murder is refused the sensationalized circulation of rumour ('*Pas de bavards*'), a point made with humour by police commissioner Faroux: 'Yeah, I've seen how tranquil your area is, for sure. So tranquil that last week a lady from the rue de Jasmin fell out of her 5th-floor window completely naked and lay *tranquilly* on the sidewalk until a milkman bumped into her' (1985, vol. 2: 158). Burma's role, of course, is to pierce through the veil of tranquillity by exposing the criminal activities being muffled by discretion. Again, cars play a central role in this mission. Madame Ailot, who has refused to report to officials the theft of her jewels for fear of scandal, owns an elegant, silent Tallemet cabriolet well-matched to her fear of noise (1985, vol. 2: 145). But Burma prefers the loud screeching brakes of a cop's *bagnole*, which shocks the lethargic rue du Ranelagh (1985, vol. 2: 163), just as he prefers to expose the criminal gangs and dirty dealings that the rich inhabitants of the sixteenth want so desperately to keep quiet. When he starts hearing more about the long history of *faits divers* that have taken place in the area, Burma is perversely delighted. The irony, of course, is that it's murders that bring the neighbourhood to 'life'. But the rhythm here, as in all the *Mystères*, is one of alternating activity and lethargy, life and death, correlating metonymically to the neighbourhood's automotive traffic, with its jolting starts and stops to circulation.

In this way, Malet's urban mysteries participate in the 'new rhythm' that Mathieu Flonneau ascribes to the mass motorization of urban populations in France during the *Trente Glorieuses* (2009). This is a rhythm that affects not only the irregular circulation of the cars themselves, but also the spasmodic changes to the city's very own infrastructure. Flonneau cites Bernard Lafay's 1954 proposal to Paris's Conseil Municipal in which he calls for aggressive urbanistic interventions in response to the city's moribund inability to deal with an influx of cars.[3] This life-and-death figuration of Paris's car crisis gets literalized in Malet's murder mysteries, in which the city's uneven development structures a herky-jerky circulation of hookers and chauffeurs, money and sex, cars and cadavers.

---

3 Flonneau's work (2009) identifies an astonishing rate of increase in the production and acquisition of cars for private use in 1950s Paris, with the number of matriculated vehicles going from 567,000 in 1948 to a million by 1958. This 'galloping motorization' strained not only the municipal road system, but also the Préfecture de Police's ability to register and track the new influx. Flonneau writes that the licence plate numbering system had to be modified three times between 1950 and 1972.

3. Citroën City: *Les Eaux troubles de Javel*

Flonneau's primary thesis on the automobile revolution is that the *Trente Glorieuses* saw a radical democratization of car culture: no longer a sign of an elite lifestyle of leisure, the privately owned automobile became a tool for working-class functionality and increased mobility. In 1946, the president of the Renault corporation announced his desire for the automobile to become a 'democratic' object, and by 1977 Louis Chevalier confirmed its fulfilment as such: 'Finally, there's the popular, working-class *bagnole*; one could almost call it a "workerist" [*ouvriériste*] car, given the role it played in that era's sociological production, engaged as it was in describing from every angle the changing conditions for the working man' (cited in Flonneau 2009: n.p.). Cars are class markers, and if in *Pas de bavards* Burma was temporarily placed by his rich client at the wheel of her discreetly elegant Tallemet cabriolet, *Les Eaux troubles de Javel* (1957) finds him back in his familiar Dugat and plonked right into the centre of the working-class car culture that Chevalier is describing.

Here, in this *quartier* of depressingly large-scale housing projects within the fifteenth arrondissement, Burma encounters Hortense Demessy, who hires him to track down her once-homeless husband, now employed as a car mechanic at the Citroën factory. For the most part in this case, Burma drives his familiar Dugat 12, but, as always, its access to the shadowy corners of Paris is limited. As Burma says in an oft-quoted section of *Boulevard... ossements*, 'Bagnoles, they're great, but when you're circulating around Paris, there's no way they'll get you exactly where you want to go. Sometimes you've got to park them a kilometre away from your end-point'.[4] In *Les Eaux troubles*, Burma reminds us of this automotive incapacity to go 'all the way' through repeated allusions to moments when he parks the car and continues to his destination on foot. The many mentions in Malet of precise driving routes and parking locations insert us directly in the material quotidian of modern car culture, but Burma's insistence on the limits of his Dugat's access, its exclusion from areas where only *pédibus* will do, indicates an ambivalence toward that very modernity. Cars take him only so far, whether in the chi-chi areas of Paris or the industrial zones of its

---

4 See Alfu (1996) and Schulman (2000: 1157). Schulman emphasizes the freedom and mobility of urban *flânerie*, the city and its characters. I'd add the alternate pole of stasis, since, yes, Malet and his story are always mobile – except when stopped short!

working class; and when it's a question of bringing his investigation into the poorest *quartiers* – as when Burma disguises himself as a *clochard* in order to roam the quayside at the end of *Les Eaux troubles*, a car would only be in the way. There are, after all, still homeless in Paris; not everything has caught up to the progressivist image of the modern capital at mid-century – and besides, Burma needs to be able to go low as well as high. His very choice of car model itself, of course, signals a certain ambivalent class-consciousness; although he associates it with a working-class refusal of ostentation, Burma adds, in typical fashion, a touch of mordant and morbid irony about the unsavoury sides of his own profession: 'Nothing luxurious. No flashy gigolo shit. A good, solid model Dugat 12, with a spacious rear trunk, enough room for two stiffs, if need be' (1985, vol. 1: 854). He's not in the system.

That peripherality is reflected when Burma drives his car to the Citroën factory where Madame Demessy's disappeared husband had last been seen working. The plant, identified to Burma by its name splayed across the top of its four-storey building in enormous blue letters, is located in the fifteenth just across the river from Renault's Boulogne-Billancourt plant. So, cars are fittingly what Burma focuses on in the description of his investigative jaunt into this industrial hub: 'On either side of the causeway, nothing but stopped cars, and all of them 2 CVs or DSs. I wondered whether my Dugat 12 would look out of place' (1985, vol. 2: 362). His car brand identifies Burma as an outsider, but he's not the only one: approaching the factory, he decides to park between two other non-Citroën automobiles, a Dauphine and a Frégate, 'which seemed to have been left there in an obvious act of provocation. Between these two cars, my Dugat would feel less alone' (1985, vol. 2: 362). Can we detect in this line the possibility of a certain mode of solidarity, made manifest through a shared resistance to the *quartier*'s dominant brand of Citroën? One might think so, but no – Burma quickly backs off any fraternal association with the working class by having his car abandon the others. It should be noted that Frégate and Dauphine are both actual cars made by Renault (i.e. the competition just across the river) while Burma's quirky Dugat 12 is a model of Malet's own invention. In this way, Burma's parking decision implies a turning his back on the whole shebang: on France's automotive industry, on the car factories that he describes as literally imbricated in the city's infrastructure, and on any sustained solidarity with the class of *ouvriers* that he identifies with ... up to a point.

That fact that Burma is a man apart from the crowd is highlighted by a tongue-in-cheek reference to his driving through the fifteenth as a 'new chapter in the *rêveries d'un automobiliste solitaire*' (1985, vol. 2: 366). Malet's repeated invocations of Rousseau make sense, as the eighteenth-century philosopher's reflections also express a tension between solitude and society; but their irony arises from the *Mystères*' modern urban setting, in which greenspaces can only appear as unidyllic *terrains vagues* crouched among car factories, ageing railway infrastructure, Métro stops and demolition sites. Burma's narration of his automotive 'promenades' emphasizes national decline and personal disappointment: as he drives through the *quartier*, he sees a sodden *tricolore* flag flapping limply in the wind and finds that the 'buildings of the Parc des Expositions were the very face, as it were, of neglect and desolation' (1985, vol. 2: 166). No progress here.

Nor has the automotive industry done that much to help the proletarian crowd with whom Burma interacts in *Les Eaux troubles de Javel*. Their exotic travels are limited to eating choucroute at the *Brasserie Alsacienne* or downing white rum at the local *Bal Colonial*; as Burma says of a bar worker, 'he must only know the Antilles through the movies' (1985, vol. 2: 374). And the auto mechanic Demessy doesn't make enough money at 'Citron' (as Burma calls Citroën, mocking its cars as lemons [1985, vol. 2: 381]) to resist getting caught up in a racket involving the traffic of car manufacturing secrets and a dangerous Algerian gun-running mob. Meanwhile, there's also his bigamy: two wives, one of them driving a luxurious 'bicolore' American car that ends up being the key to Burma's investigative breakthrough: 'The car was an American or assimilated brand, a fine vehicle, shining in the sun with all its chrome trim, a little vanilla-boring, because of its two-colour paint job, but a fine piece of machinery nonetheless' (1985, vol. 2: 411). If the famous Dumas line '*Cherchez la femme*' takes on, as Alistair Rolls demonstrates, a fetishistic logic in Malet, that logic of displaced erotic/epistemological desire makes its way in *Les Eaux troubles de Javel* not only to women's sheer stockings and fancy perfumes, but also to the cars that they drive: '*Regardez cette auto*' is the line that directs Burma's gaze to the shiny American automobile that will reveal Demessy's bigamist '*mariage blanc*' to a sexy woman seeking French citizenship (1985, vol. 2: 410). It is precisely from this supple and graceful, *bicolore* car that the high-heeled mystery-woman will step. And although her French citizenship has been held out as an ostensible prize, the underlying contrast between the 15th arrondissement's dismal industrial infrastructure and the woman's glitzy American car suggests that the *tricolore* is flagging, while the *bicolore* US model is on the rise. Try as it might to enter into the world of automotive progress, France will always be a step behind the US – perhaps, as indicated by the Algerian mob violence in *Les Eaux troubles,* because it is still caught up in the nets of its own postcolonial history.

4. No Progress: *Brouillard au Pont de Tolbiac*

If the modern cars-and-cinema nexus of the eighth arrondissement affords Burma maximum mobility in *Corrida aux Champs-Élysées,* the dingy thirteenth arrondissement of *Brouillard au Pont de Tolbiac* represents an opposite extreme: a stuck-in-the-past exclusion from automotive access typical of the lower-class underside of the 1950s Mobile Risk Society. From its very first sentence, *Brouillard* puts Burma into a state of precarity vis-à-vis modern transportation: 'With my *bagnole* in the shop, I took the Métro' (1985, vol. 2: 239). Although those of us who have read the entire story might be tempted to interpret Burma's choice of public transportation as an act of symbolic solidarity with his old anarcho-socialist days at the *foyer végétalien,* he makes it clear at this point that it's just a question of being broke. Burma's horizontal peregrinations through the different arrondissements of *Les Mystères* are also vertical class-jumps, with temporary forays into the cosmopolitan upper-crust balanced by descents, such as this one, into the constricted space of the proletariat masses. Without access to his personal car, Burma is an outsider again, one who prefers to take a public autobus rather than enter the police commissioner's cop car, but who also knows all too well what it feels like to be stuck in a 'seedy spot' late at night after the last Métro has finished its rounds (1985, vol. 2: 270–71, 286). His dependency on the city's outdated transportation system feels stifling: at the sinister cross-tracks of the Orléans railway line, 'You get a disagreeable sensation of being suffocated, crushed' (1985, vol. 2: 295). And certainly, the constant fog of the story's title reinforces the frustrating obstacles to Burma's circulation and investigation.

Teresa Bridgeman has provided a suggestive close reading of *Brouillard* that helps us situate this novel in relation to larger questions of mobility and urban space. Bridgeman identifies *Brouillard* as especially refractory to models of mastery inherited by Malet from both the rational French detective tradition and the American noir; the story's scenes of subjective memory and impressionistic alienation replace any possible spatial or narrative control. Indeed, Burma's confused, amnesiac relation to the thirteenth arrondissement makes manifest this lack of confidence, as 'purposeful freedom of movement is replaced by claustration and loss of topographical mastery' (Bridgeman 1998: 65). Not surprisingly, the city's transportation infrastructure reinforces that sense of reduced mobility. Bridgeman's rich analysis of *Brouillard* includes a number of relevant observations: Lenantais's dilapidated Ford van is 'noticeably not an icon of shiny, fast and clean American modernism' (1998: 61); the railway line emerging from the Gare d'Austerlitz belies any 'positive assertion of speed and progress', since it has fallen into disuse and appears linked to 'the uninhabitable areas of the *quartier*, the *terrains vagues*, which exclude human life' (1998: 64); and, of course, the central passage in which a corpse falls out of a van driven by Burma onto the Pont de Tolbiac figures a nightmarish loss of clarity due to the overwhelming sensorial effects of rain and fog, trains, cars and sirens (1998: 72).

Bridgeman is right to emphasize the way in which *Brouillard* imprints the space of Paris with its collective – and Burma's own personal – past. As Burma tries to unearth the layers of criminality and corruption that have transformed his old anarchist buddies into murderer-capitalists, he's sent farther back into dusty and disused alleyways, as well as the cluttered *chiffonier* depot of the murder victim Lanentais. His is the 'antediluvian Ford' that becomes the completely glamour-free mode of transport for Burma and the gypsy-girl Bélita as they drive through thickening fog with a cadaver in the back (1985, vol. 2: 299). And in addition to the sensory confusion identified in Bridgeman's reading of this scene, we also find the literal shock of cars in collision. As they pass the 'metallic bridge that straddles the Paris-Austerlitz railway tracks', Burma and his riders (one dead, one alive) become the victims of a violent hit-and-run that replaces action with jarring immobility:

> A couple more turns of the wheel and we'd be on the *quais*. I... That lousy reckless driver! He was plastered. Unbelievable! [...] he was barely a couple metres from the hood of the Ford. One less! It was like a flash. As in a dream, before the bright headlights blinded me, I saw iridescent droplets float into the atmosphere and the steel hoops of that masterpiece glisten. I braked in a panic and ran up onto the sidewalk, in loud racket of bashed-up bodywork, and stopped along the grating, the motor stalled out. [...] I sat there for a moment like a moron, under the impact of the rebound jolt. In shock [*secousse*]. (1985, vol. 2: 299)

This is the literalized shock, spasm or *secousse* of modernity's unequal pace of progress. When the 'antediluvian' Ford won't re-start, it reinforces for Burma the deathly feeling that permeates *Brouillard* – the death, perhaps, of his old friends, his old anarchist ideals, old Paris. Or maybe it's the death of any hope for future-oriented progress? After all, even when he gets the motor running again, Burma is reminded that 'new' Paris is no shinier for its less fortunate denizens; he drives the clinker car past the homeless sheltering under the bridge ('lying on the aeration grids of the urban heating system [...] some bums, deaf to the appeals of Abbé Pierre') and plans to dump the corpse in a heap of iron that fits the corpse's lowly status: 'The guy, who seemed to like junk, would feel right at home in this scrap metal salvage site' (1985, vol. 2: 300). If recuperation from the detritus of the past is the story's epistemological goal, it's a frustrated one, as Burma finds the cadaver's been jolted out of the old Ford. This is a story of failure, as his own investigations end in a confusing gunfight in and around the pillars of a Métro viaduct followed by the jolting death by stabbing of Burma's now-lover Bélita. She never stood a chance. And maybe, without the mastering mobility of his Dugat 12, neither did he.

Conclusion: Malet's Second Modernity

In *Les Nouveaux mystères de Paris*, Nestor Burma is continuously batted back and forth between the two possible states of automotive modernity that Enda Duffy (2009) describes: the empowering thrill of speeding through space and the crushing immobility of the car crash. And as I've tried to suggest here, that start-and-stop rhythm structures Malet's entire project, moving beyond the specifics of car culture and into the uneven political vagaries of modern urbanization, the life-death antimonies of criminal violence and investigation, and the hybrid explosive style of a surrealist-cum-noir narrative.[5] If the theme of mobility has been a useful tool in exploring Malet's œuvre, it is in part because social science theorizations of automotive modernity allow us to historicize Malet's aesthetic ambiguities and ideological ambivalences without reducing them to synthesizable dialectics. Burma's capital city is both solid and liquid; his movements are both free and restricted.

The precarious 'open closure' of each arrondissement – and its corresponding *mystère* – keeps this series within a transitional conceptual space that can be usefully elucidated by mobility theorists' notion of 'second modernity'. Ulrich Beck writes about an impulse to move beyond

---

5 On modern urban infrastructure and the cinematic noir, see Dimendberg. And on urban space in the contemporary *roman policier*, see Sirvent.

a modernist vision of 'globalization as a repatterning of fluidities and mobilities on the one hand and stoppages and fixities on the other' while also resisting the abstract relativism that underlies a postmodernist 'welcome [of] the fluidity of an increasingly borderless world' (1992: 32). Sven Kesselring, in his exploration of the deep interpenetration of modernity and mobility, lays out a third, intermediate, option of 'second modernity':

> Under the conditions of permanent congestion and increasing insecurity concerning social ascents and descents it becomes visible that the modern mobility of autonomous subjects through time and space is illusionary. This is a kind of disenchantment of the modern mobility imperative and the beginning of a realistic appraisal of mobility as a general principle of modernity. In line with Bruno Latour's notion of modernity it is possible to say 'We have never been mobile' and we will not be able to move totally freely and unrestrictedly. In second modernity people and institutions realize mobility as imperfect and incomprehensive, as a goal that is unattainable in total and a project which cannot be produced in completeness. (2008: 83–84)

Neither naively progressivist nor po-mo blasé, the second-modern thinker holds onto unresolved antinomies; what's at stake here is a deep ambivalence about the paradoxical effects of capitalism, of modernization, of urbanization, of speed. The self-imposed constraints of Malet's arrondissement-by-arrondissement structure, combined with the saccadic, explosive rhythm of the novels themselves, reveals a text that is neither unproblematically nostalgic for a past Paris nor breezily comfortable with a boundary-less world of flows and networks. Malet's mid-century œuvre is a hiccup, a trip, a skip-step reaction to the inevitable arrival of postmodernity.

Works Cited

Alfu (1996). *Gaston Leroux: Parcours d'une œuvre* (Amiens: Encrage).

Beck, Ulrich (1992). *The Risk Society: Towards a New Modernity* (London: Sage Publications).

Bridgeman, Teresa (1998). 'Paris-Polar in the Fog: Power of Place and Generic Space in Malet's *Brouillard au Pont de Tolbiac*'. *Australian Journal of French Studies* 35.1: 58–73.

Canzler, Weert, Vincent Kaufmann and Sven Kesselring (eds) (2008). *Tracing Mobilities: Towards a Cosmopolitan Perspective* (Farnham: Ashgate).

Dimendberg, Edward (2004). *Film Noir and the Spaces of Modernity* (Cambridge, MA: Harvard University Press).

Duffy, Enda (2009). *The Speed Handbook: Velocity, Pleasure, Modernism* (Durham, NC: Duke University Press).

Flonneau, Mathieu (2009). 'Rouler dans la ville. Automobilisme et démocratisation de la cité: surprenants équilibres parisiens pendant les "Trente Glorieuses"'. *Articulo: Journal of Urban Research* 1: n.p.

Gorrara, Claire (2001). 'Malheurs et ténèbres: narratives of social disorder in Léo Malet's *120, rue de la Gare*'. *French Cultural Studies* 12: 271–83.

— (2009). 'Dramatic and Traumatic: French Crime Fiction and the Reconstruction of France', in Louise Hardwick (ed.), *New Approaches to Crime in French Literature, Culture and Film* (Oxford: Peter Lang), 121–36.

Goulet, Andrea (2014). '*Le Soleil naît derrière le Louvre*: Malet, Surrealism, and the Modern Explosion of Paris'. *L'Esprit Créateur* 54.2: 141–58.

— (2015). *Legacies of the Rue Morgue: Science, Space, and Crime Fiction in France* (Philadelphia: University of Pennsylvania).

Gudin de Vallerin, Gilles and Gladys Bouchard (2007). *Léo Malet Revient au Bercail* (Montpellier: Actes Sud).

Harvey, David (1990). *The Condition of Postmodernity: An Enquiry into the Origins of Cultural Change* (Oxford: Blackwell).

Kalifa, Dominique, and Marie-Ève Thérenty (2015). 'Les Mystères urbains au XIXe siècle: Circulations, transferts, appropriations'. *Médias19.org*. http://www.medias19.org/index.php?id=17039 [accessed 15 November 2018].

Kaufmann, Vincent (2011). *Rethinking the City: Urban Dynamics and Motility* (Lausanne: EPFL).

Kesselring, Sven (2008). 'The Mobile Risk Society', in Weert Canzler, Vincent Kaufmann and Sven Kesselring (eds), *Tracing Mobilities: Towards a Cosmopolitan Perspective* (Farnham: Ashgate), 77–102.

Malet, Léo (1985). *Les Enquêtes de Nestor Burma et Les Nouveaux Mystères de Paris*, volumes 1 and 2 (Paris: Éditions Robert Laffont).

Rolls, Alistair (2014). *Paris and the Fetish: Primal Crime Scenes* (Amsterdam: Rodopi).

Ross, Kristin (1995). *Fast Cars, Clean Bodies: Decolonization and the Reordering of French Culture* (Cambridge, MA: MIT Press).

Schulman, Peter (2000). 'Paris en jeu de l'oie: les fantômes de Nestor Burma'. *The French Review* 73.6: 1155–64.

Sirvent, Michel (2000). 'Représentations de l'espace urbain dans le roman policier d'aujourd'hui'. *Nottingham French Studies* 39.1: 79–95.

Walz, Robin (1997). 'Nestor Burma, Détective de Choc: Les Mystères de Léo Malet Sous l'Occupation'. *Tapis-franc, revue du roman populaire* 8: 116–27.

CHAPTER EIGHT

Secrecy and Transparency in Hideo Yokoyama's *Six Four*

Andrew Pepper, Queen's University Belfast

There is a tendency to want to fix crime fiction: to fix the boundaries of what constitutes the genre, its typologies, and hence what it is and more importantly what it is not. Following Tzvetan Todorov's categorization of detective fiction into the subgenres of the 'whodunnit', the 'thriller' and the 'suspense novel', and his claim that all 'types' can be understood as an interplay between the story of the crime and the story of the investigation, where one supplants or suppresses the other (1977: 42–50), this move has spawned further attempts to refine its typologies (Malmgren 2001) and its formal and political characteristics. Crime fiction is 'fixed' either as a conservative genre that privileges, consciously or otherwise, an essentially 'bourgeois' worldview (Mandel 1984; Porter 1981) or as a deviant, radical genre, which unsettles basic presumptions about law, property and morality (Collins 1992; Hilfer 1992). Even where crime fiction is seen to move between polarities, the tendency is to see this movement as preordained – the 'victory of public knowledge and civic solidarity over the dangers of private desires' (McCann 2000: 4) – or a more general move towards 'the restitution of social order' in response to 'unease about the potential chaos of the social world' (Evans 2009: 19). There is a related tendency to want to fix crime novels according to national traditions and to identify crime fiction as exhibiting certain features or characteristics particular to these traditions. Hence we have studies of British, French, Irish, US, Japanese, Italian and Spanish crime fiction, to name a few, though it should be acknowledged that many of these studies also draw attention to the problems of a nation-centred approach and to the inherent transnationality of crime fiction as a genre (Gorrara 2009; Pezzotti 2014; Cliff 2018).

Thankfully, there has been a backlash against this move to designate, to fix, to tie down. Just as Scaggs describes crime fiction as 'unclassifiable' (2005: 1) and points to its 'generic (and sub-generic) flexibility and porosity' (2005: 2), Horsley proposes a 'dialogic approach' that emphasizes 'the ambiguity, or indeed contradictoriness, of individual texts and the different ways of reading them' (2005: 2). Hence, as McCracken tells us, even where fiction is seen as a move from order to disorder and back to order, '[m]ore often than not, we read for the uncertainties provoked by the mystery rather than the security given by the solution' (1998: 50). The present collection as a whole picks up and develops this project by underscoring how crime fiction as a genre must be seen, as noted in the editors' introduction in this collection, as 'constantly violating its own boundaries'. How this fluidity and elasticity create new hybrid forms of crime fiction requires us to think beyond traditional nation-centred categories.

In this chapter, I want to focus on a single novel by the Japanese crime novelist Hideo Yokoyama, first published in Japan as *Rokuyon* (2012) and then translated into English by Jonathan Lloyd-Davies as *Six Four* (2016), as an example of this mobility. By mobility, I am referring in the first instance to the ways in which the novel activates and moves between different generic registers, especially regarding the complex interplay between the generic requirement to reveal or make clear and a corresponding imperative to frustrate and obfuscate. But this move to discuss and problematize the mobility of genre vis-à-vis *Six Four*, as we shall see, also has important transnational implications, insofar as it requires us to think about the ways its account of investigation and policing speaks at the same time to domestic Japanese and international concerns and hence to local and global audiences. Generically, *Six Four* is a hard novel to tie down: it is a police procedural that moves far beyond basic procedure to examine the complex lifeworld of an entire bureaucratic system; it is the story of a kidnapping and the failed investigation of this kidnapping, but one in which these failures are not confined to the past and, instead, play out in the present of the narrative; and it is a story of the disappearance of the teenage daughter of the protagonist, Mikami Yoshinobu, head of Media Relations in the Prefecture D police department, and his search for her. The novel is very much located *within* contemporary Japanese culture and it gives us an insider's perspective on a closed, distinctively Japanese world. As David Peace notes in an interview with the author, 'one of the great achievements of *Six Four* is the incredible insight you give the readers into the everyday workings and structure of the Japanese police force, their political machinations and rivalries, internal, local and national, and also their relationship with the press' (2017: 641). But the novel's commercial success in the UK (where it became a best-seller) is predicated not just on its effective opening up of an unfamiliar world, i.e. giving UK readers insight into the Japanese 'real', but more significantly on its determination to use this apparently unfamiliar landscape (e.g. the internal workings of a Japanese police department) to interrogate and lay bare the essential characteristics of power and governance of a modern democratic society. Readers, therefore, move and are moved between their own and the novel's worlds, producing what Slavoj Žižek describes as a parallax view: 'the perspective shifts and in being deprived of a single point of identi-fication' the reader gains an alternative view 'bound together by a dual sense of vulnerability and solidarity' (2003).

This idea of a 'parallax' is more useful than the 'Orientalist' lens, which is typically used to understand the relationship between 'East' and 'West', whereby the exoticized East is understood as a series of projections of Western desires and fantasies and hence of a set of underlying power relations that produce these projections (Said 2003). It may be true that 'Japan has been consistently "Japanized" by the West', whereby it constitutes 'a crucial site at which white Western masculinity (re)establishes its superiority, dominance and, increasingly, innocence' (Yamamota qtd in Sarkowsky 2006: 110), but *Six Four* is a novel written for a Japanese and international audience by a Japanese author that crucially does not merely set out to overturn this Orientalist framework (thereby retaining the essential binary nature of it). The culture of police work and bureaucracy in Prefecture D may, on one level, be intriguingly different to norms and traditions pertaining to the UK (e.g. with the title *Six Four* deriving from 'the sixty fourth year of the Showa period' when the initial kidnapping took place; and where the 'issue of saving face' [Yokoyama 2017: 58, 89] would seem to carry greater cultural weight), but at the same time non-Japanese readers can understand well enough the internecine bureaucratic struggles that set individuals and departments against one another and the struggles between a central authority and peripheral units to retain control over decision-making processes. If an Orientalist perspective or its mirror, a postcolonial one, seeks to establish or overturn a fixed view of the world (i.e. whereby Western hegemony is either reaffirmed or contested), Žižek's concept of the parallax is more useful for opening up Yokoyama's novel because it allows us to hold onto and examine different perspectives at the same time and to think about the ways in which the novel moves between different positions without ever fully endorsing one or the other. Specifically, it allows us to really see and pull apart the novel's central preoccupation – the complex thematization of the relationship between secrecy and transparency whereby secrecy and transparency as procedural means and ends are both endorsed and questioned.

Defined as 'the absence of concealment' (Birchall 2011b: 8), transparency is typically characterized as a commitment to openness, accountability and unmasking, and hence the unmasking of that which is unseen or unknown, i.e. what is secret. As a means or technique of governance and an end itself, it is seen as 'a virtue, the secular version of a born-again cleanliness that few can fail to praise' (Birchall 2011b: 8) and that 'can solve all our problems' insofar as it is 'entrusted with the task of fostering accountability and strengthening participatory democracy' (Birchall 2011c: 60). By contrast, secrecy 'comes to be associated with all that is nefarious (inefficiency, corruption, malfeasance, conspiracy)' (Birchall 2011c: 66), and hence must be banished through a commitment to openness and revelation. The detective story, typically understood, is similarly aligned and presents itself as a process of unmasking (Porter 1981: 4) where secrets are 'secreted away waiting to be exposed' (Birchall 2011a: 134) by the actions of the exemplary investigator who enacts transparency – 'the absence of concealment' – through his or her method and commitment to revelation aligned to what Goodman calls 'the state's expansive public missions' (2009: 3).

A particular understanding of genre wants to fix the crime story according to the logic of public unmasking, whereby the crime story moves from one polarity, a world of secrets, to its opposite, where these secret worlds are made public. Yet Goodman's account of the genre, which understands that some secrets and private lives can be made public while others are 'unrecognizable, unrepresentable, or contradictory', accords not just with the dynamic, rule-breaking understanding of genre pursued by this book as a whole, according to which the trajectory of crime stories is not necessarily towards revelation, but also with my account of Yokoyama's *Six Four*. In other words, *Six Four* does not simply endorse this kind of unquestioning push towards revelation but also poses far-reaching questions against the logic and work of transparency and in doing so asks whether there are certain secrets that cannot or should not be known. As such, we might ask what transparency is and whether it can be achieved; whether the choice between transparency and secrecy is a false one, whereby 'both positions fail to understand their own relation not only to secrecy itself but also to each other' (Birchall 2011a: 134), and whether 'the moral discourse that condemns and rewards transparency may cause us to overlook the integral, perhaps constitutive, role secrecy (in different guises) might play' (Birchall 2011b: 12).

As Director of Media Relations, Mikami's role is to move between the often conflicting worlds of the Press Club, comprising thirteen individual press agencies, and the snake pit of Prefecture D Police Headquarters where Administrative Affairs and Criminal Investigations are vying with one another in a covert struggle for supremacy and autonomy. *'A pawn of the press. A guard dog for Administrative Affairs'* (Yokoyama 2017: 12; emphasis in the original): this is how Media Relations is typically regarded, especially from within Criminal Investigations, where Mikami used to work as a detective. His first goal as the new Director is 'reforming Media Relations' (Yokoyama 2017: 15), not by facing down the press, as his superior expects ('A tough press director, someone fierce, someone ready and able to stare them down' [Yokoyama 2017: 14]), but by leveraging personal relationships with figures in Criminal Investigations in order to secure 'intel so he could stand up to press' (Yokoyama 2017: 16). Drawing upon the logic and language of a reform-minded 'transparency', the framing metaphor for Mikami's endeavours is that of a 'window': 'It was as if there were a towering wall separating the police from the general public and Media Relations was the only window even close to opening outwards' (Yokoyama 2017: 18). In other words, in the early chapters of the novel, Mikami would seem to have bought into the arguments in favour of transparency as espoused by liberal advocates for whom greater openness equates to accountability and trust and hence to better or more efficient forms of governance (Lathrop and Ruma 2010).

Right away, however, this move towards transparency is tested and unsettled. For a start, the 'full disclosure' principle, whereby Media Relations has 'an obligation to disclose' the full details of a traffic accident involving a housewife and 'an elderly man, resulting in severe, full body injuries to the victim', is put under pressure by the competing right to privacy apparently owed to the driver, who we are told is 'eight months pregnant' and has 'been in a state of extreme distress since causing the accident', resulting in a threat to her unborn child (Yokoyama 2017: 22). Here the logic of transparency, which the liberal-minded crime story (McCann 2000) with its commitment to revelation wants to endorse, runs up against the demands of secrecy, here recast as privacy, which, as Goodman tells us, 'frames foundational ideas behind citizenship in modern democratic culture, where, by privacy guarantees firmly established by legal precedent [...] certain practices are state protected as autonomous from state intervention' (2009: 15). Notwithstanding the issue of whether secrets are secretive if they are partially known (e.g. by certain figures in the novel and by us, as readers), this dilemma, whereby the disclosure principle is set against the right to privacy, immediately puts pressure on Mikami's 'window' metaphor; as he tells the press: 'The window is still there. It's just not as big as you thought' (Yokoyama 2017: 26). Here, partial transparency (a smaller window) co-exists uneasily with partial secrecy (some know about the woman's identity; others do not), as the novel moves back and forth between the two, testing and probing the legitimacy of both sets of claims vis-à-vis the unfolding story. In this particular case, as Mikami comes to realize, the driver's name has been concealed not simply because she is heavily pregnant and in a state of distress but also because her father is Takuzo Kato, the acting chairman of King Cement 'and now in his second year as a member of the Prefecture D Public Safety Committee', after which he acknowledges, with a sense of personal shame, that 'HQ's position had been a sham' (Yokoyama 2017: 212, 123). Afterwards, we are pointedly told that 'the windows in Media Relations had no view' (Yokoyama 2017: 125).

In this case, there is a conspiratorial aspect to secrecy insofar as Administrative Affairs have deliberately acted to conceal the identity of the driver of the car at the behest of a powerful private individual who has assumed a public role within Prefecture D and has used his influence accordingly. Hence the privacy bill being proposed by central government is, for the high-ranking figures in Administrative Affairs at least, little more than a mechanism for 'seiz[ing] control of every aspect of our press reporting' (Yokoyama 2017: 120), and where exceptions to the rule (of law) at once characterize the exercise of power and expose a fundamental rottenness at the heart of the system. A consequence of this is an atmosphere of distrust and paranoia affecting all parties and the breakdown of relations between Media Relations and the press. For Mikami, the solution is an even greater injection of transparency, whereby the 'tactics' of trying to manipulate and control the press are replaced by a more radical openness defined, in the first instance, by fully implementing the disclosure principle: 'We will no longer withhold information from our press reports' (Yokoyama 2017: 408). But in order to persuade the Press Club to trust him, Mikami has to distance himself from Administrative Affairs and Media Relations and offer himself as singularity: 'I'm not asking you to put your faith in something as abstract as [the force as a whole] [...] What I'm asking you to decide is whether or not you can trust *me*' (Yokoyama 2017: 423). And to underline his credentials, Mikami proceeds to tell the press about Takuzo Kato's daughter and about the victim, Ryoji Meikawa, and indeed 'everything there is to tell' (Yokoyama 2017: 424).

There is much more to tell, however, and more that is unknown and potentially unknowable, about the larger crime and investigation that frames the novel as a whole: the unresolved kidnapping and murder fourteen years earlier of Shoko Amamiya; the continuing reverberations and implications of this event; and the police's failure to find and apprehend the perpetrator, into the present. The precipitating event in the present of the novel is the decision of the Commissioner General – 'a man who sat at the very top of the pyramid, above the 260,000 officers in the police force' (Yokoyama 2017: 36) – to visit Shoko Amamiya's father ostensibly to 'pay his respects' at the daughter's altar in order to 'inject new life into the investigation' (Yokoyama 2017: 59) and to produce a 'picture' of the commissioner and the bereaved father 'for the TV and papers' (Yokoyama 2017: 39). Mikami sees the event for what it is or what he believes it to be: 'a PR exercise' (Yokoyama 2017: 54) in which his transparency agenda runs up against a need to manage and control contingencies. As his superior makes clear, 'it would be untenable if the commissioner were to stumble over any capricious or otherwise irresponsible questions' (Yokoyama 2017: 40). Crime fiction as a genre is predisposed towards scepticism – that is, refusing to take at face value what is otherwise being presented as unequivocal; in this case the idea that this is simply an innocent PR exercise. As such, it is Mikami's task, as Director of Media Relations, to prepare for the visit, and as a former detective with a lengthy association with Criminal Investigations (and a personal involvement in the initial kidnapping), to look into the matter and see through what is self-evident in order to uncover what is really motivating the Commissioner's visit and how this relates to what happened or what went wrong during the botched kidnapping investigation fourteen years earlier.

Mikami's professed desire to turn Media Relations into a 'window' runs aground on what he does not and cannot know, i.e. what is secret, and also on the problem of transmission: for transparency to be known as transparent 'there must be some agency (such as the media) that legitimizes it as transparent: and because there is a legitimating agent which does not have to be transparent, there is a limit to transparency' (Birchall 2011a: 142). Both problems, as Mikami comes to realize through his own digging, are conjoined. To address the issue of transmission first of all: if Mikami's own efforts to orchestrate a PR exercise using the press as his instrument speak to the limits of transparency in one sense, in another, as he finds out, the press have their own agendas and their own sources of information. Hence, when abusive behaviour towards suspects in custody by the police is revealed by the *Toya* newspaper, it is not via the enactment of transparency but because this information has been secretly 'leaked' to the *Toya*'s reporter by the head of Criminal Investigations (Yokoyama 2017: 323). If this suggests that secrecy and transparency are co-determinate – i.e. that both are 'caught […] within the same commonsensical idea of the secret: one that assumes the secret is secreted away, waiting to be exposed' (Birchall 2011a: 133) – this logic of revelation is both corroborated and unravelled by the novel's internal struggle between Criminal Investigations and Administrative Affairs.

Let us return for a moment to the question of mobility that frames this chapter and this volume as a whole. In one sense, Yokoyama's novel must be careful about straying too far from the norms and expectations that readers bring to the genre, even if, as Gulddal, King and Rolls argue in the Introduction to this collection, 'crime fiction, far from being static and staid, must be seen as a genre constantly violating its own boundaries'. In part, *Six Four* moves in quite familiar ways: there is a secret and it is Mikami's role to uncover it – that is, to move the novel and the reader from a state of not-knowing to one of knowledge. In the original 'Six Four' operation run by Criminal Investigations, as Mikami discovers, by using his prowess as a detective, not only did the police detectives fail to find and apprehend the kidnapper or the ransom, or to stop the kidnapper from killing Shoko Amamiya, but they also made 'inexcusable' mistakes, such as failing to record the voice of the kidnapper when he called to issue his ransom demands, and then 'systematically covered it up and lied to the public for fourteen years' so that the Prefecture HQ 'would have no means of defence if the truth came out' (Yokoyama 2017: 256). The dilemma of transparency, then, is linked to the problem of secrecy: by keeping their failures secret for so long, Criminal Investigations have opened themselves and potentially the entire police force to greater threat if this secret is made public or brought into the open: 'It would suffer attacks that were of a different magnitude to the censure it would have received if it had first confessed to its mistake' (Yokoyama 2017: 256). Both transparency – i.e. a desire to bring this 'mistake' and cover up into the open – and secrecy (the opposing impulse – i.e. to keep this mistake hidden) are, therefore, linked to 'the same commonsensical idea of the secret'.

However, this is only one relatively minor aspect of the novel as a whole. Far more significant is the covert struggle between Criminal Investigations and Administrative Affairs, and between Prefecture D and police HQ in Tokyo, to exercise their partial and always incomplete knowledge to their own advantage. The opposition between transparency and secrecy, in this sense, is a false one, because both are impossible in the face of contingency and provisionality: what is not known or partially known and cannot therefore be unmasked through a single enactment of transparency. Returning to the issue of mobility, *Six Four* does not simply move in one direction according to the end-oriented logic of revelation; rather, it zigzags back and forth as secrets are traded, partially revealed, then partially hidden again, and so on, by different parties for different reasons and along multiple axes. The resulting perspective is not a fixed or singular one, then, but in the manner of Žižek's parallax, the novel produces multiple and at times conflicting accounts of the same events, which must be weighed up and assessed in light of changing circumstances and where no universal, objective truth can ever ultimately be produced. Furthermore, the same logic applies to the ways in which the novel moves between Japan and the world, and between the closed secretive society of Japanese policing and complexities of governance characteristic of all modern democracies without necessarily endorsing one or the other. Certainly, there is no single moment of revelation and, as such, total objectivity and total transparency are impossible because there are some secrets which cannot be known or cannot be revealed, or where secrets are simultaneously revealed and concealed according to competing and overlapping agendas. The central logic is not then an overarching dilemma of concealment and revelation but a number of smaller, interconnected questions: who knows what, and when, and whether these people know that others know and if so how they are prepared to exploit this knowledge or lack of knowledge for strategic reasons.

For Mikami, the goal is not unearthing the conspiracy but trying to figure out who is trying to use and conceal knowledge of what has been kept secret and for what reasons. As such he crosses paths with Futawatari, who is described as the 'ace' of Administrative Affairs and who 'was digging around in Criminal Investigation's weak spots' in order to unearth 'the Koda memo' (Yokoyama 2017: 169), a secreted document written by Koda following his resignation from the police in the aftermath of the botched kidnapping investigation. No one knows what the memo says or can verify its existence but the notion that it *might* exist prompts a countermove from or by Arakida, Director of Criminal Investigations, in the form of a 'gag order' preventing anyone from his division talking to anyone from Administrative Affairs, including Mikami. 'The Iron Curtain had been granted the full support of the de facto head of Criminal Investigations', Mikami realizes (Yokoyama 2017: 174). In other words, secrecy is enacted as a direct bulwark to the apparently universalizing logic of transparency (universalizing because 'who could be opposed to it?'). As Mikami and Futawatari shadow one another in pursuit of knowledge and allies, with each trying to work out what the other knows and how this knowledge might be deployed, the idea, espoused by Futawatari that 'the police force is monolithic' – i.e. that 'there are no distinctions; no headquarters, no Toyko' (Yokoyama 2017: 294) – comes under increasing pressure as rival factions within Prefecture D threaten to unravel the basic policing mandate. Certainly, as Mikami comes to realize, his agenda is fundamentally at odds with Futawatari's, even though they ostensibly serve the same boss and coexist in the same division:

> Mikami had already guessed that his interests weren't going to be compatible with Futawatari's. But he'd hoped, regardless. He'd hoped that they were both torn between allegiances, single bodies with two minds, existing in a world where hierarchy was everything; that the man's conflicted state would come to the surface if he challenged him face to face [...] But he'd been wrong. (Yokoyama 2017: 294)

The problem with Futawatari's thinking, in the larger scheme of the novel, is that he is only able to deal in or with fixities. In order to be able to move effectively through *Six Four*'s fraught, complex landscapes, Mikami needs to be able to be agile, mobile even, to see ambiguities, multiplicities, and to negotiate a careful path between competing positions, figures and loyalties; that is, to see from different perspectives in the manner of Žižek's concept of the parallax. As someone who has one foot in Administrative Affairs, due to his post as Director of Media Relations, and one foot in Criminal Investigations, following a successful twenty-year stint as detective, Mikami is uniquely placed to grasp the treacherous paths ahead of him. 'He could tell himself he was still a detective at heart', we are told, 'but, as long as he was unable to imagine the danger Criminal Investigations faced, it was impossible to see things from their perspective' (Yokoyama 2017: 362). At stake is the larger relationship between secrets, knowledge and action and the challenges to action posed by not-knowing; in this case, not knowing 'the dangers that Criminal Investigations faced'. Moreover, as Mikami's investigations move him in different directions and along different paths, the hidden motivations behind the various figures and factions might become more apparent but this does not make acting or making decisions any easier. The Commissioner's decision to visit the Amamiya house on the anniversary of the kidnapping is merely the pretext to a larger move intended to discredit Criminal Investigations, force its director to step down and bring it, and the entire Prefecture HQ, under the direct control of Tokyo. 'This is sequestration', the Director tells him, 'the NPA intends to make us a fiefdom of Tokyo' (Yokoyama 2017: 377). Mikami's understanding is even blunter – 'It was hegemony. Seizing power was an instinct of the central command' (Yokoyama 2017: 380) – and nudges him closer to the other camp: 'He could feel the blood coursing through his body. The blood of a detective. It was the only way he could parse the intensity of the emotion' (Yokoyama 2017: 380).

It is not straightforward to make connections between the work that secrecy does in Yokoyama's novel and Birchall's claim that power does not have a monopoly on secrecy and that the left 'needs to recognize secrecy as a resource' (2011c: 73). For a start, *Six Four* – while quietly critical of Tokyo's power grab – does not have or does not pursue an obvious political (whether leftist or rightist) agenda. But I would like to develop the notion of secrecy as a form of resistance to put pressure on the novel's more self-evident commitment to transparency. In response to the NPA's move to centralize power by assuming control of the key position of Director of Criminal Investigations, the secretive agenda of Arakida, the incumbent director, and other figures in Criminal Investigations, whose goal is to disrupt the Commissioner's visit, assumes a shadowy turn when another girl is kidnapped in the same manner as in the original Six Four case and the same ransom demands are issued: 'All [Mikami] was left to do was contemplate the irony, almost predestined, of the outcome. *The spectre of the Six Four ending the Six Four Inspection*' because 'the kidnapping had saved Criminal Investigations from the commissioner's visit' (Yokoyama 2017: 478, 479, emphasis in the original). Whether the new kidnapping is ironic, coincidental or predestined, and what lies behind, is not immediately clear but the secrecy at work – as Birchall puts it, 'a pervasive organizing secret which makes the commons secret to itself' (2011c: 75) – is 'radical' or 'resistant' insofar as it presumes a community characterized by 'non-belonging' (Birchall 2011c: 74): 'a space in which subjects encounter secrets qua singularities' (Birchall 2011c: 75), i.e. where secrets cannot be fully discerned and no one really knows what other people know even within larger collectives. In this sense, the conspiratorial agenda that typically animates crime stories, implying a force that keeps a secret, fails to account for what takes place in Yokoyama's novel where the state is not 'monolithic' and where secrets – both known and also unknown, and perhaps even unknowable – constitute a means of resisting a centralizing program.

Yet *Six Four* does not rest here, in effect, endorsing secrets over transparency; rather, it moves again to counter or problematize the notion of secrecy as a form of resistance. While secrecy is used to stymy Tokyo's '*coup d'état*' (Yokoyama 2017: 463), Mikami cannot endorse the related claims of anonymity over disclosure (i.e. secrecy over transparency):

> Any tale of make-believe, however far-fetched, could come alive when hidden behind a screen of anonymity. It could walk freely. Any and all developments were plausible. When it came to weaving a tale, anonymity was omnipotent, a delusion itself, one that allowed for an infinity of choice. (Yokoyama 2017: 491)

Of course, whether intended or not, this is an instructive meta-commentary on the nature of fiction and, by implication, crime fiction, at least up to the point where any number of developments are plausible and an infinity of choices remain open or possible in the manner of Žižek's parallax. Yet, just as crime stories also need to narrow possibilities and produce answers or outcomes, i.e. truths rather than the truth, even if these 'truths' or answers are only provisional or ambiguous, Mikami understands that he cannot 'allow anonymity to run wild; it was a monster, feeding on doubt to multiply indefinitely' (Yokoyama 2017: 494). Instead then, it is a form of provisional transparency he chooses – tagging along with the Mobile Command unit, as they monitor the kidnapper and ransom demands, and relaying the details back to the waiting press with a twenty-minute delay. The transparency is 'provisional' because whereas Yokoyama does give us some answers (i.e. we find out that the disgraced Koda and the bereaved father, Amamiya, have tracked down the original kidnapper, Mesaki, by calling up everyone in the telephone directory and listening to their voices, and have turned the tables by pretending to kidnap his daughter and hence subjecting him to the same kind of torment) and while the basic details of the police operation are made available to the press, they are not *yet* told of the connections between the cases. 'If Mesaki were to be arrested, make a full confession [...] The glorious press conference to mark the arrest would, at the same time, become ground zero for the explosive secret Criminal Investigations had kept hidden for fourteen years' (Yokoyama 2017: 614), a moment that is deferred in the present of the story, wherein the new Director of Criminal Investigations had 'made the department's secret his own, drawn it in close' (Yokoyama 2017: 615).

If this is an example of Birchall's claims that 'secrecy is already at work in transparency' (2011c: 71), we might ask whether the choice between secrecy and transparency is a false one or indeed whether 'both positions fail to understand their own relation [...] to secrecy itself' (2011a: 133). By this, Birchall means 'unconditional' secrets or secrets that are not just unknown but also unknowable (2011a: 135) and turning our attention back to Yokoyama's novel, we might think about the implications of one final story strand: the disappearance, at some point before the start of the narrative, of Mikami's daughter, Ayumi, and the failure of Mikami and his wife Minako, and indeed the 260,000-strong legion of police officers in Japan, to find her. By way of a conclusion, I would like to recast this disappearance and this failure as one of these 'unknowns' or something that is 'unknowable' at least to us as readers and to think about the implications for our understanding of crime fiction and the larger relationship between genre and mobility that has framed the concerns of this essay.

In one sense, of course, crime fiction as a genre moves towards revelation, and so it is with *Six Four* where the fourteen-year-old 'secret' of the initial kidnapping is cracked. But in relation to Yokoyama's novel and, I suspect, many other crime novels that similarly disrupt, in small and not-so-small ways, this idea or telos of unmasking, there is something fundamentally misguided about Evans's generalizing remarks on the genre:

> At the same time as the murderer is finally revealed, what is also restored is social order, and it is possible to see this restitution of social order as the definitive contribution of the detective story to social unease about 'origins' [...] Detection is, in this sense, a hugely healing and redemptive form of fiction and as such is immensely calming to what might be a general [...] unease about the potential chaos of the social world. (2009: 19)

This holds true only insofar as one sees or characterizes crime fiction according to the more general logic of revelation (and the fixed, unidirectional movement from disorder to order); but what we see in *Six Four*, and in the crime novels explored in this collection as a whole, is very definitely not this. Taking transparency and secrecy as its reference points, the novel moves back and forth, in complex, unpredictable ways, from one to the other, and in doing so it radically disrupts the kind of certainties that Evans wants to ascribe to the genre. If secrecy is always already present in transparency, and vice versa, any insights or knowledge that crime fiction is able to generate will only ever be partial, provisional and always open to challenge. For Mikami, who moves between the partial transparency required of him as Director of Media Relations and the partial secrecy forced upon him by his associations with Criminal Investigations, the result is an awkward, messy and ambivalent compromise, a sense of never quite being able to settle. 'I haven't sold my soul', he says defiantly, '[b]ut nor am I clinging to my past as a detective, not any more' (Yokoyama 2017: 501). And to Evans's complacent certainties, Yokoyama offers us not only these ambiguities but also what cannot be known, e.g. Ayumi's disappearance, which is not resolved or explained at the end of the novel. Moving, in this sense, is not just in the direction of explanation and unmasking, as required by the logic and demands of transparency, but also in the direction of unknowability where secrecy refuses to reveal itself to itself.

Works Cited

Birchall, Claire (2011a). '"There's Been Too Much Secrecy in This City": The False Choice Between Secrecy and Transparency in US Politics'. *Cultural Politics* 7.1: 133–56.

— (2011b). 'Introduction to Secrecy and Transparency'. *Theory, Culture and Society* 28.7–8: 7–25.

— (2011c). 'Transparency, Interrupted: Secrets of the Left'. *Theory, Culture and Society* 28.7–8: 60–84.

Cliff, Brian (2018). *Irish Crime Fiction* (New York: Palgrave Macmillan).

Collins, Jim (1992). *Uncommon Cultures: Popular Culture and Post-Modernism* (London and New York: Routledge).

Evans, Mary (2009). *The Imagination of Evil: Detective Fiction and the Modern World* (London and New York: Continuum).

Goodman, Robin Truth (2009). *Policing Narratives and the State of Terror* (Albany: State University of New York Press).

Gorrara, Claire (ed.) (2009). *French Crime Fiction* (Cardiff: University of Wales Press).

Hilfer, Tony (1992). *The Crime Novel: A Deviant Genre* (Austin: University of Texas Press).

Horsley, Lee (2005). *Twentieth-Century Crime Fiction* (Oxford: Oxford University Press).

Lathrop, Daniel and Laurel Ruma (eds) (2010). *Open Government: Collaboration, Transparency, and Participation in Practice* (Sebastopol, CA: O'Reilly Media).

Malmgren, Carl D. (2001). *Anatomy of Murder: Mystery, Detective and Crime Fiction* (Bowling Green, KY: Bowling Green State University Press).

Mandel, Ernest (1984). *Delightful Murder: A Social History of the Crime Story* (London: Pluto).

McCann, Sean (2000). *Gumshoe America: Hard-Boiled Crime Fiction and the Rise of New Deal Liberalism* (Durham, NC and London: Duke University Press).

McCracken, Scott (1998). *Pulp: Reading Popular Fiction* (Manchester: Manchester University Press).

Peace, David (2017). 'Hideo Yokoyama: Man of Mystery', in Hideo Yokoyama, *Six Four* (London: Riverrun), 637–43.

Pezzotti, Barbara (2014). *Politics and Society in Italian Crime Fiction: An Historical Overview* (Jefferson, NC: McFarland).

Porter, Dennis (1981). *The Pursuit of Crime: Art and Ideology in Detective Fiction* (New Haven: Yale University Press).

Said, Edward (2003). *Orientalism* (London: Penguin).

Sarkowsky, Katja (2006). 'Manga, Zen and Samurai: Negotiating Exoticism and Orientalist Images in Sujata Massey's Rei Shimura Novels', in Christine Matzke and Suzanne Mühleisen (eds), *Postcolonial Postmortems* (Amsterdam: Rodopi), 109–34.

Scaggs, John (2005). *Crime Fiction* (London and New York: Routledge).

Todorov, Tzvetan (1977). 'The Typology of Detective Fiction', in *The Poetics of Prose*. Trans. Richard Howard (Oxford: Basil Blackwell), 42–52.

Yokoyama, Hideo (2017). *Six Four*. Trans. Jonathan Lloyd-Davies (London: Riverrun).

Žižek, Slavoj (2003). "Parallax". *London Review of Books* 25:22 (20 November): 24–25.

Part III

Transnational Mobility

CHAPTER NINE

From Vidocq to the Locked Room

International Connections in Nineteenth-Century Crime Fiction

Stephen Knight, University of Melbourne

International Criminography

The international status of crime fiction was itself fictionalized in the suggestions by Régis Messac and Dorothy L. Sayers that the form could be traced back to the Old Testament, the classics or, more recently, Voltaire (Messac 1929: 47–99; Sayers 1972: 71–109).[1] They were inventing a dignified antiquity for their own interests by seeing the genre as primarily detective fiction, linked to clever solutions to problems through many places and times, and solved by what Messac calls 'princes subtils' (89–99). However, a genuine internationality arose in collections of true-crime stories that emerged in the eighteenth century, gathering previously separate contemporary pamphlets or ballads. The French 'Pitaval' genre was the first: François de Pitaval, a courtroom lawyer, published several volumes of *Causes célèbres et intéressantes* between 1733 and 1743. In England *The Newgate Calendar* was a series of anonymous crime anthologies, first published in 1773, taking its name from the London jail but by no means only set in that city. Germany followed suit when the legal scholar Paul von Feuerbach published *Merkwürdige*

---

1 The first four stories that Sayers reprints are, she notes, from 'the Jewish Apocrypha, Herodotus, and the Aeneid' (72), and she goes on to justify this.

Rechstfalle (1808, Noteworthy Legal Cases). America did not have an early anthology of crime stories, but many separate accounts appeared there in the same period.[2]

Equally international were the fictional accounts of crime deployed by some Romantic-period writers as ways of imagining how an individual might dissent from social forces that seemed almost criminal. It is common to see the English William Godwin's *Things as They Are* (1794) – which came to be known by its sub-title *Caleb Williams* – and the American Charles Brockden Brown's *Edgar Huntly* (1799) as archetypes, both investigating a puzzling murder in the context of social critique, but these were preceded in Germany by Friedrich Schiller's *Die Räuber* (1781), which celebrates heroic criminality, and his unfinished *Der Geisterseher* (1786–87) has an aristocrat examining mysterious events. In E.T.A. Hoffman's *Das Fräulein von Scuderi* (1819) an elderly lady explains mysterious crimes in eighteenth-century Paris. In the same city Honoré de Balzac published two novels focusing on the deeds and qualities, both good and bad, of the pirate Argow in *Le Vicaire des Ardennes* (1823) and *Annette et le criminel* (1824), both of which were inspired by international sources, such as Godwin and the Romantics Scott and Byron (Mannironi 2015: 145–60).

With criminal narratives encountering the modern hero, it is unsurprising that the first crime story, which itself became a major international influence, interwove and developed those two forces. Eugène François Vidocq, a criminal turned police informer, was so successful in the latter role that he was in 1812 appointed as the first head of the Paris Sûreté. His four-volume *Mémoires* (1828–29) were exciting, and, through his editor-cum-ghost-writer, L.F.H. L'Héritier, quite often fictitious. Vidocq's detailed and courageous involvement with the criminal world, often in disguise, gave rise to many theatrical versions and both the *Mémoires* and extracts from them were rapidly translated and reprinted across the world.

For the French, the new urban detective connected with another international innovator, J. Fenimore Cooper, in what they called *Cooperisme*, through which American frontier heroics both against the natives and also using their wiles were translocated to Paris (Messac 1929: 205–18). Eugène Sue calls Cooper 'the American Walter Scott' in his 1842–43 *Les Mystères de Paris*. Dumas would sum *le Cooperisme* up in his title *Les Mohicans de Paris* (1857–58), but Edgar Allan Poe had

2 On early American true crime stories, see Cohen (1993) and Halttunen (1998).

already reciprocated from 1841, setting his Dupin stories in the Paris he had never visited. Dumas himself responded to that connection: 'L'assassinio di Rue Saint-Roch' (1860) appeared in the Neapolitan newspaper, *L'Independente*, which Dumas edited, and features the death of two women and an investigation led by one Edgar Poe and a police surgeon called Paolo Dupin.[3]

Vidocq's influence travelled north, as is clear from the date alone of Steen Steensen Blicher's Danish *Præsten i Vejlbye* (1829, The Rector of Vejlbye, subtitled A Crime Story), and, as Yvonne Leffler outlines (2015: 161–81), the new tradition thrived in Scandinavia, with Carl Almqvist's Swedish *Skällnora kvarn* (1838, Skällnora Mill) and the Norwegian Mauritz Hansen with *Mordet på Maskinbygger Roolfsen* (1839, The Murder of Engine Maker Roolfsen, subtitled A Crime Anecdote from Kongsberg), while Zacharias Topelius's *En natt och en morgen* (1843, A Night and a Morning) was the first Finnish crime novel, written in Swedish. These are all novellas focused on investigations, two by judges, two by members of the public; they all expose a murderer who is pretending innocence; Leffler sees them as examples of the 'Romantic crime story', both Gothic and moral, focusing on 'repressed desire and emotional conflicts' (Leffler 2015: 175–80).

The earlier German moves towards crime fiction were confirmed in the year of Vidocq's *Mémoires*, with Adolph Müllner's *Der Kaliber* (1828, The Caliber), in which, Mary Tannert comments (2016: 36), as well as the detective detail suggested by the title, 'much space is given to romantic themes (the forest, fratricide, the inevitability of fate, the redemptive power of love)'. Others followed: Otto Ludwig von Puttkammer's *Der Tote von St. Annas Kapelle* (1839, The Dead Man of St Ann's Chapel) offers the Gothic pattern of a wife tried for murdering her husband, but it turns out he killed himself and wanted her blamed. Most of the criminals in early German crime fiction are, like this, deranged, not the cunning agents of bourgeois malice whom the English preferred, and the German investigators tend to be magistrates, as in the work of J.H.D. Temme, a Swiss liberal judge who wrote more than three dozen detective stories, notably the forest-located *Wer war der Mörder?* (1873, Who Was the Murderer?). Temme's routinization of the genre in

---

3 The story reappeared in 2012 as an e-book. This version was edited by Ugo Cundari and published in Milan by Baldini and Castoldi. I am grateful to Maurizio Ascario for this information: in an email dated 5 August 2016 he describes the story as 'a playful act of plagiarism'.

German was followed by many, such as Adolf Streckfuss, who started with *Der Sternkrug* (1870, The Star Tavern), though here too the pattern is not simple. An undercover police detective nearly arrests the wrong man, falls in love with his daughter, and having found the right man gives up detecting in a manner reminiscent of E.C. Bentley's *Trent's Last Case* (1913) (Tannert 2016: 42).

Though these languages are localizing a genre which had come to them through English, French and American sources, there remains a world focus to the developing crime fiction genre. When Eugène Sue began his very popular and influential *Les Mystères de Paris* in 1842, he did not use a detective hero, but the centre of the action, and the dominant force for good against widespread criminality, is a German, Prince Rodolphe of Gerolstein. The story was imitated around the world, with 'Mysteries' reaching from St Petersburg to Melbourne and into most of the Eastern American cities,[4] and internationalism remained thematic. George Reynolds in his *The Mysteries of London* (1844–48) moved the action to a city teeming with body-snatchers, corrupt businessmen and MPs, but his hero Richard Markham, son of a failed banker, loves an Italian girl, helps her refugee father regain his territory, and becomes the commander of the Castelcicalan armies and then Prince Ricardo, a radical liberator fifteen years before Garibaldi.

Others followed the trend. Paul Féval, in a frenzy of French internationalism, made his *Les Mystères de Londres* (1843–44) focus on Irishman Fergus O'Brian, who escapes from transportation in Australia, becomes, as the Marquis of Rio Tinto, a rich world-ranging pirate and finally plans to blow up the Bank of England and the Houses of Parliament and install in charge the currently captive Napoleon, including as lord of newly French India. Féval's somewhat calmer detective novel, *Jean Diable* (1863), also starts in London, with Scotland Yard's Gregory Temple, who works on a case that zooms through England, France and several German states; a central figure, French nobleman Henri de Belcamp (who is also English Percy Balcombe and perhaps others too) possesses doctorates from several European universities. Much the same hyperbolic multi-locationism is found in the first part of Féval's *Les habits noirs* (1863, The Black Coats), in which, while Italy is the source of criminal power, Paris is the major location, and characters travel to London and elsewhere.

4 For an account of the main worldwide Mysteries, see Knight (2012).

Anglophone Internationalism

Throughout the century reference to Europe is very strong in English culture, and Europe and even transatlantic connections became familiar in crime writing. When *All the Year Round* was printing Collins's novel *The Woman in White* (1860), which has a good deal of detection in it, the magazine also reprinted extracts from Vidocq's *Mémoires*, as if to assert a Europe-wide sense of the crime fiction genre. Ascari has drawn attention to the multiple-nation contexts of early crime fiction (2007: 94–109). He shows how the 1827 Blackwood's story 'Le Revenant', set in London despite its French title, was reprinted in 1838 in France, now with an American setting – it was classically one of the stories that inspired Poe, who was himself both plagiarized and celebrated in Paris by the dubious 'Émile Forgues' (Paul-Émile Daurand), and then canonized by the influential Charles Baudelaire.

Ascari also identifies French sources for English crime stories, such as Mary Braddon's *The Trail of the Serpent* (1861) and Thomas Taylor's very successful play *The Ticket-of-Leave Man* (1863), which made 'Hawkshaw' a popular synonym for detective; he shows how the English mid-century police detective stories, like those by the still pseudonymous 'William Russell',[5] both used French characters and locations and also were routinely translated into French. Finally he notes how Collins was also celebrated by 'Forgues' as early as 1855 in a long essay in *Revue des deux mondes*, in response to which Collins gratefully dedicated *The Queen of Hearts* (1859) to 'Forgues'.

In the context of Collins, Ascari also raises the issue of how the plots of many English crime novels make, like Reynolds and Féval, major use of Europe-based elements. This matter of location is the widest-ranging and most striking of all the elements of internationalism in nineteenth-century crime fiction and goes back to the formation of the self-conscious genre. Edward Bulwer created *Pelham* (1828), a murder mystery that starts in high-style Paris, moves to the world of London gentry – Pelham himself becomes an MP – and resolves the story with a brave venture into one of London's criminal no-go areas.

Internationalism of setting remained central as the crime novel developed. The reverse of Bulwer's Anglo-French narrative mix is found in Catherine Crowe's *Susan Hopley* (1841) where a woman servant calmly

---

5 Recurrent suggestions he was the William Russell who famously reported the Crimean War for *The Times* are definitely wrong.

observes exciting events starting with murder in the English provinces and moving through aristocratic romance in Paris to a sequence of crimes by two rogues in the Dordogne. The pattern continued: though Bulwer (now surnamed Bulwer Lytton) based *Lucretia* (1846) on Thomas Wainewright, the English serial murderer who had been transported to Tasmania, he made him a Frenchman, Gabriel Honoré Varney. Wilkie Collins was also consistently internationalist in his narratives. He looked recurrently to Italy and France, but in his early mystery *Hide and Seek* (1854) Matthew Grice returns from America to solve a family mystery: the pioneer-like name he has taken on, Mat Marksman, and the remarkable fact that he has been scalped make him a clear instance of English Cooperism. A version of this recurs in *The Woman in White* (1860), when the meek drawing teacher Walter Hartright returns from an adventurous journey to Honduras as a strong, active person and takes over detecting from the enfeebled Marian Halcombe. Cooperized masculinism also appeared in Collins's 'The Diary of Anne Rodway' (1856).

Not only the admiration of 'Forgues' connected Collins to France. He made the French Revolution the context for the 1855 novella 'Sister Rose', which develops a police element as the family's land-steward becomes a Chief Agent of Police under Robespierre. Collins was, moreover, influenced by Maurice Méjan's *Recueil des causes célèbres* (1808–14), an updating of Pitaval, which not only provided him with the basic plot of *The Woman in White*, but also stimulated much in the method of what would be Collins's breakthrough success (Ascari 2007: 104–05), whose action concludes in Paris where the evil genius Count Fosco is found dead in the morgue. Collins's later crime fiction novels were often international with plots that traverse the West Indies, France, Italy, America, India and the Pacific.

Other English writers followed Collins more fully both in his sensationalist and partly crime fiction mode and also his recurrent internationalism. Ellen Wood's major success *East Lynne* (1861) has a beautiful aristocratic English lady, Isabel Vane, leave her respectable lawyer husband to live in France with a man who turns out both bad to her and a murderer: after a disfiguring railway accident she returns as her own children's governess, to live out a sad repentance. The plot and settings reverse the pattern of Mary Braddon's equally successful *Lady Audley's Secret* (1860), in which a woman's husband deserts her for the Australian goldfields and she marries up bigamously into the gentry. When the husband returns, predictably rich, she pushes him down a well, but he survives and she is finally revealed as a villainess in spite of her sweetly enticing beauty – and, still the opposite of Isabel Vane, is packed off to a Belgian *maison de santé*, where she will soon conveniently die.

The trip to Australia was a popular theme in mid-nineteenth-century fiction (Lansbury 1970). Early stories tell how a young man not doing well at home makes the long journey, usually without the compulsion of the law, grows rich from cattle, sheep or, from 1851 on, gold, and returns home in charitable glory. Féval's super-plotter Fergus O'Brian was an extreme example of this, but Reynolds also joined in, though not even Lansbury knew of his contribution. Early in *The Mysteries of London* Crankey Jem is transported for theft, very improbably escapes and returns, to avenge himself on the multi-villainous Resurrection Man who fingered him – but Jem also saves Queen Victoria from attack.

Other English fiction visited the distant colony: Dickens used the idea of Australian wealth as an ironic explanation of Pip's inheritance in *Great Expectations* (1860), but he set none of Magwitch's activity, criminal or enriching, in the distant colony. Bulwer Lytton wrote a classic money-and-crime colonial adventure in *The Caxtons* (1849), emphasizing, in that pre-gold-rush period, moral weakness rather than actual crime. Charles Reade went further and welcomed six shiploads of new Australian gold that arrived early with his play *Gold!* (1853). Then in a novel which largely reworked the plot of *The Caxtons*, *It is Never too Late to Mend* (1856) he celebrated colonial wealth returning to Britain, though the actual criminal figure John Meadows tactfully stays in Australia. Henry Kingsley's novel *The Recollections of Geoffrey Hamlyn* (1859), which employed 'every known cliché of Australian life' (Lansbury 1970: 118), focuses on respectable English gentlemen gaining large amounts of money and bringing it home, though the overtly criminal bushranger and murderer George Hawker remains far distant from English civility.

Most Australian crime fiction was primarily international through the immigrant status of most of the authors; though it was also often published either solely or jointly in Britain, the emphasis is on the unique Australian settings and activities. A major figure was Marcus Clarke, author of *His Natural Life*, which in 1871–73 as a monthly serial told powerfully how a transported man survives his brutal context and settles to Australian prosperity. This was revised and published in book form, with a strikingly new – or perhaps old – 'return to England' happy ending in 1874, a version which became known as *For the Term of His*

Natural Life (1885). International in a merely biographical way was the remarkable Mary Fortune, born in Scotland and married in Canada, who as 'Waif Wander', or 'W.W.', published hundreds of high-quality stories set in rural Victoria or Melbourne, mostly using police detection, in *The Australian Journal* for some forty years from 1866.

There were exotic elements of Australian internationalism, like *Les Voleurs d'Or* (1857), a melodramatic story by the Comtesse de Chabrillan, a Parisian dancer whose aristocratic husband was sent in disgrace as a consul to Melbourne in 1854. The native-born John Lang, a Cambridge-trained barrister, left Sydney for India in 1842: living in Meerut, he edited *The Moffusilite* newspaper and wrote some India-set crime adventures and others, usually published in London, about both English and Australian crime, notably *The Forger's Wife* (1855), with George Flower as a convincing Sydney-based investigator into convict society.

In America there are early and sometimes negative elements of international connections – Brockden Brown uses Godwin's model in a positive mode but also depicts disruption from overseas: though Carwin in *Wieland* (1798) is American-born he is educated in trouble-making ways in Europe, and the bossily intrusive Sarsfield in *Edgar Huntly* (1799) is also a world-traveller. Cooper and Poe would in different ways return a positive influence to the old world, but the dominant American pattern until the later part of the century was eager transplantation of European material, notably in the Mystery mode, but also in adventurously pirated reprints: both *The Confessions of an Attorney* (1852) and *The Recollections of a Police-Officer* (1853) appeared in collected form in America before they did in London. But before long fully American crime fiction appeared, like the 'Jem Brampton' stories from 1865 by James B. Williams about a New York police detective, and the series of Allan Pinkerton novels starting with *The Expressman and the Detective* (1874) which, though written by a Scottish-born private detective, were entirely American in their concerns.

That was to be the American pattern – Harriet Prescott Spofford started with a Poe-like Paris-set jewel-theft story in 1859, but adopted the Brampton-like American Mr Furbush as her detective in 1865. From then on occasional international references were made at times, but they tended not to be positive – in *The Dead Letter* (1867) by 'Seeley Regester' (Metta Fuller) the villain finally gets away to Mexico, and the criminals in the later 'Old Sleuth' and 'Nick Carter' dime-novel tradition were often non-American. In contrast, in *The Leavenworth Case*, the more sophisticated Anna Katharine Green makes the point that the murdered

Mr Leavenworth's hatred of the English was a mistake, and the British immigrant Henry Clavering is ultimately a romantic hero.

The English sensational writer Mary Braddon was even more internationalist than Collins. Always closely interested in French fiction, she early on said Balzac's realization of the 'morbid-anatomy school' was her 'especial delight' (Woolf 1979: 127). Her *The Trail of the Serpent* (1861) deals with events in Paris, as does, *The Cloven Foot* (1879), while *Eleanor's Victory* (1863) uses French settings, and she maintained the French connection: *Phantom Fortune* (1883) is an experiment in Zolaesque naturalism, in part based on his *La Curée* (1872), but relocated entirely to mysterious events in England and across Europe. *Under the Red Flag* (1883) is set entirely in the Communard Paris of 1870, though it is also a story focusing on two Irish sisters, and the whole of the politically complex 1850s novel *Ishmael* (1884) occurs in Paris.

Braddon also travelled beyond France for some of her settings – to Belgium in *Birds of Prey* (1867) and to Venice in *The Black Band* (1862), *One Life, One Love* (1890) – which also visits Paris – and in *The Venetians* (1891). But she also goes further: *Henry Dunbar* (1864) and *The Story of Barbara* (1880) have important sequences in India, while *Sir Jasper's Tenant* (1865) visits Africa and *The Octoroon* (1862) is set entirely in the American south. *Lost for Love* (1874) develops the pattern of *The Caxtons*, by her much-admired correspondent Bulwer Lytton, in that a central figure returns from Queensland a very rich man. He dies quite soon from heart disease, but a younger Australia returnee, an artist, becomes involved in criminal activity, then a near murder; he has relationships with two women who are first cousins, and finally he and the favoured cousin leave for abroad.

Another of Braddon's internationalist books found its way into Australian tradition: *Wyllard's Weird* (1885), her novel that most closely resembles a classic murder story. It has European connections – a young French woman falls to her death from a train in Cornwall, and this traces back to events of the early seventies, when the central figure in the novel, now a Cornish solicitor, was a very successful financial operator on the Paris Bourse. But to see how this very capable mystery novel links to Australia and a wider internationalism, it is first necessary to trace the development of the crime novel itself.

The International Mystery Novel

Among his remarkable and sometimes improbable achievements, Paul Féval can claim to be the foster-father of the international mystery novel, as he led its real father, Émile Gaboriau, towards the form. In 1862 while writing *Jean Diable*, Féval employed Gaboriau as a secretary; before long he was editing Féval's magazines, notably the one named after the success of the novel *Jean Diable*. Gaboriau probably ghosted some of Féval's work, but certainly picked up his techniques and focused them rather better. His first mystery, *L'Affaire Lerouge* (1866) uses an elderly bookish amateur detective, Tabaret, but there is also a young policeman called Lecoq, which had been the name of the master-criminal in Féval's *La Forêt de Paris*, who is eventually beheaded by the hero in fine Févalian mode, using a safe door as his implement.

Gaboriau retired Tabaret, though he is at times consulted in later books, which focus on Lecoq as a young, energetic, insightful Parisian police detective, capable of both deep disguise and close detection. It is likely that the numbers of mid-century London police detective stories, well known in France, influenced Lecoq's official status, but it is also clear that French authors and readers did not share the English class hostility to police as mere proletarians (Trodd 1989: 12–44; Knight 2017). While working on his masterpiece, *Monsieur Lecoq* (1869), Gaboriau's publishers persuaded him to produce in quick succession the shorter novels *Le Crime d'Orcival* (1867), *Le Dossier no. 113* (1867) and the less mystery-focused *Les Esclaves de Paris* (1868). Unlike Féval's work, these are not international in their settings and characters – in *Le Dossier no. 113* a missing heir goes to England, dies there and is replaced by the aristocratic villain, but none of the real action occurs outside France. The internationalism of Gaboriau's work, however, lay in its acceptance and its imitation overseas, first, and most, in America, where Gaboriau was quickly translated or reworked: a version of *Le Dossier no. 113* is *The Steel Safe*, set in America, and published as early as 1868 under the name of Henry Llewellyn Williams, usually a translator from French.

A better-known and itself internationally influential American response to Gaboriau was in the work of Anna Katharine Green, whose first mystery *The Leavenworth Case* (1878) was clearly influenced by Gaboriau: she picks up his use of a map of the murder scene, and extends this technique with a facsimile of a letter. She also uses a police detective in a capital city, this time New York; though Ebenezer Gryce lacks the vigour and disguises of Lecoq, he is just as patient and attentive, as able to undertake historical searches and regional travel. She also retains Gaboriau's use of a romantic subplot.

The Leavenworth Case was the first mystery novel to sell in really large numbers – initially in America, as it was not published in London until 1884. Britain was moving rather slowly in the development of the crime novel: there were examples like *The Notting Hill Mystery* (1865, serialized 1862–63) by the publisher Charles Warren Adams, writing as 'Charles Felix', but the provision of mystery in the sensational form, as well as the weight of the three-volume novel, and no doubt some publishing snobbery, seem to have retarded the English development. Gaboriau himself was not translated there nearly as quickly as in America, though he was clearly known in the 1870s, presumably in French or in copies brought in from America.[6] In the early 1880s Henry Vizetelly, a London publisher of French origin, started producing his novels in English, where they sold very well. Indeed, this process, inspired this time by Braddon's *Wyllard's Weird*, generated the major international sensation of the new mystery novel, which would have dramatic influence on the genre through its huge sales in London in 1887–88, Fergus Hume's *The Mystery of a Hansom Cab*.

Born in England and growing up in New Zealand, Hume wrote for the stage and newspapers before he moved in 1886 to Melbourne, a busy city still enjoying the riches of the gold-rush. His play-writing was not taken seriously: a bookseller advised him that Gaboriau was selling very well, and Hume later said he bought some copies to imitate (Sussex 2015: 75). Yet the policing is by no means as decisive as Lecoq's – the two police detectives are quite minor figures, one plump and semi-competent, the other nervy but at least insightful: a lawyer and the first suspect's girlfriend do much of the investigation. It seems clear that in the original form of *The Mystery of a Hansom Cab* Hume had used as a model *Wyllard's Weird,* which appeared in serial form in the Melbourne newspaper *The Leader* when he arrived there. In both stories a wealthy man is challenged by a visitor from abroad about his dubious

---

6 Gaboriau's 'ingeniously constructed novels' are referred to on page 3 of *The Morning Post* (11 January 1873); page 2 of *The Dundee Courier* (14 November 1873), a notably literary newspaper, has a passing reference to his work; on 2 January 1877 *The Times*, in a review of 'Light French Literature', comments on the 'explanatory episodes which used to break the sensational thread of the story in Gaboriau's more pretentious works' (3).

past; he murders the challenger; a young man he knows well is suspected, but his girlfriend and a lawyer sort things out.

Hume found it impossible to place the book with a publisher, and later claimed they only wanted overseas material (Sussex 2015: 97) – so he published it himself, with skilful publicity by a friend, Frederick Trischler. It sold strongly and went into several editions in Melbourne. A well-crafted story, it is rich with reference to the city's busy life and this must have seemed very up-to-date: the novel hardly refers to the wide rural acres that had long been central in Australian fiction, including crime fiction. Trischler obtained funds to take the novel to London, where just before Christmas 1887 it appeared, with the words 'A Sensational Melbourne Novel' on the cover. Sales were themselves sensational: 340,000 copies sold in less than a year (Sussex 2015: 159–60). While Trischler's publicity was certainly good, much of the success must be due to the mix it offers of a briskly told, fairly short mystery novel and its setting in a colonial city well known by reputation at least to many Londoners – internationalism strongly at work. It is not true, though often asserted, that Hume's novel was the first best-selling crime novel – *The Leavenworth Case* had sold more copies in the previous ten years than Hume would overall. It was, however, the first London best-seller, and the speed of its success alerted publishers to the new mystery novel genre that had emerged now in Britain, after America, France and Australia.

Something else appeared for Christmas 1887: Arthur Conan Doyle's *A Study in Scarlet* came out in *Beeton's Christmas Annual*. He later said he finished it by mid-1886 and had to wait for publication, so it seems impossible that he knew Hume's novel, which appeared in October 1886 in far-off Melbourne. But Doyle also used Gaboriau as a discarded influence, dismissing Lecoq as 'a miserable bungler' (1999: 25). Hume did, however, do something for Doyle. Hume's worldwide success – including by piracy in America – seems to have alerted publishers to the new possibilities of the crime genre, and though Doyle did not place much value on his first detective novella, in 1889 another was commissioned by the American *Lippincott's Magazine*. *The Sign of the Four* appeared there in 1890 and led fairly directly to the first of the Holmes short stories in *The Strand Magazine* in early 1891 and in America immediately afterwards.

The Holmes stories were, especially early on, frequently international in reference. The plot of *A Study in Scarlet* depends on events in America which are retrospectively recounted. This use of the past had been a pattern for Gaboriau, but a closer general source was R.L. Stevenson's very recent *The Dynamiter* (1885). Doyle continued this pattern with *The Sign of the Four*, which originates in colonial India where a treasure has been stolen and then charts the aftermath in England, much like Collins's *The Moonstone*.

The Holmes stories are often rural or suburban, but can have wide international reference. The first involves the King of Bohemia, and others deploy a conflict from the Australian goldfields ('The Boscombe Valley Mystery'), a maritime drama involving the Indian Empire and the American south ('The Five Orange Pips'), and others present men who have worked in empire returning to Britain troubled and dangerous: Dr Roylott in 'The Speckled Band', the colonel in 'The Crooked Man' and Colonel Moran in 'The Empty House'. America is an important context in 'The Noble Bachelor', 'The Dancing Men' and 'The Yellow Face', but Doyle also offers non-Holmes internationalist themes and threats. This started in 'The Gully of Bluemansdyke', an Australian-set goldfields story published in *London Society* in 1881, which features Chicago Bill, a shrewd American able to read a horse as well as Holmes would interpret people. Much tenser in its imperial themes is *The Mystery of Cloomber* (1889): the retired English general once murdered a Buddhist holy man and is finally dealt with by 'three avenging Buddhist chelas', reminiscent, again, of *The Moonstone* (Barsham 2003: 71). A little earlier, but still written after *A Study in Scarlet,* Doyle's story 'The Mystery of Uncle Jeremy's Household' primarily centres on a dishonest secretary who is after both his master's money and a young governess with a criminal past who is half-Indian, the daughter of a prince. She is rescued from the secretary by a mysterious visiting Indian.

As the Holmes stories continued, there were rather fewer distant and imperial international alarms. The European threats that had appeared early in 'The Greek Interpreter' and 'The Adventure of the Six Napoleons' tend to accelerate with growing tensions and the approach of war, and the two remaining novellas re-assert the early transatlanticism: in *The Hound of the Baskervilles* (1901) Sir Henry has the good influence of North America, while his murderous relative Stapleton has been in South America, and *The Valley of Fear* (1914) is like *A Study in Scarlet* in its detailed use of American conflict as the basis of the story.

Locking the Generic Room

By the end of the nineteenth century the single-volume crime story had become very common and would generate two new strongly international modes. Following Anna Katharine Green is a series of novels by women writers which are essentially classic murder mysteries with clues, a surprise outcome, a detective and some element of romance, though usually not for the primary narrating character. Mary Roberts Rinehart is the best known of these authors, but one worth remembering is Carolyn Wells, who not only wrote many mysteries but also produced *The Technique of the Mystery Story* (1913), setting out the classic shape of what is usually called the Golden Age mystery pattern. She refers to five other American women writers of the period as well as two British and one Austrian (1913: 225).[7]

But though American masculinist commentators feel the classic mode is essentially English, there were American men as well as women who would produce some of the finest classic mysteries, 'S.S. Van Dine' from 1926, 'Ellery Queen' from 1929 and the non-pseudonymous Rex Stout beginning in 1934. Another male writer in the classic mode was the Londoner Israel Zangwill, who, though now remembered with honour as a major scholar of Jewish tradition and a shaper of modern Zionism, also wrote the relatively short *The Big Bow Mystery* (1892): Bleiler calls it 'one of the landmark novels in the history of the detective novel' (1978: xiii). It transpires that the detective himself did the murder after he broke into the locked room – but Gaston Leroux made the explanation even more complicated in what became the best-known locked-room mystery, *Le Mystère de la chambre jaune* (1907).

Agatha Christie no doubt read Leroux and also Wells's book; this latter work appears never to have been published in Britain, but Christie seems to have carefully followed Wells's recommendations when writing her first mystery novel in 1916. Christie would become the most widely purchased and translated of all crime writers around the world, in part because her simple writing style made her ideal reading for learners of English. Christie also created in her Belgian detective, who is the antithesis of Sherlock Holmes, an emblem of internationality that flourishes still in film and television form. But she also did something else – she consistently wrote books in the espionage genre, the second of the two new turn-of-the-century modes of crime fiction, after the woman-focused mystery. The essentially international espionage form of crime fiction had been a possible domain for Sherlock Holmes's activity,

7 The four Americans in addition to Rinehart are Mary E. Wilkins (Freeman), Natalie Lincoln, Stella M. Düring and A.M. Barbour; the English are Baroness Orczy and Florence Warden; the Austrian is Augusta Gröner.

but developed into a firm generic novel-based form with specialist authors like William Le Queux and E. Phillips Oppenheim. It realized its first classic example in Erskine Childers's *The Riddle of the Sands* (1903) and then became increasingly published and was felt to be urgently contemporary as world politics deteriorated through the twentieth century, especially during the Cold War.

In these ways, as in so many others, Doyle and Christie epitomized the crime fiction of the century of their birth, being in success, reputation, materials and overall attitudes truly worldwide: both of them summarized and sublimated the international characteristics of the genre that they brought to its full and continuing form.

Works Cited

Ascari, Maurizio (2007). *A Counter-History of Crime Fiction: Supernatural, Gothic, Sensational* (London: Palgrave Macmillan).

Barsham, Diana (2003). *Arthur Conan Doyle and the Meaning of Masculinity* (Aldershot: Ashgate).

Bleiler, E.F. (ed.) (1978). *Three Victorian Detective Novels* (New York: Dover).

Cohen, Daniel A. (1993). *Pillars of Salt, Monuments of Grace: New England Crime Literature and the Origins of American Popular Culture, 1674–1860* (New York: Oxford University Press).

Doyle, Arthur Conan (1999) [1887]. *A Study in Scarlett*, in *The Penguin Complete Sherlock Holmes* (London: Penguin), 13–86.

Dumas, Alexandre (2012). *L'assassinio di Rue Saint-Roch*. Ed. Ugo Cundari (Milano: Baldini and Castoldi).

Halttunen, Karen (1998). *Murder Most Foul: The Killer and the American Gothic Imagination* (Cambridge, MA: Harvard University Press).

Knight, Stephen (2012). *The Mysteries of the Cities: Urban Crime Fiction in the Nineteenth Century* (Jefferson, NC: McFarland).

— (2017). *Towards Sherlock Holmes: A Thematic History of Crime Fiction in the Nineteenth-Century World* (Jefferson, NC: McFarland).

Lansbury, Coral (1970). *Arcady in Australia: The Evocation of Australia in Nineteenth-Century English Literature* (Melbourne: Melbourne University Press).

Leffler, Yvonne (2015). 'Early Crime Fiction in Nordic Literature', in Maurizio Ascari and Stephen Knight (eds), *From the Sublime to City Crime* (Monaco: LiberFaber), 161–81.

Mannironi, Giacomo (2015). 'Criminal Ambitions: The Young Balzac and the Influence of British Romanticism', in Maurizio Ascari and Stephen Knight (eds), *From the Sublime to City Crime* (Monaco: LiberFaber), 145–60.

Messac, Régis (1929). *Le 'Detective Novel' et l'influence de la pensée scientifique* (Paris: Champion).

Sayers, Dorothy L. (1972). 'Introduction to *The Omnibus of Crime*', in Howard Haycraft (ed.), *The Art of the Mystery Story: A Collection of Critical Essays* (New York: Carroll and Graf), 71–109.

Sue, Eugène (1843). *Les Mystères de Paris*, 4 vols (Paris: Gosselin).

Sussex, Lucy (2015). *Blockbuster: Fergus Hume and 'The Mystery of a Hansom Cab'* (Melbourne: Text).

Tannert, Mary (2016). 'The Emergence of Crime Fiction in German: an Early Maturity', in Katharina Hall (ed.), *Crime Fiction in German: Der Krimi* (Cardiff: University of Wales Press), 33–50.

Trodd, Anthea (1989). *Domestic Crime in the Victorian Novel* (London: Macmillan).

Wells, Carolyn (1913). *The Technique of the Mystery Story* (Springfield, IL: The Home Correspondence School).

Wolff, Robert Lee (1979). *Sensational Victorian: The Life and Fiction of Mary Elizabeth Braddon* (New York: Garland).

CHAPTER TEN

Brain Attics and Mind Weapons

Investigative Spaces, Mobility and Transcultural Adaptations of Detective Fiction

Michael B. Harris-Peyton, The University of Delaware

The adventures of Sherlock Holmes and John Watson begin at the end of Watson's personal mobility. He has 'gravitated to London, that great cesspool into which all the loungers and idlers of the Empire are irresistibly drained', with his health, and his career as a colonial medic, 'irretrievably ruined' (Doyle 2006: 14). Watson, curious about his new flatmate's profession, makes a list of his new friend's unique specializations and areas of ignorance – Holmes possesses a precise knowledge of London and the surrounding suburbs and an encyclopaedic catalogue of crime and chemistry, but knows little else (34). Holmes's unconventional occupation is revealed not in some dramatic conversation about a crime, but through his particular beliefs about the brain's ability to store a finite amount of information, like an 'attic' belonging to a 'workman' (32). Sherlock Holmes, with his carefully stocked 'brain attic', is a domestic detective and so his skills are described in domestic terms. The 'attic' is immobile; his skills are limited and specialized; and his knowledge of London's geography is not transferrable to another locale. He is so narrowly specialized that we (and even Watson) might say he is provincial.

The irony in calling Sherlock Holmes provincial is that his province, his region or specialty, is London as the Victorian imperial centre. Holmes is an ideal late-Victorian scientist taken to a distinctly un-Victorian extreme of specificity. And yet, this strange, provincial character is central both in imperial space, as London's superdetective, and in the international genre of detective fiction writ large, as a prototype of 'the great consulting detective'. Holmes's empire over the genre is wide but the character's abilities as a detective are decidedly narrow.

There is a parallel relationship between how a great detective's skills are described and how the space they inhabit relates to imperial-cultural centres. A Holmes-like detective whose investigative space includes a different type of space or place might choose a different metaphor than 'brain attic' to describe their investigative toolkit, as their relationship to their space is different. Adapting a genre's conventions or tropes to local conditions and conventions is a well-studied phenomenon. What is not often discussed, and what is revealed by these subtle changes to Holmes-like detectives, is the politics inherent in this practice.

Critical commentary on transnational genre dissemination and genre adaptation is invested with hierarchy – the original or earlier manifestation is typically somehow superior to its mobilized and transplanted descendants, its 'local variants' subordinated to an ostensibly (though usually not actually) nonlocal, central paradigm. Like Holmes himself, the paradigm of the genre is both central and provincial, its local specialization disguised by the fallacious notion that those qualities are universal and formulaic. However, paying attention to how the metaphors for detective skill and the character's spatial mobility are reconfigured exposes a process where the local, oft-subordinated, 'regional' text demands and obtains the authority to make changes on equal terms to textual predecessors; it reveals, in other words, an assertion of ownership over a global genre. It also throws into contrast the efforts at localization made in the predecessor, questioning the claimed nonlocality or universality of the predecessor's features. This fundamentally challenges the popular notion of crime fiction as a British or American cultural product and draws attention to crime fiction's history as a genre that was always already transculturally adapted.

As the genre travels and becomes more mobile, the metaphors for the detective character's intellectual tools also become more portable, more mobile and more achievable by the readership. In the three examples that follow, I examine how each text is positioned critically, identify the language the text employs to describe the detective's skills, and explore how that descriptive language is informed by the detective's locales – their spaces and places of work. The descriptive objective is straightforward: the metaphor used to describe investigative skills is radically altered by the nature of the investigative space. The comparative objective is less straightforward but more revealing: there are gaps between the way the text is described in relation to other members of its genre, and the way the text itself describes its relationship to those members. Attention to those gaps reveals the text's arguments for its own authority in that genre, and thus, the genre's continuous movement and development – a notion that opposes the idea that crime fiction is a Western cultural formula exported as a complete, finished product. Here, I work chronologically backwards, emphasizing an act of relating back to and adapting the predecessor that occurs even in Doyle's own *A Study in Scarlet* (1887).

The first reading is thus the most contemporary example: Satyajit Ray's Feluda mysteries, Holmes-style cases set in postcolonial India. My objective is to illustrate how careful examination of these 'localizations' produces conclusions that fit uneasily with the texts' critical presentation as a 'local Holmes'. The second reading, of Cheng Xiaoqing's Huo Sang mysteries, written forty years prior, highlights how the text makes changes to the genre on equal, rather than subordinate terms. The final reading, of Doyle's first Holmes mystery, *A Study in Scarlet*, argues that Holmes is explicitly adapting an already international formula to local conditions, rather than being some pure British or universal product from which all other Holmes-like detective fiction texts must descend.[1]

A Mind Weapon in India

The relatively barebones Wikipedia entry for Satyajit Ray's detective character Feluda relies heavily on direct comparison to Sherlock Holmes. The authors of the entry assert that

> Ray had deep interests in crime fiction and he read all of Sherlock Holmes fictions in his school days. And when Ray himself started writing crime fiction, unsurprisingly, the character Sherlock Holmes inspired his writings. Feluda's character resembles Sherlock Holmes and Tapesh/Topshe's character resembles Dr. Watson. ('Feluda' Wikipedia)

Notably, the source that the article cites for this point is the introduction to a 2011 comic book spinoff of Ray's series – neither the art nor the story of *The Criminals of Kailash* are by Ray; it is instead written by Subhadra Sen Gupta and illustrated by Tapas Guha. By no means, however, are these comic book authors, or the authors of the Wikipedia entry, alone

---

1 For more on this point, see Harris-Peyton (2017).

in this easy comparison. The canonical short story 'Feluda in London' (1989) includes an attempt to locate 221B Baker Street in order to pay respects to the 'guru' of all private consulting detectives (Ray 2000: 554).[2] However, 'Feluda in London', like Ray's other Feluda stories, never suggests that Holmes and Feluda are analogous. In the Wikipedia article's most humorously incorrect supposition, the authors assert that '[l]ike Sherlock Holmes, he has a voracious reading habit [...] which add[s] up to his enormous general knowledge' (Wikipedia), even though, as expressed in Doyle's *A Study in Scarlet*, Holmes is a voracious but *narrow* reader and his enormous body of knowledge is carefully curated, rather than general. It is perhaps most accurate to say that Feluda, along with his sidekick and narrator, Topshe, are translations or translocations of the concept of Holmes, 'reincarnations', as Suchitra Mathur asserts (2006). The characters function analogously and are connected, but they are not identical, nor even are they particularly similar.

The collapse of the distinction between the two detectives is likely a symptom of Stephen Knight's idea that criticism or commentary on detective fiction assumes that the genre is intensely formulaic, and thus fails to 'pay attention to the voices of the texts themselves' (2015: 3–4), combined with an observation that I have made elsewhere that detective fiction produced in postcolonial, non-British spaces is consistently assumed to be derivative and subordinate to British cultural products (Harris-Peyton 2017: 216). It is assumed that Ray's mysteries call upon an older text, the product of a colonial overlord, for cultural cachet. Feluda's 'magajastra', or 'mind weapon', can easily be seen as a form of the Holmesian 'brain attic'. But even cursory attention to the distinction between the terms – why translate the concept as 'mind weapon' in Bengali, instead of keeping the Holmesian 'brain attic'? – reveals that *something* has changed from the Holmes paradigm and that the text is advertising that change, even if its forewords, prefaces and Wikipedia entries are not.

Feluda's reading habits and the metaphor he chooses to refer to his own methods of investigation are directly connected to his mobility in India and India's changing relationship to the old imperial centre. With the city of Kolkata as the characters' home base (and the centre of Bengali ethnic geography in India), the rest of India is arranged peripherally around it, at most a few days away by train or car. Comparing this directly to Holmes's London and its suburbs, while tempting, is

---

2 The term is transliterated, but not translated, from the Bengali 'guru', or 'teacher'.

facile – India does not exist, even in the stories, at the same scale or degree of familiarity as London. Feluda is routinely unfamiliar with the geography, language and social terrain of the investigative destination and must rely on a broad general knowledge of India's languages and cultures, and particularly a voracious reading of tourist guidebooks, since many of the mysteries occur while the characters are travelling. Feluda cannot be a specialist in local soils or street layouts – his skills must be portable and transferable, literally translatable, and thus less specialized.

A 'mind weapon' is metaphorically more mobile than a 'brain attic' – a weapon is quite literally more portable. Likewise, rather than resembling those of a specialist consultant, the wide range of Feluda's interests and research figure him as a sort of Indian Renaissance Man, intellectually flexible and broadly educated. The first Feluda mystery offers a typical model of how the detective's relationship with investigative spaces necessitates a different sort of skill set. 'Danger in Darjeeling' (1965/66) begins, as the title suggests, with Feluda and his narrator-cousin Topshe on vacation in Darjeeling. Rajen Babu, a Bengali lawyer-turned-antique-collector retired to Darjeeling, has received a threatening note. Rajen Babu's house functions as a guesthouse, and so the mystery's settings include Rajen Babu's house, the guesthouse Feluda and Topshe are staying in, and several public parks and shops in Darjeeling. Portability is key to his methodology: Feluda must operate entirely in permeable, public and unfamiliar spaces and much of the action takes place while he is walking from one of these spaces to another.

The permeability of semi-public places (like guesthouse bedrooms) forms the crux of the 'danger' in 'Danger in Darjeeling' as well: Rajen Babu is visited, one night, by a masked figure and nearly scared to death. Of the three suspects for this crime, all are hypermobile and operating in public or semi-public spaces: a local doctor who is constantly on the move; an antique dealer (strongly implied to be an antique smuggler working for a European artefact syndicate), who by his own admission does not 'stay in one place very long' (Ray 2000: 8); and Rajen Babu's estranged son, who, having 'fallen into bad company' (15), has fled to London and become involved in the curio business with the same antique dealer/smuggler. The son never exists in any coherent domestic space – he was literally ejected from his father's home during their falling out, and now sports a suit from London, a tie from Paris and shoes from Italy, and is staying in a local Darjeeling hotel meant for foreigners (13–14). When Feluda encounters him, it is a chance meeting in Darjeeling's famous

Chowrasta Mall – a crowded intersection of public streets – outside a curio shop, rather than a planned encounter.

The story so rarely returns to any specific location and involves such frequent public movement and travel that Feluda's ability to explain his deductive conclusions to Topshe is impaired: he routinely aborts telling Topshe what he thinks because they might be overheard (11, 19). Notably, the story uses the presence of highly mobile doctors and European-based curio salesmen as a red herring: a fourth suspect is revealed at the end of the narrative. Rajen Babu's current houseguest, Tinkori Babu, is the man who has sent the note and broken in with the mask. His crime is unplanned and has nothing to do with international antiquities smuggling or the estranged son – the threatening note and night-time masked intrusion are meant to disturb Rajen Babu's peaceful retirement in revenge for long-forgotten childhood cruelties. These cruelties were not avenged in childhood, Tinkori Babu later explains, because Tinkori Babu's father had been obligated by work to move the family to a different town; thus, the schoolyard showdown was prevented by a change of domestic situation, another instance of intrusive mobility (22–23). Furthermore, Tinkori Babu escapes any punishment for his revenge by virtue of travel arrangements. Using the difficulty of train travel as an excuse, the suspect slips away, later confessing via letter. Feluda is prevented from ever physically locating Tinkori Babu again, tellingly, because he fails to provide anyone with a real home address.

As is typical of Ray's Feluda mysteries, the mystery occurs almost entirely in public or touristic spaces and hinges on the ease or difficulty of movement in those spaces to create the mystery itself. As a detective, Feluda is more tourist or travelling investigator than solver of specialist, domestic mysteries, and so a 'mind weapon' forms a much more apt metaphor for his skill set than a 'brain attic' might. The skill sets, and the metaphors, diverge primarily in approaches to specialization and location. In 'Feluda in London', the city of London and the city of Kolkata are linked by a mystery involving Anglo-Indian and Indian expatriate families. The detective and his travelling companions, functioning in their typical touristic mode, solve a crime in London just as easily, and just as nonchalantly, as they do in Kolkata – London requires no special localized 'brain attic', as Feluda's mind weapon is more than adequate to the task.

Tellingly, while in London, Feluda and company cannot resist the touristic impulse and go in search of 221B Baker Street. The search for Holmes's fictional address and the nature of the mystery occasioning their visit reveal that the city's importance is based on a shared heritage of fiction and economics, rather than a hierarchy of centre and periphery (London is important enough to necessitate the search for a real 221B Baker Street, but never offers a suitable consolation prize to Feluda or Topshe). The function of London as the inspiration for a fictional version of itself, home to the fictitious 'guru' of Feluda's profession, leaves the 'real' city feeling culturally and narratively bland, reinforcing the notion that the city is not immune to Feluda's generalized detective and tourist experiences. The story de-centres London while also making an assertion about the text and detective's relationship to the genre's paragon: they are connected, and indebted, but definitely not reflections or subordinates.

Pedagogical Aims in Shanghai

Cheng Xiaoqing's Holmes-like mysteries featuring the investigator Huo Sang and narrator-sidekick Bao Lang are particularly interesting because of Cheng's relationship with the Sherlock Holmes stories. Cheng Xiaoqing was among the first translators of Doyle's Sherlock Holmes mysteries into Chinese, and he had a specific and explicitly pedagogical aim in translating Holmes and inventing Huo Sang. The parallels are so openly available that the English translation of the Huo Sang stories by Timothy C. Wong is entitled *Sherlock in Shanghai*. The back cover of the paperback edition of that translation devotes its lead paragraph to emphasizing the relationship between Huo Sang and Holmes and noting that the inclusion of Bao Lang as a 'Watson-like I-narrator' is a 'rare instance of so direct an appropriation from foreign fiction' in Chinese literature (2007: back cover). Cheng's aim in inventing Huo Sang as a Chinese Holmes, 'to introduce' an implicitly Western version of 'critical thinking to his readers', is bound up with his decision to merge the structural characteristics of Holmesian mystery with more 'traditional' Chinese 'sensationalism'. The back cover's three small paragraphs engage in a complex balancing act, emphasizing how Holmes-like these stories are while demonstrating how they have been modified to fit Chinese tastes, employing 'recognizably native elements even as he espouses more globalized views of truth and justice'. An inherent hierarchy is clear: Holmes is the original; Huo Sang is the subordinated local variant. And yet, that hierarchy is instantly subverted by the focus on cultural adaptations, the reliance on a long Chinese literary tradition, and the implication of the author's right to translate and bend a transnational genre to local audiences and his own pedagogical aims.

Wong's introduction to the collection notes that Cheng's earlier translations of Arthur Conan Doyle's Holmes mysteries, and Cheng's later 'adaptation' of the model to China with the Huo Sang mysteries, were part of an early-twentieth-century Chinese cultural modernization project meant to introduce Chinese readers to more scientific ways of solving problems. This occurred, Wong notes, through the translation of Western fiction. Cheng's move from translation to 'a certain [kind of] adaptation' or 'another kind of translation' in writing the Huo Sang mysteries (Wong 2007: viii), is never quite termed 'authorship' in Wong's introduction; instead, the terms 'producing', 'publish[ing]' and engaging in 'China's native condition of *fiction making*' are used (vii, vi, author's emphasis), alongside other various translation- and adaptation-inflected terms. Even so, Cheng's translations of Holmes are so well adapted to local conditions that they have been considered 'essentially undistinguishable from contemporary native creations' and his subsequent Huo Sang mysteries are 'contemporary native creations' (Wong 2007: viii).

Even as Wong's introduction copes with complicated notions of modern and traditional forms – and the relationship between authorship, translation and adaptation – the texts of the stories themselves make it very clear that Huo Sang is no clone of Sherlock Holmes. The Western critical fallacy of assuming that a formulaic genre is inherently conservative or derivative and that Western generic models are *the* default, nonlocal versions of those models joins with Cheng's complex role as both translator and author within a specific genre to make the Huo Sang mysteries easy targets for accusations of knock-offery. Indeed, the mysteries' surface conditions make the texts a hard case – Huo Sang is a rational but sometimes idiosyncratic detective, Bao Lang his tireless companion, roommate and first-person narrator, and the two characters have a contentious relationship with the local metropolitan police for whom they consult. The influence of Holmes is apparent.

And yet, the language used to describe Huo Sang's investigative skills and his relationship with Shanghai as a space reveal that these stories are not a direct transposition of some universal model; instead, they are as indistinguishable from their locality as the Holmes stories are from theirs. The Huo Sang mysteries join their generic forebear in being strongly domestic and precisely local, but the demands of Huo Sang's Shanghai domestic spaces require a different set of investigative skills and metaphors. The first Huo Sang mystery, 'The Shoe' (1923), is a conventional murder mystery: a woman has been killed in her apartment at night, and the normally locked Shanghai house is found unlocked by the chauffeur-doorman in the morning. The only outside object in the crime scene (a locked bedroom), which the Shanghai police claim to be the only clue, is an ostentatious men's shoe. Thus, the Shanghai police believe that locating the owner of the shoe will reveal the murderer, and Huo Sang is called in to assist (Cheng 2007: 3–8).

By all accounts, the setup of the mystery and its apparent inscrutability hinge on the closed nature of domestic spaces: the only potential witnesses are the household staff. Narratively, too, the entire text of the story occurs within a chain of well-contained domestic spaces – the scene of the crime and the apartment shared by Huo Sang and narrator Bao Lang. In fact, all the parts of 'The Shoe' that might occur outside these two spaces are described after-the-fact by characters rather than dramatized, creating the impression that Bao Lang simply inhabits one domestic space or the other with no transition in between. Huo Sang, too, is not visibly mobile: his activities outside the crime scene or his shared home are described only in terms of what information was obtained and are precisely documented in terms of realistic Shanghai addresses but never otherwise described. Huo disappears from his narrator's view for hours and returns with new information; but unlike in the Holmes stories, the relationship between Huo and Bao is more congenial and less hierarchical: they share inside jokes and sarcastic remarks when investigating (6), and Bao is routinely trusted with note-taking, interviews and research. Both characters are essential to Huo's practice – an especially remarkable change to the formula when compared to Watson's perpetual incredulity and cluelessness when it comes to Holmes.

This change in the detective's methodology and relationship with his narrator is necessitated by the story's explicitly pedagogical aim, and this aim requires changes to how the narrative handles space, which has a further effect on the detective's described methodology. Extensive descriptions of real places within Shanghai are unnecessary; the target audience for Cheng's mysteries is the Shanghai literate elite. In 'The Shoe', only the domestic interior of the crime scene is described (2–8). Unlike the Feluda stories, the Huo Sang mysteries give addresses and real nearby landmarks, but not much description – just enough to orient a Shanghai resident without adding local trivia. The Huo Sang mysteries are structurally dedicated to presenting the crimes as rational puzzles set in defined, confined spaces, and to illustrating how rational thinking can solve them. The parts of the text are likewise labelled with their illustrative purpose – 'The Scene of the Crime', 'A Premature Conclusion' and 'The Point of Dispute', for example – to facilitate presenting the mystery as a reader-solvable puzzle. The larger locality informs, but does not interfere with, the core logical puzzle. This does, however, change the personality and metaphorical dressing of the detective character. Huo Sang cannot be a superdetective and cannot possess a specialist knowledge of sensational crime because his readers must learn his practical methods. Huo Sang's investigative acumen is remarkable but ostensibly achievable. Thus, he can have no metaphorical 'brain attic' or 'mind weapon' at all and cannot afford to keep new information away from his narrator, Bao Lang, for dramatic effect. Covering the method in an explanatory metaphor defeats the pedagogical objective of the text.

In the case of 'The Shoe', the object lesson of the story is how outlandish details are often red herrings: the titular shoe, as the foreign object in the room, demands the attention of the Shanghai police at the expense of smaller, domestic objects and events that are out of place (ash from a burned letter, the lack of stolen items, the moving of the body from the floor to the bed, the absence of the murder weapon, and the bizarre move to lock the already sleeping maid in her room before committing murder). The shoe, as it turns out, entered the crime scene by being thrown on the balcony by an intoxicated passer-by – the intrusion of public space into the private, domestic apartment. Its presence is incidental to the actual murder. The burned letter revealing a financial crisis, the locked door, and the disparity in age and attractiveness between wife and (long-distance) husband lead Huo Sang to implicate the husband while police are still fixated on the sensational footwear. Huo Sang's logical method is thus able to solve the puzzle even with the happenstance contamination of the domestic puzzle space (42–43). The juridical consequences of the puzzle, as irrelevant but entertaining details, occur outside the scope of the logical exercise: the capture of the husband and the owner of the shoe and their punishments are described by a police detective in the closing lines of the story (43–44). Huo Sang and Bao Lang, like the reader, are meant to be more concerned with the story's pedagogical demonstration of the method than with its judicial or social consequences. Compared to Holmesian stories, where contextually superhuman deductive feats and the capture of the criminal are key narrative components, Huo Sang's cases are sensational (they frequently include a bizarre and lurid murder) but rarely emphasize judicial or even physical action, instead favouring the careful accumulation of material evidence.

These significant departures from the Holmesian formula are obscured by an overvaluation of Cheng's status as Holmes translator, which in turn overemphasizes the distinction between translation, adaptation and authorship. The local cultural circumstances, including both locale and the purposes and audiences for the texts, have a profound impact on these two detectives' interactions with space and with how their skill sets are presented to their audience. In a move shared by Ray's and Cheng's detectives – and, as we shall see in the next section, shared even with Sherlock Holmes – each successive detective in a Holmesian tradition acknowledges his predecessor (either explicitly or through reference) but attempts to be more 'realistic'. In Huo Sang's case, as is the case for Feluda and others, this increased realism is actually an adaptation to local generic conventions and cultural circumstances: Feluda is more mobile and less specialized than Holmes; Huo Sang is less superhuman and more approachable than Holmes; and Holmes argues that he is more empirical and efficient than his cited predecessors.

A Quaint Brain Attic in London

Sherlock Holmes's nigh-provincial, highly specific knowledge of London as a place and his intensely restricted body of interests become all the stranger if London is understood *not* as some monolithic centre of quintessential Britishness, but instead as the imperial microcosm. While Holmes's intense Londoner-ness and archetypal Britishness are a popular motif in commentary and criticism on the character, the actual texts of Doyle's Holmes mysteries imagine London less as a British location than as a 'cesspool' of the empire, as Watson so aptly puts it in the early lines of *A Study in Scarlet*. Holmes's mysteries deliberately undercut the apparent wholesomeness of London's suburbs and the English countryside, revealing an undercurrent of colonial economics, greed and scandal. His relationship to London's environs is essentially domestic and intimate, but that intimate domestic environment is uniquely vulnerable to, and dependent on, colonial commerce and contamination. The plot of *A Study in Scarlet,* for instance, hinges on the arrival in London of an American revenge drama. Other stories, like 'The Speckled Band' (1892) and *The Sign of the Four* (1890), rely specifically on middle-class Londoners making money in the colonies before returning home, marked in the process by some criminal, colonially dependent enterprise. London and its suburbs are more colonial than central; or, we might say, the centre is a colonial patchwork, the home of 'loungers and idlers' not just from Britain, but from the whole empire. Likewise, its detective and his sidekick are complicated collages of Englishness and colonial foreignness.

This complex model of locality highlights a critical fallacy common to discussions of genre fiction generally, and to the Holmes model of crime fiction intensely: the notion that the prevailing Western model is the normative or 'default' model, a universal, nonlocal paradigm to which all other instances must relate as specifically local sub-varieties. Holmes's specific knowledge and his ability to move through London in perfect disguise challenge that assumption: London is not like anywhere else, but is connected to everywhere else as a coherent, knowable place. It is not, in other words, transportable, universal or generic, but specific. That London does not transfer with the generic model: the knowledge and skills that work in London do not work in Shanghai or Kolkata. Holmes is as adapted to London's conditions as each new Holmes-like detective is to his own space. This adaptation makes the politics of the process clear: Holmes may be a model for these later works, but their authors do not feel particularly beholden to reinterpret their city as London or to describe their detective's skills as a 'brain attic'.

The 'brain attic', in this context, is deeply connected to the requirements of the text's London: it may be a carefully curated domestic space, rather like Huo Sang's Shanghai, but the tasks for which it is configured are decidedly both domestic and colonial, as the domestic space is irretrievably bound up with the larger empire. The structure of the first Holmes narrative, *A Study in Scarlet*, demonstrates this point particularly well: only the first part of the text is centred on Holmes and set in London; the second half is an imported narrative, told primarily from the perspective of the criminal and set in the western United States. Holmes and Watson dominate the domestic narrative but they depend on the perspective and honesty of another, much more mobile character to complete both the mystery and the text. London is the nexus of the narrative, to be sure – it contains the solvable crime – but the narrative requires additional geographic mobility. The guilty party, once captured in London, willingly explains his role in a long-term, transnational revenge quest over the course of the first six chapters of the text's second part, before the 'Reminiscences' of Watson (as the primary narrative thread is termed) pick back up, detailing the British juridical aftermath. Ultimately, Holmes and Watson need not leave London or its periphery to solve this crime; rather, they are dependent on imports for the reader-satisfying context.

In fact, Holmes's whole described method of operating is predicated on extrapolating larger unseen or unexperienced context from local proxies or domestically available analogues. After Watson's first inquiry, where Holmes coins the metaphor of the 'brain attic' and describes his deliberate attempts to eliminate extraneous knowledge from it, Watson peruses Holmes's reading material and comes across an article entitled 'The Book of Life'. Watson summarizes as follows:

> 'From a drop of water,' said the writer, 'a logician could infer the possibility of an Atlantic or a Niagara without having seen or heard of one or the other. So all life is a great chain, the nature of which is known whenever we are shown a single link of it' (2006: 40)

Watson calls this theory 'ineffable twaddle' before Holmes reveals that he wrote the article and depends on such methods for his 'bread and cheese' (41). The choice of example in Holmes's article is rather telling – the inference of geographic phenomena outside of his home space using a minuscule, domestically available clue. The science of deduction can only ever be applied to cases set in environments where Holmes's knowledge of local conditions is guaranteed.

Immediately thereafter, Watson draws on prior fictional detectives as examples for understanding his new acquaintance, and all his examples are decidedly not British: he cites Poe's Dupin and Gaboriau's Lecoq as potential models for his friend's methods (42, 43). This constitutes one of the most interesting, and critically overlooked, moments in the Holmesian canon: Doyle's acknowledgement of transnational textual and generic lineage via an in-narrative critique and dismissal of those predecessors by Holmes. This citation-by-disavowal argues for equal membership in, and thereby the right to modify, a complex international genre. The citation reveals that Doyle (and Holmes and Watson in the narrative) have read the requisite books and know the rules well enough to innovate upon them locally. Having made the appropriate references to earn membership in this genealogy of great detectives, the new member is free to adapt, improvise, deviate and critique as local conditions demand. And so, Holmes's particular skills are described in terms of Lecoq's and Dupin's shortcomings (43).

Holmes's (and Doyle's) conceit here is a familiar one: he asserts authority over and membership of an intellectual field by virtue of prolific citation and critique. Like an academic – and like many participants in the crime fiction genre – Holmes asserts his authority as a detective, and Doyle his authority as an author in the genre, by illustrating an ability to reference, correct, adapt and innovate in a specialist role, rather than an ability to provide universal modes or to subordinate himself to existing paradigms. Universal tropes can be inferred, but only local realities can be confirmed. And so, the grandiose truths of 'The Book of Life' must be made to fit the practical needs of a specialist's 'brain attic', as the vagaries of international crime fiction must be fitted to London.

Conclusion

As we have seen throughout the three examples, each detective – Feluda, Huo Sang and Holmes – uses empirical and rational methods for solving crime, but how these are presented and explained to readers changes radically according to location and the chosen spaces of investigation. Even in the very first Holmes text, this adaptive process is already, unabashedly present. In two of the three cases presented here, changes to the generic pattern necessitated by transcultural or geographic movement of the detective fiction genre are de-emphasized in commentary on the text to illustrate a continuity and conformity with Sherlock Holmes. Commentary on the Holmes stories themselves, incidentally, does the opposite: changes are emphasized, and the texts they are changing *from* are forced into a subordinate position, thereby creating the impression that Holmes is central or unique while all others in the genre are dependent, derivative or not fully developed. These moves compete with the texts' own self-positioning: continuity is discussed and may even offer comparison or criticism, but is not necessarily always hierarchical. The actual relationship between text and predecessor evinced in these texts is far more complex. The politics, the arrangement of generic authority and power, is therefore also complex. The nature of the key change traced in this analysis is particularly useful because it is tied directly to space, movement and place – to geography, history and cultural context – and so the reasons for the changes are theoretically traceable. The contrast between textual and paratextual presentations of genre politics, when viewed jointly with subtle changes to the detective character's abilities and description, highlights the complex method of asserting power in a genre: claiming the fluency to identify tropes and 'rules', and asserting the role of author necessary to implement fundamental changes while still claiming textual continuity. There is a substantial difference in power between repeating something and adding to it where authorship is concerned, and this difference must be managed carefully.

The great danger of a critical overemphasis on the distinction between authorship and adaptation – between generic originator and generic participant – is that it draws attention away from the historical movement of genres across cultures. By over-distinguishing 'universal' canonical texts and local variants, we create the notion that genres are national or cultural properties, made in one place and exported to others as a finished product. Attention to paratextual commentary, like back covers and scholarly introductions, suggests that this immobile notion has academic and cultural cachet, even as it is subverted by the text it seeks to describe. Attention to 'localizations' in the texts themselves, however, asserts something quite different: that there is no completed form or instance of the genre, no central canon or paragon, and that all participants must adapt and iterate the genre. If this is true even of the allegedly formulaic Holmes-style detective story – as popular, numerous, and superficially similar as members of that genre can be – the same may be true of crime fiction writ large, and of other genres.

Attention to the mobility of the genre, and to the mobility of its central character, highlights the unstable and artificial immobility of notions like national literatures or static genres. These notions are particularly unsuited to detective fiction, whose actual history of continuous development, global popularity, perpetual localization and cultural mobility mark it as a world genre. My analysis here suggests that it is impossible to approach the genre of crime fiction accurately as anything *but* a world literature, since to do so would be to erase the genre's developmental history and the particularities of its central characters.

Works Cited

Cheng Xiaoqing (2007). *Sherlock in Shanghai: Stories of Crime and Detection*. Trans. Timothy C. Wong (Honolulu: University of Hawai'i Press).

Doyle, Arthur Conan (2006). *The New Annotated Sherlock Holmes: The Novels* (New York: W.W. Norton).

'Feluda'. *Wikipedia: The Free Encyclopedia*. Wikimedia Foundation, Inc. 24 September 2017 [accessed 27 September 2017].

Harris-Peyton, Michael B. (2017). 'Holmes Away from Home: The Great Detective in the Transnational Literary Network', in Louise Nilsson, David Damrosch and Theo D'haen (eds), *Crime Fiction as World Literature* (New York: Bloomsbury), 215–32.

Knight, Stephen (2015). *Secrets of Crime Fiction Classics: Detecting the Delights of 21 Enduring Stories* (Jefferson, NC: McFarland).

Ray, Satyajit (2000). *The Complete Adventures of Feluda*. Trans. Gopa Majumdar (New Delhi: Penguin Books India).

Mathur, Suchitra (2006). 'Holmes's Indian Reincarnation: A Study in Postcolonial Transposition', in Christine Matzke and Susanne Mühelen (eds), *Postcolonial Postmortems: Crime Fiction from a Transcultural Perspective* (New York: Rodopi), 87–108.

Sen Gupta, Subhadra and Tapas Guha (2011). *Satyajit Ray's Feluda Mysteries: The Criminals of Kailash* (New Delhi: Puffin Books India).

Wong, Timothy C. (2007). 'Preface', in Cheng Xiaoqing, *Sherlock in Shanghai: Stories of Crime and Detection*. Trans. Timothy C. Wong (Honolulu: University of Hawai'i Press), vii–xi.

CHAPTER ELEVEN

The Reader and World Crime Fiction

The (Private) Eye of the Beholder

Stewart King, Monash University

In *Through Other Continents: American Literature across Deep Time* Wai Chee Dimock asks us to imagine a literary history 'divided, not into discrete periods, and not into discrete bodies of national literature'. What would such a field look like, she asks, and '[w]hat other organizing principles might come into play' (2006: 73)? This chapter engages in the sort of literary imagining that Dimock proposes. Taking genre as a case study, this chapter treats crime fiction as a transnational phenomenon and examines how we might conceive of relationships between crime writers, readers and texts that eschew the common categorization of a universal British-American tradition, on the one hand, and, on the other, localized national traditions. The aim of imagining different forms of textual kinship that I propose in this chapter is not to fix new taxonomies, to demobilize a genre that is inherently mobile; it seeks instead to produce innovative reading strategies that validate new organizational principles beyond the traditional foci of nation and history. With this in mind, the chapter develops a reading practice of world crime fiction that acknowledges local specificity and also allows for the emergence of new transnational and trans-historical readings. This practice is centred on the reader – here the private eye of the beholder from the chapter title – whose conscious engagement with a variety of texts from around the world can make possible the sort of global literary imagining promoted by Dimock.

The Study of Crime Fiction

With the exception of a few recent publications that are mentioned below, the study of crime fiction tends to be bound by the discrete periodization and national identification that Dimock urges us to overcome. *The Cambridge Companion to Crime Fiction* (2003) serves as a clear example of this, with chapters dedicated to the genre's chronological development (chapters 1–3, 9–10) and to different national traditions, which are limited to France, Britain and America (chapters 4, 9–10).[1] This collection, and others like it, points moreover to another important categorization in crime fiction studies. That is, the separation between a British-American tradition that acts as a universal norm and a subset of peripheral national traditions. While differences do exist between British and American crime fiction, in general they are treated as two sides of the same coin which, like the greenback, acts as an international currency against which all other crime fiction traditions are valued and compared. Lee Horsley's *Twentieth-Century Crime Fiction* (2005), for example, only examines British and American texts while *A Companion to Crime Fiction* (2010), edited by Horsley and Charles Rzepka, dedicates only two of its forty-seven chapters to non-anglophone crime fiction, one to a specific author, Argentinian Jorge Luis Borges, and the second – a scant twelve pages long – to the diversity of foreign-language crime fiction – and even then it is restricted to European crime fiction available in English translation. Although the editors recognize that the genre has 'a thousand faces' (Rzepka and Horsley 2010: 91), in their collection at least, it speaks almost exclusively in one tongue – English.

This division has consequences for how we read and interpret specific texts. Outside the British-American 'norm', crime fiction is in the main framed within the national context in which it was produced. Thus, we have studies of Australian, Catalan, Cuban, French, German, Italian, Japanese, Mexican, Swedish as well as transnational Nordic crime fictions. While these studies have expanded our knowledge of the diverse practice of mystery fiction globally, they rarely engage with the genre's international dimensions. Instead, they tend to delimit their subject to

---

1 Other chapters in the *Cambridge Companion* are categorized according to different organizing principles, including genre, identity and media, with chapters on Golden Age, private eye, spy and thriller fiction, as well as so-called literary detective fiction (chapters 5–8, 14), women detectives (chapter 11), black crime fiction (chapter 12), and film and TV crime narratives (chapter 13).

specific national or regional literary traditions by passing briefly over British-American and, occasionally, French influences before settling on the production of autochthonous crime narratives that treat themes and issues of particular relevance to the specific national literary polysystem which is the subject of the study. Such nationally focused studies treat their subject like a locked-room mystery: they are hermetically sealed from the outside world, and the clues and answers to the mystery are considered to reside within. Readers of crime fiction know, however, that under close scrutiny by the detective, the locked room is anything but.

National-bounded approaches tend to be the norm in literary studies. We do, after all, still live in a Herderian world. In the case of crime fiction, national specificity is particularly reinforced through the focus on the strong sense of place that connects crime novels to particular nations, regions and cities. Indeed, place has become a central feature of so many crime novels that it is considered one of the genre's defining characteristics. Eva Erdmann, for example, argues that place is so important that it trumps even the nationality of the author and the language in which the text is written. She posits that 'the distinguishing feature of Scottish or Greek crime fiction is not that it is written by a Scot or a Greek, but that it attempts to convey a Scottish or a Greek atmosphere' (2009: 22). This is because, in her reading, the genre 'has assumed the task of describing local cultures and, in addition to the constant restoration of justice, does the work of cultural representation' (2009: 25).

Crime fiction's connection to place is more than just atmospheric. It also manifests itself through a given community's legal and moral system which the criminal transgresses. As the narrator of Brazilian novelist, Alberto Mussa's *The Mystery of Rio* claims, 'It is not the geography, it is not the architecture, it is not the heroes, or battles, much less so the chronicles of customs, or the fantasies conjured up by poets. No, what defines a city is the history of its crimes' (2013: 9). Mussa's perhaps hyperbolic claim is not restricted to urban centres alone; crimes also define societies more broadly. To explore this through a concrete example, the murder of twin babies in the Ibo society represented in Chinua Achebe's *Things Fall Apart* (1959) is not treated as a crime because it forms part of the Ibo worldview in which twins are considered devils. In contrast, in Kishwar Desai's *Witness the Night* (2010) systemic female infanticide in Punjab is a crime against Indian law and it is duly investigated and exposed by her social worker-cum-detective Simran Singh. In the way fictional crime stories implicitly promise to provide knowledge about a particular place, to reveal what is hidden, they offer readers a means of exploring the connection between crime and community.

While this is true of all crime fiction, for texts written in foreign languages or peripheral English-language literatures these cultural aspects take on greater prominence when the text travels beyond the linguistic or cultural tradition in which it was produced. This results in the local becoming a fixed interpretative framework that is reminiscent of Fredric Jameson's prescriptive reading of so-called Third-World fiction as inherently political and (nationally) allegorical (1986).[2] Alberto Mussa's novel, cited above, is a good example of how the local is foregrounded when fiction is translated and travels afield: the novel's Portuguese title *O senhor do lado esquerdo* (The Master of the Left Side) is re-*placed* by *The Mystery of Rio*. The cover with its newly blazoned Rio-ness, and hence its Brazilianness, shapes anglophone readers' horizon of expectation before they have even cast an eye over its opening lines.

It is only recently that scholars have begun to recognize the limitations of framing crime fiction texts through self-contained national and local referents. Maurizio Ascari (2007: 8), Stephen Knight (2015: 4) and Andrew Pepper (2016: 7–8), for example, have acknowledged the genre's transnational and multilingual origins, while several edited collections – *Globalization and the State in Contemporary Crime Fiction* (Pepper and Schmid 2016) and *Crime Fiction as World Literature* (Nilsson et al. 2017) – as well as my own earlier interventions in the field (King 2014; King and Whitmore 2016), have sought to account for the genre's international engagement beyond the monolingual and largely monocultural British-American canon. These emerging world literature approaches to crime fiction seek to account for 'the presence of the world within the nation'; that is, the way in which seemingly nationally bounded novels engage with the world beyond the nation in which they originate and how readers experience the world – and world literature – from within 'the national context in which they live' (Damrosch 2014).

Recognizing crime fiction as a form of world literature has also required scholars to redefine exactly what constitutes world literature (King 2014: 11–12), a field that has traditionally ignored popular fiction forms in favour of so-called literary greats. This is despite the fact that

2 For a discussion of the multiple ways in which crime fiction can function as a national allegory, see the individual contributions to 'Translating National Allegories: The Case of Crime Fiction', a special issue of *The Translator*, edited by Rolls, Vuaille-Barcan and West-Sooby (2016).

much popular fiction – the majority of translated literature (D'haen 2012: 132) – is inherently mobile. Taking the example of crime fiction, if we consider world literature 'a mode of circulation and of reading' (Damrosch 2003: 5), then the genre is clearly a form of world literature. From its diverse origins in China, the Middle East, Germany, France and the United States, it has become a global phenomenon, crossing borders and languages as writers throughout the world have adopted and adapted the genre and as readers have embraced it.

The relative lack of attention by scholars of world literature to popular genres like crime fiction is perhaps unsurprising for a number of reasons. The first is the peripheral place occupied by popular fiction genres in the academy in general. Second, although popular fiction circulates with great ease beyond its originating culture, which is one of the more commonly accepted definitions of world literature (Damrosch 2003: 4), world literature is usually restricted to so-called literary fiction. Finally, until fairly recently genre as an organizational or classificatory category has largely been absent from the debates about world literature (Siskind 2011: 345).

Mariano Siskind argues that the neglect of genre can potentially limit our understanding of the interconnectedness of texts across cultures. In making a case for a transnational, trans-historical study of genres, Siskind is not interested in the traditional generic categories of novel, short story, poetry, theatre or even tragedy and epic; instead, he argues for *'the genres of world literature'* that introduce questions of novelty and specificity (2011: 347; emphasis in the original). Siskind maintains that 'world literature produces [...] new generic formations, constellations of texts whose identity is defined in accordance with new needs and new critical and aesthetic desires translated into new organizing principles' (2011: 347). He identifies three such principles, the first of which seeks to bridge 'the different historical and geopolitical ways in which texts are inscribed and classified locally and globally within mappings made up of uneven power relations'. The second draws attention to 'the *worldly* in world literary texts – in other words, discovering the *universalizable* potential of akin texts'. The final organizing principle attempts to 'account for the ways in which texts mutate as they travel across cultures and languages, and therefore elude the generic fixity of yesteryear' (2011: 347). Siskind lists six examples of many such new formations, including magical realism, cosmogonic epics, *Bildungsromanen*, travel narratives, ghost stories and *Ghazal* poetry (2011: 347–48). I suggest that crime narratives – in the broadest sense of texts that deal with transgressions

– constitute another major formation. Following Siskind, I am interested in the way in which new paradigms can open up innovative ways of reading and understanding crime fiction.

Reading World Crime Fiction

It is here that we come to the role of the crime fiction reader. Whereas much scholarship has traditionally sought to produce readings of texts within specific national contexts, I propose an alternative practice that pays attention to the local concerns that are central to national readings while also exploring the possible transnational connections that exist when we read crime fiction in a worldly way. To do so, I draw on Jorge Luis Borges's reflections on Poe's contribution to the development of detective fiction in 'El cuento policial' (The Detective Story), the fourth of five lectures he gave at the Universidad de Belgrano in Buenos Aires in 1978.[3] Borges's lecture, I contend, provides us with a way of developing a reading practice that moves from the local to the global, embracing both simultaneously.

In 'The Detective Story' Borges treads the well-worn path of crime fiction scholarship by attributing the genre's invention to Edgar Allan Poe. As soon as he does so, however, Borges begins to raise doubts about the very subject of his lecture. 'Before speaking of the genre', he says, 'there is a small prior question that should be discussed: Do literary genres exist?' (1999: 491). In typical Borgesian fashion, he responds in the affirmative, but follows this with a caveat: genres do exist, but not as they are generally conceived. While the study of genre is traditionally textually based, a means of classifying works considered to share certain recognizable characteristics that distinguish them from other textual groupings, Borges flips this by suggesting that 'literary genres may depend less on texts than on the way texts are read' (1999: 491). For Borges, the 'aesthetic event requires the conjunction of reader and text; only then does it exist' (1999: 491). Accordingly, 'The Murders in the Rue Morgue' is important not just because Poe invented a new way of writing, but because in inventing the detective story, 'he subsequently created the reader of detective fiction' (1999: 492).

Readers of detective fiction have traditionally been treated rather shabbily by literary scholars, who tend to dismiss them as unsophisticated

3 I wish to thank Prof. Emron Esplin (Brigham Young University) for providing me with details on the context of Borges's lecture.

consumers who seek both to evade reality and to satisfy cheap thrills. Edmund Wilson is perhaps the most extreme holder of this view. In his (in)famous *New Yorker* essay, 'Who Cares Who Killed Roger Ackroyd?', he berates readers of detective fiction for their 'lax mental habits', lack of 'imagination and literary taste', and he goes on to describe them as akin to alcoholics and opium addicts who waste their time and degrade their intelligence with such 'rubbish' (1945: 61, 65–66).

Borges, however, has in mind a different, more positive image of crime fiction readers. The readers that Poe has created approach stories in a particular way that aims to dispel the mystery or mysteries contained within. If crime fiction is 'the art of framing lies' (Sayers 1988: 31), as authors are deliberately loose with the truth in order to throw the reader off the track of the criminal until that point at which the detective reveals him or her to us, then readers are trained to develop what Dr Sheppard in Christie's *The Murder of Roger Ackroyd* describes as '[r]ather a suspicious attitude' (2002: 156). In response to the deliberate duplicity of the mystery writer, crime fiction readers learn to interrogate the way information is presented to them. Thus, the genre produces particular sorts of readers, whose cognitive capacity is challenged first to 'store information under advisement and, then, once the truth-value of this information is decided, to think back to the beginning of the story and to readjust [their] understanding of a whole series of occurrences' (Zunshine 2006: 132). As Dr Sheppard puts it, '[e]very new development that arises is like the shake you give to a kaleidoscope – the thing changes entirely in aspect' (Christie 2002: 236).

Borges's observations on Poe's contribution to literary history and interpretation prefigure an important shift from texts to readers that occurred in the study of crime fiction in the late 1990s and early 2000s. Like Borges before him, Andrew Pepper argues that 'meanings, and indeed genres, are not fixed within texts, as most criticism seems to assume, or secured through the interaction of text and critic, but are constantly being made and remade by readers' (2000: 14). Paul Cobley likewise maintains that '[t]exts may be shown to possess the internal textual organization that genre theorists have discerned [...] but repeatedly, reception theory has shown that textual meaning derives in large part from what the reader has imported him/herself' (2000: 55). These observations on the role of the reader in the construction of meaning have important consequences for reading crime fiction in either national or transnational frameworks. Whereas traditional approaches to crime fiction attribute nationality to works written in the national language by authors, the reader-centred approach that I am proposing here draws attention to the porosity of such borders and points to the coexistence of the nation and the world beyond and within it. In other words, where we read from is just as important as the origins of the text itself.

As a reader on the literary periphery, Borges is cognizant of the appeal of 'The Murders in the Rue Morgue' to a transnational readership beyond the American or English-language readers for whom Poe initially wrote. The reader that Poe created, according to Borges, numbers 'in the millions' and 'may be found in every country in the world' (1999: 492). The international popularity of Poe and other crime writers points to the disconnection that often exists between readers and the national tradition in which a crime novel was produced. While authors often consciously write within a specific national literary tradition and with a particular audience in mind, few readers read only those novels written by their compatriots and set in their home country, as evidenced by the international popularity of Nordic noir. There are, after all, fewer than ten million Swedes, but Henning Mankell has sold over 35 million copies of his Wallander series while the first volume of Stieg Larsson's Millennium trilogy, *Män som hatar kvinnor* (2005) (*The Girl with the Dragon Tattoo* [2008]), has sold over 30 million alone. This phenomenon is not limited to works from small literary polysystems. The estimated one billion sales of Agatha Christie's novels in translation is evidence that English-language crime fiction is also read outside the culture in which it is produced. What we have then is a global readership that often enjoys crime novels set in – from the reader's perspective – a range of foreign locales.

Of all the variants of the crime genre, Borges's preferred novels were of the intellectual, clue puzzle variety of the so-called Golden Age of crime writing. Since Chandler published 'The Simple Art of Murder' in 1944, these novels have often been accused of ignoring the great socio-economic and political issues of the time.[4] Much crime fiction since then, however, very much embraces the world, its contradictions, inequalities and asymmetrical power relations. In this regard, international crime fiction can be considered a particular form of travel literature, through which readers seek to experience what lies behind the tourist image of particular cities and countries via the detective's investigation. While Borges was dismissive of this type of fiction, this explicitly engaged, worldly, crime fiction allows us to take Borges's reflections on readers

---

4 The theory of the apolitical nature of the classic detective novel has been debunked by scholars such as Knight (2004), Horsley (2005), and Pepper (2016).

further. What we have now is a transnational community of 'detectory' readers, who, in their 'unlimited *serial* reading', that is, the return to a familiar structure – near identical scenes, tropes, characters, etc. (Rushing 2007: 3, 15; emphasis in the original) – have become trained to read detective fiction, to acknowledge and appreciate departures from the texts and cultural and historical contexts with which they are already familiar. Through these differences, readers are able to identify 'how symbolic power varies from place to place' (Moretti 2000: 66).

While it is impossible to make any general observations about crime fiction readers without undertaking a substantive qualitative and quantitative survey of their experience when reading local and world crime fiction, what I propose here is the potential for a worldly reading practice that emphasizes the interconnectedness of crime texts from around the globe as opposed to their separation into discrete national blocks in much traditional scholarship. Indeed, when we recognize crime fiction as a transnational phenomenon, it becomes a way of reading texts and contexts from around the globe that opens up 'a new vantage point on our moment' (Damrosch 2003: 300) and 'urges on us the entire planet as a unit of analysis' (Dimock 2001: 175). For the reader, such an approach 'yields a geography that is fluid rather than fixed' (Prendergast 2004: 1), mobile rather than static. When we develop a global viewpoint the limitations in Eva Erdmann's nationalizing project, through which crime novels are classified according to their setting, becomes more evident.[5] Indeed, the novels of Donna Leon and Henning Mankell, whom she cites as examples of the importance of the national *locus criminalis*, actually resist the nationalizing reading Erdmann proposes (2009; 2011). While readers do, indeed, enter into the place represented in the novel, they follow the foreign flatfoot with one foot planted at home. The first in Donna Leon's Commissario Guido Brunetti series, *Death at La Fenice* (1992), provides an example of the way in which the novel embraces the shift between the local and the universal, the strange and the familiar, when introducing the protagonist:

5 It is worth noting that Erdmann's focus on the local and the regional has the potential to unsettle the primacy of the nation as an interpretative referent, such as occurs in Catalan crime fiction (King and Whitmore 2016). However, as can be seen in her definition of Scottish and Greek crime fiction discussed above, Erdmann nationalizes texts that by the very fact of being set in one place and written by a non-national author and in a language other than that of the locale where the action is set are inherently transnational.

Brunetti [...] was a surprisingly neat man: tie carefully knotted, hair shorter than was the fashion; [...] His clothing marked him as Italian. The cadence of his speech announced that he was Venetian. His eyes were all policeman. (2004: 7)

In this passage we see how the perspective initially seems to confirm Erdmann's reading of place, as readers encounter differing degrees of foreignness: first, the familiar Italianness of Brunetti's clothes, then his localized Venetian accent, acting as a mark of identity rooted very much in a particular place, before expanding out through his profession. While speech is an outward marker of identity, the eyes are – as the cliché goes – the windows to the soul. Moreover, the eyes of the private or in this case public eye of the policeman provide the framework through which readers will encounter the other; an other that is made familiar through the investigation. In Leon's introduction of her protagonist we can appreciate a universalizing impulse that stands beside the local and the national and which makes the transnational experience possible. While her detective's ability to read the signs of his city, to uncover its secrets can be attributed to his localized vision, for Leon's readers this vision is experienced transnationally.

Set in Italy, but written in English for an international English-speaking audience, Donna Leon's novels, like Poe's Paris-centred mysteries, have transnationality in their DNA. Transnationality, however, is not limited to pseudotranslations. The interconnected nature of the global and the local is also present in novels in which the alignment between place, language and author is more traditionally national. Henning Mankell's *Villospår* (1995) (*Sidetracked* [1999]) illustrates the ways in which the world is present in the nation. Situated of course in Sweden, the novel includes multiple murders as well as various suicides and acts of self-harm by children and adolescents. When confronted with the knowledge of young children taking their own lives in gruesome ways, Wallander responds incredulously:

'That just isn't possible [...]. Not here in Sweden'.

'It was here, alright', she [a doctor] said. 'In Sweden. In the centre of the universe. In the middle of summer'. (Mankell 2012: 65)

Sweden thus becomes the centre of the reader's universe for the duration of the investigation, in particular, into what Wallander calls 'the Age of Failure':

Something the Swedish people had believed in and built had turned out to be less solid than expected. All they had done was raise a monument to a forgotten ideal. Now society seemed to collapse around him, as if the political system was about to tip over, and no-one knew which architects were waiting to put a new one in place, or what that system would be. (2012: 272)

Yet, as will be discussed below, Sweden is not self-contained or cut off from the rest of the world; its borders are porous. Indeed, its national distinctiveness, the very thing that is supposedly important in nationally bounded readings, is beginning to collapse in the wake of the increasingly global flow of capital, goods, people, information and, here, crime.

By drawing attention to the way in which the novel resists acting as an allegory of Sweden, I do not wish to suggest that the national context has no relevance for the novel. Globalization has, after all, failed to do away with nations and national identification (Cooppan 2009: chapter 1). National- and world-focused readings are not necessarily antithetical and reading a crime novel as world literature should not be a question of downplaying the importance of the local, but one in which the global and the local coexist simultaneously. As Wallander realizes later in the investigation, place is not fixed; it is conditional and elastic. The revelations he has begun to uncover change how he and we readers view the world. As he says, it is as if the 'world had shrunk and expanded at the same time' (Mankell 2012: 135). If this is true for a Swedish cop in his own country, it is also true for Borges's international reader of crime fiction.

Wallander's simultaneous expanding and shrinking world is central to the experience of transnational readers of crime fiction. 'The work of world literature', Damrosch argues, 'brings us into a world very different from ours', creating a 'doubled experience' (2003: 164). This doubled experience is what Slavoj Žižek calls the 'parallax view': the displacement of an object when viewed from two different perspectives. When crime fiction is read from afar, 'the perspective shifts, and in being deprived of a single point of identification, the reader gains a whole family, a collective identification bound together by a dual sense of vulnerability and solidarity' (Žižek 2003: 24). In this shift from a national to a transnational reading 'an alliance of readership' emerges that makes possible a global consciousness (King and Whitmore 2016: 147), as the convergence of two national contexts – that of the crime novel and that of the crime reader – creates a doubled experience. Vilashini Cooppan's analysis of W.E.B. Du Bois's theory of the doubled identity of African

Americans is pertinent here to understand the ways in which readers of world crime fiction negotiate between the local and the global:

> Divided within itself, linked outside itself, endlessly moving between the space and time of the self and the other, double consciousness [...] expresses an idea of the psyche – divided within, connected without – that maps not just racial and national consciousness but global consciousness too. (2009: chapter 3)

For the transnational reader of crime fiction, then, a global perspective emerges through the convergence of two locals – that of the reader and that of the text. In this way of reading, the specific becomes universal or, in other words, all we have are 'local universalisms' (Lazarus 2011: 134). Returning to the Sweden represented in Mankell's fiction, while the country provides the scene of multiple murders, these crimes make sense when the lens pans back to reveal a much larger and more complex world, one in which foreign readers are also able to position themselves. From a Swedish perspective perhaps, the novel draws attention to the multiple ways in which Sweden is connected to the rest of the world: serial and random killings by unknown assailants, common American phenomena, are beginning to appear in Sweden and for which assistance from foreign law enforcement agencies is required; crime rings from the former Eastern-bloc frequently penetrate the nation's borders; Swedish criminals are involved in trafficking women from Third-World countries; and the novel reflects on refugees in Sweden and Swedish engagement with alleviating the plight of refugees abroad. For non-Swedish readers, these same phenomena serve to connect the rest of the world to Sweden. As Barry Forshaw argues, Mankell's international popularity can be attributed to his detective's investigation into 'issues that transform (for better or worse) society [...] common to us all' (2016: 70). In other words, Mankell's success is due to the ways in which the reader, negotiating between a here and there, makes sense of the larger world through the Sweden represented in Mankell's text.

If crime fiction in general develops a 'detectory' practice in readers, then the experience of world crime fiction results in a form of 'relational thinking', through which, as Cooppan argues, citing Stuart Hall, 'the global/local reciprocally re-organise and re-shape one another' (2009: Introduction). For Cooppan, when we develop relational thinking, the national and the global become 'tandem ideas, twinned identifications, and doubled dreams' that are at the heart of world literature (2009: Introduction). This relational thinking allows readers of world crime fiction to make sense of crimes and their impact in and between different places. It facilitates the worlding both of the place from which readers read and the place represented in the novel. To return to Kishwar Desai's *Witness the Night* as an example, while the novel can be interpreted within a local or a national context as a damning indictment of the treatment of women in patriarchal Punjab, when read in a worldly way the systemic oppression of women that the novel addresses can be situated at one point on a continuum of male violence against women that much women's crime fiction seeks to expose and denounce. In turn, the sort of worldly reading that I propose here can potentially question the relevance of and provide greater complexity to a model of women's crime fiction that has emerged largely from the experience of women in British and American contexts.

In some ways the spectacular success of world literature as a category of analysis over the past fifteen years can be attributed to the exciting new relationships that are forged by bringing together texts from across a range of what have been previously considered discrete national, cultural and linguistic contexts. Rather than reinforcing national distinctiveness as an interpretative framework, when we identify the profound connections between the local and the global, we recognize the inherent transnational mobility that has characterized the genre since its inception. The difference between an approach that favours national readings and one that opens up the text to the world can perhaps best be summed up by returning to 'The Murders in the Rue Morgue' in which Poe's detective, Dupin, dismisses his French progenitor Vidocq because '[h]e impaired his vision by holding the object too close. He might see, perhaps, one or two points with unusual clearness, but in doing so he, necessarily, lost sight of the matter as a whole' (Poe 1984: 412). While Dupin, like Holmes after him, is quick to find fault with the methods of his forebears, I am more reluctant to repudiate the sort of interpretations that arise from previous critical practice. As I have argued here, it is not necessary to undermine or, indeed, reject the local or the national in order to embrace a more global approach to the genre. The two are brought into parallel with one another through the confluence of text and reader. The national and the global, then, exist in the private eye of the beholder.

Works Cited

Achebe, Chinua (2001) [1959]. *Things Fall Apart* (London: Penguin).

Ascari, Maurizio (2007). *A Counter-History of Crime Fiction: Supernatural, Gothic, Sensational* (New York: Palgrave Macmillan).

Borges, Jorge Luis (1999). 'The Detective Story', in Eliot Weinberger (ed.), *Selected Non-Fictions* (London: Penguin), 491–99.

Chandler, Raymond (1995) [1944]. 'The Simple Art of Murder', in *Later Novels and Other Writings* (New York: Library of America), 977–93.

Christie, Agatha (2002) [1926]. *The Murder of Roger Ackroyd* (London: Harper).

Cobley, Paul (2000). *The American Thriller: Generic Innovation and Social Change in the 1970s* (New York: St Martin's Press).

Cooppan, Vilashini (2009). *Worlds Within: National Narratives and Global Consciousness in Postcolonial Writing* (Stanford, CA: Stanford University Press).

Damrosch, David (2003). *What is World Literature?* (Princeton, NJ: Princeton University Press).

— (2014). 'World Literature as Figure and as Ground', in *The 2014–2015 Report on the State of the Discipline of Comparative Literature* (American Comparative Literature Association). https://stateofthediscipline.acla.org/entry/world-literature-figure-and-ground-0 [accessed 15 November 2018].

Desai, Kishwar, 2012 [2010]. *Witness the Night* (New York: Penguin).

D'haen, Theo (2012). *The Routledge Concise History of World Literature* (London and New York: Routledge).

Dimock, Wai Chee (2001). 'Literature for the Planet'. *PMLA* 116.1: 173–88.

— (2006). *Through Other Continents: American Literature across Deep Time* (Princeton, NJ: Princeton University Press).

Erdmann, Eva (2009). 'Nationality International: Detective Fiction in the Late Twentieth Century', in Marieke Krajenbrink and Kate M. Quinn (eds), *Investigating Identities: Questions of Identity in Contemporary International Crime Fiction* (Amsterdam: Rodopi), 11–26.

— (2011). 'Topographical Fiction: A World Map of International Crime Fiction'. *The Cartographic Journal* 48.4: 274–84.

Forshaw, Barry (2016). 'Inspector Kurt Wallander', in B. Forshaw (ed.), *Detective* (Bristol: Intellect), 68–77.

Horsley, Lee (2005). *Twentieth-Century Crime Fiction* (Oxford: Oxford University Press).

Jameson, Fredric (1986). 'Third-World Literature in the Era of Multinational Capitalism'. *Social Text* 15: 65–88.

King, Stewart (2014). 'Crime Fiction as World Literature'. *Clues: A Journal of Detection* 32.2: 8–19.

King, Stewart and Alice Whitmore (2016). 'National Allegories Born(e) in Translation: The Catalan Case'. *The Translator* 22.2: 144–56.

Knight, Stephen (2004). *Crime Fiction 1800–2000: Detection, Death, Diversity* (Houndmills: Palgrave Macmillan).

— (2015). *Secrets of Crime Fiction Classics: Detecting the Delights of 21 Enduring Stories* (Jefferson, NC: McFarland).

Lazarus, Neil (2011). 'Cosmpolitanism and the Specificity of the Local in World Literature'. *Journal of Commonwealth Literature* 46.1: 119–37.

Leon, Donna (2004) [1992]. *Death at La Fenice* (New York: Dark Alley).

Mankell, Henning (2012) [1999]. *Sidetracked*. Trans. Steven T. Murray (London: Vintage).

Moretti, Franco (2000). 'Conjectures on World Literature'. *New Left Review* 1: 54–68.

Mussa, Alberto (2013). *The Mystery of Rio*. Trans. Alex Ladd (New York: Europa).

Nilsson, Louise, David Damrosch and Theo D'haen (eds) (2017). *Crime Fiction as World Literature* (London: Bloomsbury).

Pepper, Andrew (2000). *The Contemporary American Crime Novel: Race, Ethnicity, Gender, Class* (Edinburgh: Edinburgh University Press).

— (2016). *Unwilling Executioner: Crime Fiction and the State* (Oxford: Oxford University Press).

Pepper, Andrew and David Schmid (2016). 'Introduction: Globalization and the State in Contemporary Crime Fiction', in Andrew Pepper and David Schmid (eds), *Globalization and the State in Contemporary Crime Fiction* (Houndsmill: Palgrave Macmillan), 1–19.

Poe, Edgar Allan (1984) [1841]. 'The Murders in the Rue Morgue', in *Poetry and Tales* (New York: The Library of America), 397–31.

Prendergast, Christopher (2004). 'The World Republic of Letter', in C. Prendergast (ed.), *Debating World Literature* (London and New York: Verso), 1–25.

Priestman, Martin (ed) (2003). *The Cambridge Companion to Crime Fiction* (Cambridge: Cambridge University Press).

Rolls, Alistair, Marie-Laure Vuaille-Barcan and John West-Sooby (2016). 'Translating National Allegories: The Case of Crime Fiction'. *The Translator* 22.2: 1–10.

Rushing, Robert A. (2007). *Resisting Arrest: Detective Fiction and Popular Culture* (New York: Other Press).

Rzepka, Charles J. and Lee Horsley (eds) (2010). *A Companion to Crime Fiction* (Chichester and Maldon, MA: Wiley-Blackwell).

Sayers, Dorothy (1988). 'Aristotle on Detective Fiction', in Robin Winks (ed.), *Detective Fiction: A Collection of Critical Essays* (Woodstock, VT: The Countryman Press), 25–34.

Siskind, Mariano (2011). 'The Genres of World Literature: The Case of Magical Realism', in Theo D'haen, David Damrosch and Djelal Kadir (eds), *The Routledge Companion to World Literature* (London and New York: Routledge), 345–55.

Wilson, Edmund (1945). 'Who Cares Who Killed Roger Ackroyd?' *The New Yorker*, 20 January: 59–66.

Žižek, Slavoj (2003). 'Parallax.' *London Review of Books* 25.22: 24.

Zunshine, Lisa (2006). *Why We Read Fiction: Theory of Mind and the Novel* (Columbus, OH: The Ohio State University Press).

Index